Dynamism, Rivalry, and the Surplus Economy

Dynamism, Rivalry, and the Surplus Economy
Two Essays on the Nature of Capitalism

János Kornai

UNIVERSITY PRESS

Oxford University Press is a department of the University of Oxford.
It furthers the University's objective of excellence in research, scholarship,
and education by publishing worldwide.

Oxford   New York
Auckland Cape Town Dar es Salaam Hong Kong Karachi
Kuala Lumpur Madrid Melbourne Mexico City Nairobi
New Delhi Shanghai Taipei Toronto

With offices in
Argentina Austria Brazil Chile Czech Republic France Greece
Guatemala Hungary Italy Japan Poland Portugal Singapore
South Korea Switzerland Thailand Turkey Ukraine Vietnam

Oxford is a registered trade mark of Oxford University Press
in the UK and certain other countries.

Published in the United States of America by
Oxford University Press
198 Madison Avenue, New York, NY 10016

© Oxford University Press 2014

All rights reserved. No part of this publication may be reproduced,
stored in a retrieval system, or transmitted, in any form or by any means,
without the prior permission in writing of Oxford University Press,
or as expressly permitted by law, by license, or under terms agreed with the
appropriate reproduction rights organization. Inquiries concerning reproduction
outside the scope of the above should be sent to the Rights Department,
Oxford University Press, at the address above.

You must not circulate this work in any other form
and you must impose this same condition on any acquirer.

Library of Congress Cataloging-in-Publication Data
Kornai, János.
Dynamism, rivalry, and the surplus economy : two essays on the nature
of capitalism / János Kornai.
    p.   cm.
Includes bibliographical references and index.
ISBN 978–0–19–933476–6 (alk. paper) 1. Capitalism. 2. Socialism.
3. Surplus (Economics) I. Title.
HB501.K583 2014
330.12'2—dc23
                                                                    2013012762
9780199334766

1 3 5 7 9 8 6 4 2

P

CONTENTS

List of Figures viii
List of Tables ix
Preface xi

FIRST ESSAY: Innovation
1. Introduction 3
2. Capitalism, Socialism, and Technical Progress 5
   2.1. Revolutionary new products 5
   2.2. Following the pioneers, the diffusion of innovation 11
   2.3. Innovative entrepreneurship under capitalism 12
   2.4. The impossibility of innovative entrepreneurship under socialism 18
   2.5. Political factors and technical progress 22
   2.6. First summary: systems and technical progress 23
3. Transformation and the Acceleration of Technical Progress 25
   3.1. New innovator entrepreneurs 25
   3.2. The acceleration of follow-up and diffusion 27
   3.3. Creative destruction 31
4. Reflection of Historical Reality in People's Minds 36
   4.1. The basic phenomenon: lack of understanding 36
   4.2. The responsibility of the economic profession 39
   4.3. The responsibility of politicians 41
   4.4. Interconnectivity and democracy 42
5. Concluding Remarks 47

SECOND ESSAY: Shortage Economy—Surplus Economy
1. Introduction 51
   1.1. Impressions 51
   1.2. A first approach to clarification of concepts 53
   1.3. The place that the approach taken in the essay occupies in economic discourse 54
   1.4. An advance look at the boundaries and structure of the subject-matter 55

2. The Market for Goods and Services: The Mechanism for the Reproduction of Surplus   57
    2.1. An example from economic history: the U.S. telephone system   57
    2.2. Supply-related processes   60
    2.3. Demand-related processes   67
    2.4. The pricing process   68
3. The Market for Goods and Services: The Conceptual Apparatus and Measurement Methods   70
    3.1. "Pure," easily handled cases   70
    3.2. The first difficulty: continual mutual adjustment of supply and demand   76
    3.3. The second difficulty: parallel occurrences of excess supply and excess demand   78
    3.4. Diversion: observing the obstacles to and micro constraints of production   78
    3.5. The third difficulty: distinguishing "necessary" from "superfluous" stocks   81
    3.6. The fourth difficulty: unjustified aggregation   84
    3.7. Pragmatic suggestions for measurement and a conceptual apparatus   85
    3.8. Formation of synthetic indicators or "composite indices"   86
4. The Labor Market: The Mechanism for the Reproduction of Surplus   88
    4.1. Conceptual clarification and measurement   88
    4.2. The shock to the labor market caused by the change of system   92
    4.3. "Keynesian" unemployment   95
    4.4. Structural unemployment   98
    4.5. Mismatched adjustment, frictional unemployment, and demand   100
    4.6. The efficiency wage   103
5. A Summary of the Positive Description and Causal Analysis   106
    5.1. The workability of the concept of "equilibrium"   106
    5.2. Asymmetry   111
    5.3. A summary account of the two demand–supply regimes   113
    5.4. The generation of a surplus economy by the capitalist system: the causal chain   118
    5.5. Genetic propensities   122
6. The Effect and Assessment of the Surplus Economy   125
    6.1. A view of the effects and the value judgments   125
    6.2. Innovation   126
    6.3. The sovereignty and manipulation of the consumer   127
    6.4. Productivity and coordination   128

- 6.5. Adaptation   *129*
- 6.6. Distribution of income and wealth   *129*
- 6.7. "Materialistic" and "spiritual" values   *130*
- 6.8. The direction of corruption   *131*
- 6.9. The advantages and drawbacks of capitalist competition, through the example of the automotive industry   *132*
- 6.10. A stand in favor of capitalism and the surplus economy   *135*
- 6.11. The scope for a theoretical synthesis and its constraints   *137*
- 6.12. The demand for mathematical models with explanatory power   *141*
7. Departures from the General Scheme   *144*
- 7.1. Fluctuations of the business cycle   *144*
- 7.2. The war economy   *149*
- 7.3. Historic changes and lasting tendencies in modern capitalism   *150*
- 7.4. Market-oriented reforms under socialism and the postsocialist transition   *158*
8. A Personal Postscript   *161*
Appendix   *163*

References   *169*
Index   *181*

LIST OF FIGURES

First Essay: Innovation

2.1 Penetration of modern technology: steel-industry, oxygen steel   *13*

3.1 Firms' entry and exit rates in the 1990s   *33*

3.2 The evolution of gross and net firm flows in transition economies   *33*

Second Essay: Shortage Economy—Surplus Economy

2.1 Telephone main lines and cellular phone subscribers per 100 inhabitants in the United States, 1990–2010   *59*

3.1 Rate of capacity utilization, United States, 1965–2011   *75*

3.2 Rate of capacity utilization, France, 1965–2005   *75*

3.3 Rental and homeowner vacancy rates, United States, 1994–2011   *76*

3.4 Impediments to manufacturing production, Hungary, 1987–2012   *79*

4.1 Activity rate and the degree of economic development, 1980   *93*

4.2 Activity rate and the degree of economic development, 2009   *94*

4.3 Job vacancies and the number of persons searching for a job in Poland, 1964–1988   *95*

4.4 The rate of the economically inactive population and the unemployment rate in three "old" capitalist countries, 1989–2010   *102*

5.1 Illustration of the shortage economy and the surplus economy   *113*

5.2 Factors generating surplus economy: the causal chain   *120*

6.1 Excess capacity in the automotive industry, 1990–2008   *133*

6.2 Business executives of the automotive industry about the global excess capacity, 2006–2008   *133*

LIST OF TABLES

First Essay: Innovation

2.1 Revolutionary innovations   6

2.2 Time-lag in following the leaders of innovation: plastic materials   11

2.3 Time-lag in following the leaders of innovation: controlled machine tools   12

2.4 Penetration of modern technology: steel-industry, continuous casting (percent)   13

3.1 Telephone lines: comparative data (number of lines per 1,000 people)   28

3.2 Penetration of modern communication technology in EU countries: 15 old EU member states (EU15) versus 10 new postsocialist member states (EU10)   28

3.3 Penetration of modern communication technology in EU countries: five Visegrád countries (V5) versus three South European countries (S3)   29

3.4 Penetration of modern communication technology in Russia and some other countries   30

4.1 Evaluation of technical progress   37

4.2 Expectations concerning the impact of new technologies (percent)   37

4.3 Satisfaction with the current system: population divided into users and nonusers of the Internet   43

4.4 Evaluation of the pre-1989 economic system: population divided into users and nonusers of the Internet   43

4.5 Evaluation of the socialist economic system: population divided into users and nonusers of the Internet   44

Second Essay: Shortage Economy—Surplus Economy

2.1 Fixed telephone lines per 100 inhabitants in some socialist countries and in the United States, 1980–1988   *59*

3.1 Ratio of capacity utilization: international comparison, 1978–2008   *74*

3.2 Ratio of input and output stocks: international comparison, 1981–1985   *83*

4.1 Linkages between concepts used in this book and those used in labor market statistics   *91*

4.2 The rate of unemployment and job vacancies in Eastern Europe, 1989–2010   *96*

4.3 The rate of economically inactive population, unemployment, and job vacancies: international comparison, 1989–2010   *101*

5.1 The two sides of coordination mechanism: a summary of terminology   *111*

6.1 Advertisement expenditures in developed countries, 1975–2007 (advertisement expenditure to GDP ratio, percent)   *128*

6.2 The elements of positive synthesis with respect to the theme "shortage economy–surplus economy"   *139*

7.1 Waiting time in Western European health-care sectors, 2004 (number of weeks)   *151*

7.2 Waiting lists for telephones in Central and Eastern European countries, 1971–2007   *159*

A.1 Impediments to production in the Hungarian industry, 1987–2012   *163*

PREFACE

"János Kornai is sort of gentle Jonathan Swift: a humane man who knows Western economics, lives in an Eastern economy, and observes clearly. Just think: next time he might write about us." So wrote Robert Solow, one of the great economists of our time, in a kind recommendation on the cover of my book, *Contradictions and Dilemmas*, which appeared in English in 1986.

"Next time" has been quite a while coming: twenty-six years. I began to delve into the attributes of the *socialist* system over half a century ago, and from the outset I compared it with capitalism—in my mind and in my works—but for decades my examination remained focused on the socialist system. My constant comparisons were enriched on increasingly frequent visits to the West, and intensified further in the period when I came to spend half my time there, commuting between Hungary and the United States, which allowed me to be acquainted with capitalism personally, not just through reading matter and statistics. That continual juxtaposition of the two systems deepened my knowledge and understanding of both.

Those comparisons gained new force as the Berlin Wall was pulled down and the Iron Curtain drawn aside. Now I could not only compare the socialist and capitalist worlds separately, but experience the drama of the change of system, with all its joys and sufferings. I have witnessed in my life how the two great systems follow each other over time: first socialism replacing capitalism, then capitalism superseding it again.

Such experiences take time to digest. I kept putting off the task of describing how I see the capitalist system. I cannot deny that I was held back from expressing my ideas by the immensity of the literature on the subject, and by the intellectual warfare between the superlative minds of excellently prepared experts on the subject. "I still have to read this book," I would think. "I have to wait out the course of this fresh development." Such considerations hindered me in expressing my thoughts.

Now I fear I am running out of time. "Next time," as Solow put it in 1984, cannot be postponed any longer. I have often imagined producing a comprehensive new work, a pair to *The Socialist System*, to summarize methodically all I know and think about capitalism. I do not have the strength for that. I must content myself with a publication that is a far more modest undertaking.

This volume contains two separate essays, with little overlap between them. Each can be read separately. Better still, they can be read one right after the other, for there is a close, complementary relation in their content.

The volume covers several themes, of which I would like to emphasize three in this Preface:

1. Most economists agree that the socialist system was dominated by a shortage economy with chronic excess demand. However, most discern in the capitalist system a balancing out of supply and demand, with fluctuations around the equilibrium. The view taken in this book is that capitalism is marked by chronic excess supply, a continual state that I have termed the surplus economy.
2. The mature socialist economy exhibits a shortage not only of products and surpluses, but of labor as well. The capitalist economy exhibits in parallel abundance of goods *and* unemployment—permanent underutilization of physical capacities and human resources. There is no elimination of chronic shortage on the goods market without a chronic surplus appearing on the labor market.
3. The explanation for both types of asymmetric state can be found on the micro level, in the motivations, driving forces, and behavioral regularities of the economic actors. These shape the propensities of the system, making up its immanent, innate "genetic programs," and ultimately *the nature of capitalism*, as the subtitle of the book makes plain. The natural propensities of the system may be strengthened or weakened by fiscal and monetary policy, the macroeconomic policy of the government, but given the political structure and the ownership relations of the system, the natural propensities of the system are given as well.

The title of the book emphasizes three phenomena. It sets out to convince readers that these very three phenomena (interdependent in many respects) are the most conspicuous and have exceptionally important explanatory force in illuminating the way capitalism operates. The capitalist system is innovative and *dynamic*, whereas the socialist system is slothful, just tottering along the path of technical progress, and inclined, rather, to copy the innovations made in the capitalist world. In a capitalist economy there is *rivalry* among producers and providers to gain the market. Furthermore, as I have noted in point 1, there is a *surplus economy* in the capitalist world, with instances of surplus supply found almost constantly. The surplus economy and the rivalry of sellers for buyers are almost interchangeable expressions, highlighting two sides of the same phenomenon. The first refers to the underutilization of resources and the second to the relations of the producers and sellers acting within the economy.

Examination of these phenomena forms a leitmotif throughout the two essays in this volume. This provides a chance to rethink some fundamental questions of economic theory, clarify some important concepts, and take a fresh look at some aspects of the measurement of economic phenomena.

These two longer studies appeared in Hungarian along with two shorter ones. I dedicated the Hungarian edition to an outstanding intellectual workshop of the young economists of Budapest, Rajk College, in the hope that their thinking had not yet ossified and they would be prepared to look critically at the syllabus they are taught at the university. I would very much like to see the English edition also reach young people still at university or just beginning their careers as economists. The better prepared the teachers who teach them and the more gripping the textbooks they read, the greater their gain from reading a work that takes a critical approach and discusses some big issues of economic theory from an angle unfamiliar to them.

Of course I will be delighted if not only the young, but also older colleagues take up this book. I fear more from them, because, in my experience they find it difficult to step out of their accustomed schemes of thinking. What if my anxiety is unfounded, however? After all, doubts arise in the minds of many experienced, learned economists about the dogmas that have impressed themselves most on us. Perhaps some of them at least may meet me on the same wavelength.

Let me underline here in the Preface that the subject of this volume is *not* the current financial crisis or the associated depression or recession. The book does *not* set out to take a stance on the Euro zone, American monetary and fiscal policy, or the Chinese rate of exchange. It does *not* attempt to advise governments or international organizations. Those interested in these questions (or solely interested in them) need read no further.

Luckily there is a division of labor among the researchers. These two studies set out to view the economy of today from a greater distance. I seek to understand the *lasting* features of the capitalist system. To the extent that I succeed in penetrating them, I do my best to convey my understanding to the readers—not just to the economists' profession in the narrow sense, but also other educated readers intrigued by the basic questions of capitalism. Though noneconomist readers may skip some pages that are harder to understand, I am certain they will manage without great difficulty to follow the book's line of thought and most of its arguments.

Readers now encounter a Gulliver from another world, a visitor from afar, who marvels at the lands of dwarfs and giants, absent-minded scholars, and honest horses, and describes how he sees capitalism, not, sadly, in the engaging style or acerbic irony of Swift, but in the dry language of economics.

*

Several people helped me both in my research that this book is based on and in the final formulation of the studies. The first footnote of each essay lists those supporting its preparation. I owe thanks not only to people whose names I know, but also to the four anonymous referees who my publishers called on to read the manuscript. From them, too, I received much valuable advice.

Here, at the end of the Preface, I would like to express my gratitude to those helping me the most in preparing the present volume. First let me mention my two assistants, Rita Fancsovits and Andrea Reményi, who contributed their continuing efforts and conscientious work in editing the text. I am grateful to my old friend, Brian McLean, translator of most of my works, who translated the texts with full attention and patience. My thanks are due to Hédi Erdős, Klára Gurzó, Boglárka Molnár, Anna Patkós, Ildikó Pető, Éva Szalai, Katalin Szécsi, and László Tóth for their help in various ways. And as always, I thank my wife, Zsuzsa Dániel, for her encouragement (much needed in my moments of discouragement), the many constructively critical remarks, and her good advice.

While it was still alive and its doors did not close in 2011, Collegium Budapest Institute for Advanced Study guaranteed ideal working conditions and an inspiring intellectual environment. I feel deep gratitude toward Corvinus University of Budapest for welcoming and helping me in continuing my work in the intellectually encouraging milieu of its faculty and students. My thanks are also due to Harvard University, where I taught and did research till my retirement in 2002; discussions with colleagues and students there inspired several of my ideas.

It is a great pleasure and honor to have this volume brought out by Oxford University Press, a publisher to which I have strong personal ties. It was Oxford who took on my first work, as an unknown author, in 1959, not long after the Hungarian edition. It placed in the hands of Western readers my book *Overcentralization of Economic Administration*, which, having been written to the east of the Iron Curtain, had to be smuggled out of Hungary in those difficult, stormy times. It was on the initiative of Oxford University Press that a second edition of this first book of mine appeared 35 years later. In 1993, Oxford, in conjunction with Princeton University Press, published my book *The Socialist System*, in which I summed up several decades of my work on socialism. I feel that now, having my two essays on capitalism published by Oxford closes a circle that has been drawn over half a century. My sense of familiarity was reinforced by the encouraging openness with which my manuscript was received. I am deeply grateful to Terry Vaughn, Scott Paris, Cathryn Vaulman, Michelle Dellinger, and their colleagues, and to the four anonymous reviewers. Their all-embracing attention and thoroughness, and their many valuable pieces of advice, have been of invaluable help to me.

Budapest, February 2013

FIRST ESSAY

Innovation

SECTION 1

Introduction[1]

The essence of postsocialist transformation can be easily summarized in a few words: a large set of countries moved from socialism to capitalism. This shift itself is the strongest historical evidence of the superiority of capitalism over socialism. Nevertheless, it is the obligation of the economic profession to continue the impartial and unbiased comparison of the two systems. I would like to spell out only one virtue of capitalism: its innovative and dynamic nature. In the first part of the essay I argue that rapid innovation and dynamism are not a random phenomenon, which may or may not occur, but a deeply rooted *system-specific property* of capitalism. The same can be said about its opposite, the socialist system. Its inability to create great revolutionary new products and delay in other dimensions of technical progress are not due to some errors in policy but, rather, is a deeply rooted system-specific property of socialism. Unfortunately, this highly visible great virtue of capitalism does not get the appreciation it deserves. It is completely ignored by most people and even by most professional students of alternative systems, and I feel angry and frustrated watching that neglect, motivating me to choose the theme of this essay.

---

1. I express my gratitude to Philippe Aghion, Wendy Carlin, Julian Cooper, Zsuzsa Dániel, Karen Eggleston, Zsolt Fekete, Thomas Geodecki, Balázs Hámori, Philip Hanson, Jerzy Hausner, Judit Hürkecz, László Karvalics, Zdenek Kudrna, Mihály Laki, Lukasz Mamica, Tibor Meszmann, Gerard Roland, Dániel Róna, András Simonovits, Katalin Szabó, Tibor Vámos, and Chenggang Xu, for their valuable comments and their devoted help in collecting data and readings.

An earlier version of this essay was presented at the UNU-WIDER conference "Reflections on Transition: Twenty Years after the Fall of the Berlin Wall" (Helsinki, September 18–19, 2009). In 2010 a later version appeared in the journal *Economics of Transition* (18[4]:629–670). The text published in the journal is a thoroughly revised version of the 2009 paper.

Entering the world of capitalism creates the conditions of innovative processes and faster technical progress, and also *increases the chances* that the country will take this opportunity. It does not, however, guarantee full success immediately. Sections 2 and 3 of this essay will discuss problems of the transition period.

The Great Transformation was an ensemble of several processes. First, there were changes in the *political* domain: the transition from a single-party dictatorship to a multiparty democracy. This transformation put an end to the state-protected privileges of the Marxist-Leninist ideology, and it gave the green light to the competition of various schools of thought. Then there were changes in the *economic* domain: the predominance of state-ownership was replaced by the predominance of private ownership. Associated with the transformation of ownership forms, the relative influence of various co-ordination mechanisms also went through radical changes. The impact of centralized bureaucratic control became much smaller, and the influence of market coordination and other decentralized procedures increased dramatically. These profound political and economic changes associated with several other changes jointly mean the change of the *system,* that is, the transition from socialism to capitalism.

The postsocialist region has experienced another class of changes in the domain of technical progress as well. Although, due to its familiarity, I apply the term *technical progress,* in my interpretation, it is a much wider phenomenon. Based on the stream of new products and new technologies, its effects go far beyond the technical aspects. It is a part of modernization, generating profound changes on our lives. This meaning of the term *technical progress* will unfold in the context of this essay. Technical progress was going on, of course, all the time, also before 1989, but following 1989 it has accelerated spectacularly.

All the experts on postsocialist transition have been concentrating their attention on the study of political, economic, and social changes as part of the Great Transformation. Let us confess frankly, we perhaps briefly mention technical progress once in a while, but we have not studied thoroughly the interaction between changing the system on the one hand, and changing our profile in generating and using new products and new technologies, on the other. I, myself, have certainly missed this point before. I have written two studies summarizing the main consequences of the changes after 1989, but discussing only political and economic changes and their interaction (Kornai 2001 and 2006b). With this essay I start to make up what I missed before. Thus, the subject of Sections 2 and 3 of this essay is the interaction between the post-1989 change of the system and the acceleration of technical progress.

SECTION 2

Capitalism, Socialism, and Technical Progress

2.1 REVOLUTIONARY NEW PRODUCTS

The complex process of technical progress is composed of several subprocesses. Let us begin with the great, breakthrough, revolutionary innovations, illustrated by 111 examples given in Table 2.1.[1] As we take a look at the role of socialist countries in creating revolutionary new products, we have to go back in time to the birth of the Soviet Union, the first socialist state. Therefore, the period covered by the list starts in 1917.

Since 1917, many innovations of great significance have been born. It is debatable why exactly these 111 are included in the table, because we could perhaps find 20 or 50 additional ones of no less significance. The selection is arbitrary, yet the list seems to be apt to demonstrate that all the innovations mentioned here in a narrower or wider scope fundamentally change the everyday practice of people's lives, work, consumption, recreation, and their relationships to others.[2] The office and the factory, transportation, shopping, housework, education have all changed. The tie between the home and the workplace differs, and travel has changed as well; we could continue listing, at great lengths, the effects of innovation causing permanent upheaval and the

---

1. The literature on technical progress and innovation distinguishes new *products* and new *technologies*, although the appearance of these two categories is often intertwined. For example, although the Xerox machine is a new product, it has also introduced a new technology of printing. Table 2.1 lists new *products*, because of their salience in everyday life.

2. Certain classes of innovation were excluded at the selection. Criteria of exclusion are explained partly in the note at the bottom of the table, and partly in later sections of the study.

Table 2.1. REVOLUTIONARY INNOVATIONS

Innovation	Year	Country	Company
Computer, Information, Communication			
Transistor	1954	USA	Texas Instruments
Integrated circuit	1961	USA	Fairchild
Touch-tone telephone	1963	USA	AT&T
Fax	1966	USA	Xerox
Optical fiber cable	1970	USA	Corning
Pocket electronic calculator	1971	USA	Bowmar
Word processing	1972	USA	Wang
Microprocessor	1974	USA	Intel
Laser printer	1976	USA	IBM
Modem	1978	USA	Hayes
MS-DOS operating system	1980	USA	Microsoft
Hard disk drive	1980	USA	Hard disk drive
Graphical user interface	1981	USA	Xerox
Laptop	1981	USA	Epson
Touch screen	1983	USA	Hewlett-Packard
Mobile telephone	1983	USA	Motorola
Mouse	1984	USA	Apple
Web search engine	1994	USA	WebCrawler
Pendrive	2000	USA	IBM
Skype (peer-to-peer phone)	2003	Estonia	Skype
YouTube video sharing website	2005	USA	YouTube
iPad tablet computer	2010	USA	Apple
Household, Food, Clothing			
Tea bag	1920	USA	Joseph Krieger
Hair dryer, hand held, electric	1920	USA	Hamilton Beach
Wall plug	1920	UK	Rawlplug Co.
Spin-dryer	1924	USA	Savage
Automatic pop-up toaster	1925	USA	Waters Genter Co.
Steam electric iron	1926	USA	Eldec
Electric refrigerator	1927	USA	General Electric
Air conditioning, home	1928	USA	Carrier Engineering Co.
Neon light	1938	USA	General Electric
Instant coffee	1938	Switzerland	Nestle
Electric clothes dryer	1938	USA	Hamilton Manufacturing Co.
Nylon	1939	USA	DuPont
Espresso machine (high pressure)	1946	Italy	Gaggia
Microwave oven	1947	USA	Raytheon
Drive-through restaurant	1948	USA	In-n-Out Burger

Table 2.1. (*continued*)

Innovation	Year	Country	Company
Saran plastic wrap	1949	USA	Dow Chemical
Polyester	1953	USA	DuPont
Tefal kitchenware	1956	France	Tefal
Hook-and-loop fastener (Velcro)	1957	USA	Velcro
Athletic shoe	1958	UK	Reebok
Halogen lamp	1959	USA	General Electric
Food processor	1960	USA	Roboot-Coupe
Tetra Pak	1961	Sweden	Tetra Pak
Beverage can	1963	USA	Pittsburgh Brewing Co.
Health			
Adhesive bandage (Band-aid)	1921	USA	Johnson&Johnson
Streptomycin, the first effective treatment for tuberculosis	1939	USA	Merck
Streptococcal septicemia with penicillin	1942	USA	Merck
Artificial intraocular lens	1949	USA	Rayner
Transistor hearing aid	1952	USA	Sonotone
Chlorpromazine (contribution to neuropsychopharmacology)	1953	USA	Smith Kline & French (today's GlaxoSmithKline)
Combined oral contraceptive pill (COCP)	1957	USA	G. D. Searle & Company
Ultrasonography for medical purposes	1963	United States	Physionic Engineering
X-ray computed tomography (CT) scanner	1969	United Kingdom	EMI
Magnetic resonance imaging (MRI) scanner	1980	United States	Fonar
Mevacor (Lovastatin), used for lowering cholesterol to reduce risk of cardiovascular disease	1987	United States	Merck
Retrovir, antiretroviral drug for the treatment of HIV	1987	United States	Burroughs Wellcome (today's GlaxoSmithKline)
Celebrex, first (COX-2) inhibitor	1998	United States	Monsanto Company
Drugstore Items			
Facial tissue (Kleenex)	1924	USA	Kimberley-Clark
Paper towel	1931	USA	Scott Paper Co.
Electric shaver	1931	USA	Schick
Aerosol container	1947	USA	Airosol Co.
Disposable diaper	1949	USA	Johnson&Johnson

(*continued*)

Table 2.1. (continued)

Innovation	Year	Country	Company
Roll-on deodorant	1955	USA	Mum
Disposable razor	1975	USA	BIC
Liquid detergent	1982	USA	Procter&Gamble

Office

Innovation	Year	Country	Company
Adhesive tape (pressure sensitive Scotch tape)	1930	USA	3M
Ball point pen	1943	Argentina	Biro Pens
Correction fluid	1951	USA	Mistake Out
Copy-machine	1959	USA	Haloid Xerox
"Post-it"	1980	USA	3M

Leisure

Innovation	Year	Country	Company
Technicolor motion picture process	1922	USA	Technicolor Co.
Dynamic Loudspeaker	1926	USA	RCA
Television	1928	USA	Jenkins, General Electric
Drive-in cinema	1933	USA	Hollingshead
Instant camera	1948	USA	Polaroid
TV Remote control	1956	USA	Zenith
Plastic construction toy	1958	Denmark	Lego
Barbie doll	1959	USA	Mattel
Quartz wristwatch	1969	Japan	Seiko
Video Casette Recording (VCR)	1971	The Netherlands	Philips
Walkman	1979	Japan	Sony
Rubik's cube	1980	USA	Ideal Toys
CD	1982	The Netherlands, Japan	Sony, Philips
Portable video-game	1989	Japan	Nintendo
Digital camera	1991	USA	Kodak
Book trade on the Internet	1995	USA	Amazon
Computer animated feature film	1995	USA	Pixar, Walt Disney
DVD	1996	Japan	Philips, Sony, Toshiba
iPod portable digital music player	2001	USA	Apple
iTunes digital "music shop"	2001	USA	Apple
eBook Kindle	2007	USA	Amazon

Transport

Innovation	Year	Country	Company
Escalator	1921	USA	Otis
Synthetic rubber	1932	USSR	State-owned plants

Table 2.1. (*continued*)

Innovation	Year	Country	Company
Parking meter	1935	UK	Dual Parking Meter Co.
Scooter	1946	Italy	Piaggio
Automatic transmission	1948	USA	GM Oldsmobile
Jet-propelled passenger aeroplane	1952	UK	Comet
Black box (for aeroplanes)	1958	UK	S. Davall & Son
Airbag with crash sensor	1968	USA	Ford
Hybrid vehicle	1997	Japan	Toyota
Commerce, Banking			
Supermarket	1930	USA	King Kullen
Shopping cart	1937	USA	Humpty Dumpty Supermarket
Shopping mall	1950	USA	Northgate Mall
Charge card	1950	USA	Diners Club
Credit card	1958	USA	Bank of America
Automated Teller Machine (ATM)	1967	UK	Barclays Bank
Express shipping	1973	USA	Federal Express
Bar code	1974	USA	IBM
e-commerce	1998	USA	eBay

Note: Entries are selected out of a larger set of innovations surveyed in various collections and lists of relevant inventions and innovations. The main inclusion criterion was the relevance for large groups of users, well-known to the majority of people, and not only to small groups of experts. The list contains only Schumpeterian-type innovations. Accordingly, innovations initiated and/or financed mainly by the military are excluded. (For the explanation of the concept see pp. 15–18.)
Sources: The source of several entries were Ceruzzi (2000), Harrison (2003 and 2004), and Vámos (2009). The source of each entry is on record, and is available from the author at request.

reorganization of life. The modern world is made dynamic by the perpetual flow of innovations. We consider our times more dynamic compared with earlier periods, because many more revolutionary innovations are being introduced, which are generating much deeper changes in our everyday life.[3]

3. The sense in which the expression "innovative process, creating revolutionary new products" is used in this essay is closely akin to the concept of "disruptive innovation" associated with the very influential, fruitful work of Clayton M. Christensen. (See Bower and Christensen 1995; Christensen 1997.)
  I would like to add a personal observation here. When I wrote this essay, I was not familiar with Christensen's work. It was only drawn to my attention at the last moment, when the copy-editing phase was over, and so I could not really make use of it. I obviously have myself to blame for this. Yet it is not an unprecedented case, for it exemplifies a gulf that separates many economists from "business economics." The Department of Economics at Harvard University, where I taught for many years, stands on one side of the Charles River, and on the other the Business School, where Christensen teaches. We never met. There are many bridges across this narrow river, but still proves to be a deep divide.

Out of the 111 innovations about 25–30 are related to computers, digital equipment, and information. This subset attracts the most intensive attention of the public and the academic world. A large and fast-growing literature is studying the social effects of the information society.[4] This essay cannot penetrate deeply into this exciting subject, because I would like to cover a wider set of innovations. Around 60–70 of 111 in the list are innovations unrelated or not closely related to the revolution in the information–communication sphere and to digital technologies. Admitting wholeheartedly the extraordinary importance of information and communication, there have been and there will be innovations in many areas outside this area. For the poorest inhabitants of a poor Albanian or Siberian village, the introduction of the refrigerator or the appearance of a supermarket might contribute to relevant changes in lifestyle; the use of the computer might come later. I would like to discuss certain issues of technical progress as a whole, that is, the technical change related and unrelated to the revolution of information and communication.

Innovation is preceded by invention. The first step is made by the inventor: the professional or amateur researcher, the academic scholar, or the company's engineer is the one to whom the new idea occurs. However, the originality of the idea, its novelty, and its ingenuity are not at all enough. In the second step, the invention becomes an innovation; the practical introduction begins, that is, the organization of production and the diffusion of the new product or the application of a new organizational form. (See Freeman and Soate 2003, furthermore Szabó 2012, and the literature cited in her study on the distinction between invention and innovation.) If we turn our attention toward this second phase, to the practical execution of the change (Table 2.1 indicates the country in which the innovator company is operating), we will, with only one exception, read the names of capitalist countries here.[5] Because the time period captured in the table includes the entire era during which the socialist system existed, it is clear that—except for a single case—path-breaking revolutionary innovations did not occur in a socialist country.[6]

---

4. Perhaps the most influential work in this area is Castells (1996–1998). See also Fuchs (2008).

5. Sometimes it is unclear which company can be considered to be the introducer of the innovation, and what date can be considered to be the actual event. A product of revolutionary importance is often introduced in several steps, more than one company experimenting with its distribution (Baumol 2002; Hámori and Szabó 2012). Frequently, however, a company surfaces as the one reaching breakthrough mass success.

Several companies and dates listed in Table 2.1 can be questioned, but changing the name of one capitalist company with another would not influence the general conclusions reached in this essay.

6. Table 2.1 excludes innovations initiated in the military sector of the economy. The military sector produced innovations appearing first in a socialist country. I will return to that point later.

2.2 FOLLOWING THE PIONEERS, THE DIFFUSION OF INNOVATION

Although revolutionary innovation is the most important component of technical progress, there are other components as well. The pioneer has followers. Beside the first innovator, after some time lag, various other organizations participate in minor quality improvements, implementation of small but not negligible inventions, and, in the process, of *diffusion*. The innovation appears first in a certain country, but then followers show up in other countries as well.

The socialist system, in numerous spheres, followed the pioneering inventions born in capitalist countries, and took diverse forms. Sometimes it was just imitation. The mere reproduction of the model, perhaps its makeshift copying, was simple. Breaking up the secret was a relatively more difficult task. The reinvention of the innovations protected by patents and business privacy virtually developed into an art in socialist economies. Industrial espionage, the stealing of intellectual property, was a further possibility.[7] However,

Table 2.2. TIME-LAG IN FOLLOWING THE LEADERS OF INNOVATION: PLASTIC MATERIALS

Product	Innovator		First Follower		Second Follower		Soviet Union	Delay behind Innovator (years)
Cellophane	France	1917	USA	1924	Germany	1925	1936	19
Polystyrene	Germany	1930	USA	1933	Italy	1943	1955–59	25–29
PVC	Germany	1931	USA	1933	Japan	1939	1940	9
Silicon polymers	USA	1941	Germany	1950	Japan	1951	1947	6*
Epoxy resins	Switzerland	1936	USA	1947	Germany UK	1955 1955	1957–59	21–23
Polypropylene	USA Germany Italy	1957 1957 1957	UK	1959	France	1960	1970	13

* In this case, the Soviet Union followed the pioneering country faster than the capitalist economies.
Source: Amann, Cooper, and Davies (1977, 272–285).

7. Stealing Western intellectual property in the high-tech sphere was hindered by various barriers, for example, by strictly enforced prohibition of exporting certain products to communist countries—the so-called Coordinating Committee for Multilateral Export Controls (COCOM) list of products used for military purposes. In spite of strict prohibitions, the cooperation of smart spies and technical experts was successful enough to slip through the holes of the barriers.

Table 2.3. TIME-LAG IN FOLLOWING THE LEADERS OF INNOVATION: CONTROLLED MACHINE TOOLS

	Reached by USSR in	USSR (+ in advance, −behind) in relation to			
		USA	UK	Japan	FRG
Start of research	1949	−2	−1	+ 4	+ 6
First prototype	1958	−6	−2	–	–
Start of industrial production*	1965	−8	−2	+ 1	−1
First machining center	1971	−12	(−10)	−5	−10
First third-generation control system	1973	−7	(−5)	(−5)	(−5)
First use of computer for control	1973	−6	(−4)	−5	(−4)

* Fifty units or more per annum.
Note: Values in parentheses represent estimates.
Source: Amann, Cooper and Davies (1977, 41).

despite the diverse attempts regarding these processes, the socialist economy sluggishly trudged behind the capitalist economy.

Let me draw your attention to two details. First, in the socialist countries, this delay, the followers' time lag behind the pioneers, was significantly longer than in the capitalist countries; see for example the data given in Tables 2.2 and 2.3. Examining a longer time period, the lag was mostly growing instead of shrinking.

Second, the diffusion of new products and new technologies was much faster in the capitalist economies than in the socialist ones; for example, see Table 2.4 and Figure 2.1.

The tables and figures shown here are only illustrations. The large amount of empirical evidence in the comparative economic literature also supports the proposition that the socialist system was sluggish in following the pioneering innovations.[8]

2.3 INNOVATIVE ENTREPRENEURSHIP UNDER CAPITALISM

Capitalism produced almost all the breakthrough innovations and was much faster in other aspects of technical progress—historical experience grants irrefutable evidence. Nevertheless, let us add the causal explanation of that crucial systemic difference. In capitalism, the entrepreneur plays a distinguished

---

8. The most important empirical works on the subject are the books by Amann and Cooper (1982), and Amann et al. (1977). See also Berliner (1976); Hanson (1981); Hanson and Pavitt (1987).

Table 2.4. PENETRATION OF MODERN TECHNOLOGY: STEEL-INDUSTRY, CONTINUOUS CASTING (PERCENT)

Country	Continuous casting per total production		
	1970	1980	1987
Socialist Countries			
Bulgaria	0	0	10
Czechoslovakia	0	2	8
East Germany	0	14	38
Hungary	0	36	56
Poland	0	4	11
Romania	0	18	32*
Soviet Union	4	11	16
Capitalist Countries			
France	1	41	93
Italy	4	50	90
Japan	6	59	93
Spain	12	49	67
United Kingdom	2	27	65
United States	4	20	58
West Germany	8	46	88

* Measured in 1986.
Source: Finansy i Statistika (1988, 109).

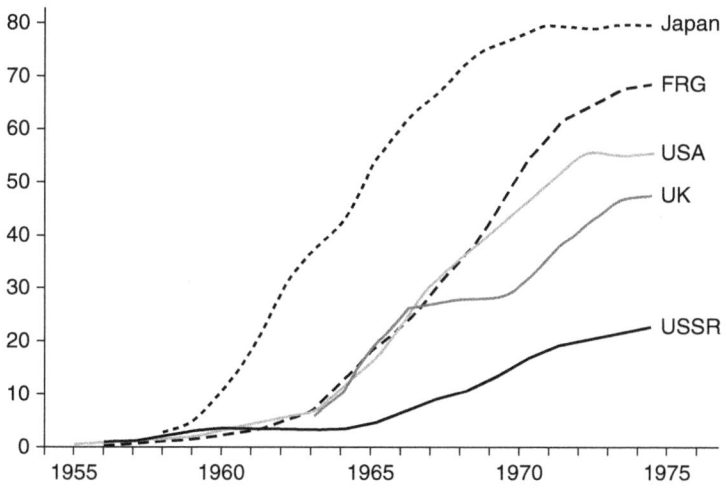

Figure 2.1.
Penetration of modern technology: steel-industry, oxygen steel (oxygen steel as a proportion of total steel output, percent of total)
Source: Amann, Cooper, and Davies (1977, 97).

role.[9] My study adopts this term in the sense used by Joseph Schumpeter (1968 [1912]). Beyond terminology, Schumpeter's theories about development and the nature of capitalism leave their mark on the message of this essay.[10]

Innovative entrepreneurship is a *function*, a role that can be fulfilled by an individual alone, or by teaming up with one or more partners, or with the support of a small firm. Even a large firm can function as an entrepreneur. The main point is that entrepreneurs are the ones who bring together the necessary financial and personal conditions that the innovation calls for, in other words, the human resources, the physical instruments, and the financial resources essential to the activity. They are the ones who find the place of application; they direct the execution of the change. Often, much time passes before a promising invention is taken up by a true entrepreneur.[11] Probably, it is a frequent occurrence that an invention or discovery and an entrepreneur do not find each other. Fortunately, it is quite frequent that the match *is* made.

From Table 2.1 it emerges how many different types of innovation are possible—not only new products or new production technologies, but new organizational forms as well. In most cases the Schumpeterian entrepreneur drives the innovation process during the first realization of the revolutionary innovation. Entrepreneurs also mostly drive diffusion, that is, the process following the pioneering innovation.

At the beginning of the sequence, the initiative appears. For example, in 1996 Larry Page, a PhD student at Stanford, was searching for a dissertation topic. Some specific issues about browsing the Internet attracted his attention. He teamed up with another student, Sergey Brin, and they developed a "search engine." On the Stanford homepage it is named "google.stanford.edu." In this story, these two men unite the two usually separated roles: they are the inventors and, simultaneously, they are the innovators. Skipping over all the intermediate stages, let us jump to where we are right now. Google is one of the world's largest and wealthiest companies.[12] Its worldwide network used about 900,000 servers in 2011. I would not like to play lightly with words, but the influence of Google has proved to be of revolutionary significance.[13] I will

---

9. Not all entrepreneurs are innovators (Baumol and Schilling 2008). This study is focusing on one extremely important class, the entrepreneurs engaged in the process of innovation.

10. On Schumpeter's contributions to social science, see Heertje (2006) and McCraw (2007). See also Baumol (2002)—the very title of this book catches the real essence of the phenomenon I am going to discuss: *The Free-Market Innovation Machine: Analyzing the Growth Miracle of Capitalism.*

11. One can find numerous examples for this delay in Rogers (1995). See also Freeman and Soate (2003).

12. For a concise introduction to the Google story, see the company's own brief summary (Google 2013) and the entry on Google in Wikipedia (2009a).

13. Based on my personal experience, I admit that it has changed my research habits as well. It is different to be a researcher in the Google age than it was earlier, in the Gutenberg era.

return to the Google story, but only to illustrate the general characteristics of the innovation process that is taking place in the capitalist environment.

Let me summarize the specific characteristics of the capitalist economy that not only make the innovation process possible, but also induce, constantly develop, and propel it:

A. *Decentralized initiative.*—Larry Page and Sergey Brin did not receive any orders from their superiors to solve a specific innovational task. They did not have to ask for permission from their superiors to work on a special direction of an innovative action. The individuals and the decision makers of small firms, or the chief executives of large companies—in other words, the separate entities functioning inside the system—determine for themselves what they want to do.[14]

B. *Gigantic reward.*—Today Page and Brin are among the richest men of the world.[15] It is not the task of this essay to analyze the difficult ethical dilemmas of income distribution. How large is the reward that is "proportional" to performance? One point is certain: the most successful innovations usually (not always, but very often, with a high probability) result in enormously large rewards.[16] The range of the reward spreads rather unevenly. At the end of the scale, one finds the owners of gigantic wealth: people like Bill Gates or, in the older generations, the Fords or the Duponts. The entrepreneur leading the technical progress is able to gain a huge monopolistic rent. It is worth being the first, even temporarily, because it creates a monopoly position. The enormous financial reward is usually accompanied by prestige, fame, and reputation.

C. *Competition.*—This is inseparable from the previous point. Strong, often ruthless competition is taking place to attract customers. The faster and more successful innovation is not the exclusive instrument for that purpose, yet a highly important one to gain advantage over one's competitors.[17]

---

14. Acemoglu et al. (2007) argue in a recent paper both theoretically and empirically that pioneering innovation requires decentralization.
15. According to the well-known ranking of *Forbes* magazine, they tie for fifth rank in the United States.
16. The Google story can be considered a unique case, in which the pioneering inventor and the role of the innovator are played by the same people. In the more frequent instance, when these roles are separated, in some cases inventors do, in others they do not attain benefits from the invention or the discovery. The latter was the fate of the computer mouse. The inventor Douglas Engelbart has received no financial reward for his ingenious invention. Apple, the innovator company pioneering the mass introduction, has produced the enormous profit on this innovation.
17. The environment of strong competition and rapid technical progress has a powerful impact on the strategic management of firms. Success depends on promoting technological, organizational and managerial innovation inside the firm (Teece, Pisano, and Shun 1997).

D. *Extensive experimenting.*—There must have been hundreds, perhaps thousands, of entrepreneurs wanting to find tools suitable to search the Internet. Only a few achieved almost as great a breakthrough as the founders of Google. However, others have also been able to realize innovations with fairly large, medium, or small success. And there must have been many, or at least a good few, who have tried but failed. Moving beyond the example, so far no one has assessed the volume of innovational attempts constantly occurring in all spheres under capitalism and the distribution of their success and failure. Those gaining an impression about this highly important activity can only intuitively sense the huge number of attempts, compared to the rare spectacular successes like the story of Google, Microsoft, Tetra Pak, Nokia, or Nintendo. Many highly talented people are motivated toward innovation precisely because—although with quite a small probability—a phenomenal success is promised, and even with a larger probability, a more moderate yet still substantial success materializes, and that is why it is worth taking up the risk of failure.[18]

E. *Reserve capital waiting to be invested: the flexibility of financing.*—The two founders of Google gained access to financial resources that enabled them to launch the innovative activity, the distribution. Successful researcher and innovator Andy Bechtolsheim (who also happened to be a wealthy businessman) at the very beginning of the process reached into his pocket for his checkbook and signed a $100,000 check. An innovative enterprise is rarely realized solely from the innovator's own resources. Although there are examples of this, resorting to outside resources is much more common.[19] The diverse forms of finding resources include a bank loan, investors willing to take part in the business, or "venture capital" institutions specialized in particularly high-risk and, in case of success, high-reward projects (Bygrave and Timmons 1992). Basically, flexible disposable capital is needed to realize the pioneering introduction and quick diffusion of innovations, which include wide-range experimentation, some of which is ultimately unsuccessful.

I do not claim that Schumpeterian-type entrepreneurship is the only way to generate innovative processes in a capitalist system. Let me mention only three of the several other non-Schumpeterian frameworks.

---

18. On the importance of experimentation see Thomke (2003).
19. Undoubtedly, there is a connection between the economic booms of the great innovative periods and the increase in the available amount of credit. Easily accessible money helps technical progress, but it also allows the danger of a bubble formation. It is timely to re-read Schumpeter when analyzing history preceding the current crisis (Schumpeter 1939, especially Chapter IV). The great temptation to discuss this aspect is regrettably limited by the available space.

1. In several instances, an important innovation is initiated, financed, and implemented by the military. For example, in the 1960s, there was a strong demand expressed by the Pentagon to generate a completely decentralized mailing service to assure that the destruction of the center of the postal system would not lead to a breakdown of written communication. This requirement of the military and the generous financial support of research in that direction led to a revolutionary innovation, the creation of e-mail, a completely decentralized "invisible hand" device for communication. Although at a later stage, the free-of-charge, nonprofit e-mail system, intertwined with more commercial profit-oriented activities, it is still a classical example of a non-Schumpeterian innovation.

    Although, under socialism, competition was eliminated in the centralized, bureaucratically managed civilian economy, the Soviet Union and its allies were deeply involved in the military race with the West, primarily with the United States. This life-and-death competition put the innovative process under sufficient pressure for generating great innovation. The first satellite, the Sputnik, was created by the Soviet Union. The sluggishness of technical progress in the civilian sector was overruled by the overall objectives of the leadership, to keep pace with, or even jump ahead of, the development of the Western military forces. However, when it came to the civilian utilization of a military innovation, the inferiority of the socialist system showed up again. In the United States, pioneering military applications were followed by the use of satellites for civilian purposes, leading to rapid quality and efficiency improvements in all areas of telecommunication. In the Soviet block, the civilian application followed only after a long delay. The example of the satellites demonstrates that focused action in a highly centralized bureaucratic system might produce spectacular results—but without the same strong spillover effect as great innovations appearing in decentralized, entrepreneurial capitalism.

2. In certain instances, important research and, later, the diffusion of the invention are initiated and financed by civilian, nonmilitary sectors of the government, for example, the agencies in charge of medical care. There are good examples in which intelligent, competition-friendly government policy is promoting targeted innovation (for instance, to protect the environment).

3. In several instances, important innovations are initiated, and also executed, by an ad hoc ensemble of researchers, or by associations or nongovernmental and nonprofit organizations. That is how, for example, one of the most significant, truly revolutionary innovations, the World Wide Web started; see the memoirs of the pioneer Berners-Lee (1999). Many other important innovations in the sphere of computers, digital applications, information, and communication started in this civilian, nonprofit, associative way of the non-Schumpeterian innovation.

Notwithstanding the relevance of non-Schumpeterian processes, most breakthrough innovations follow the Schumpeterian path. That is certainly true for the innovations targeted at the market of consumer goods and services for practical use in everyday life. Even the non-Schumpeterian starts are followed typically by many profit-oriented applications, and innovators with a commercial orientation execute the larger share of wide diffusion.

2.4 THE IMPOSSIBILITY OF INNOVATIVE ENTREPRENEURSHIP UNDER SOCIALISM

Moving on to socialism, let us begin by stepping back to the preceding phase of innovation, namely *invention*. Creative minds lived in the socialist countries as well. Excellent scientists and engineers worked there, who made important discoveries and inventions that were of revolutionary significance, with potential to be applied in industry and commerce. The first example is the Soviet physicist Abram Joffe, who is regarded in the history of science as one of the pioneers of semiconductors, which today play a fundamentally important role in the electronics industry. He had already come forward with his discoveries during the 1930s, but the economic environment simply did not allow for the introduction of their industrial applications. Much later, the manufacturing of semiconductors became dominated by the United States, Japan, Taiwan, and South Korea; the Soviet Union trailed behind among the slow followers of the leaders.[20]

Jacek Karpinski, a Polish engineer and scientist invented the first minicomputer between 1971 and 1973. His name is recognized among the great pioneers of computer technology. However, his invention did not become a widely dispersed innovation while he lived on Polish soil. Karpinski later emigrated, and his invention, in competition with similar discoveries, became a widespread innovation in the capitalist world.

The most famous Hungarian example is the story of Rubik's cube. I listed this ingenious toy among the breakthrough innovations, and it certainly has a legitimate place there. The inventor, Ernő Rubik, tried to initiate worldwide distribution, after seeing the enthusiastic reaction of those familiarizing themselves with this intellectual masterpiece, but he had only a rather moderate effect. Later Rubik's cube became a fantastic success when a well-known, truly entrepreneurial American toy company bought it and started worldwide marketing.

---

20. Joffe was first showered with the highest state awards, and received high academic honors, but during the last years of Stalin's terror, he was removed from his high positions as a "Zionist." Whether up or down, his discoveries never turned into a revolutionary innovation.

Even in Hungary only a few know that a Hungarian engineer, Marcell Jánosi, invented the floppy disc, the plastic covered simple data storage device for personal computers used by millions. After inventing it in 1974, Jánosi offered the well-functioning prototype to the Hungarian industry and exporters in vain; the leaders of the socialist industry did not see the great business opportunity in the invention. They felt reluctant to risk mass production and worldwide distribution, and they did not even support the extension of its patent protection. The inventor was not allowed to take the marketing of his intellectual product into his own hands. At the end, a Japanese firm "reinvented" it, and it was there that the innovative process of mass introduction developed.[21]

After these sad stories of frustrated inventors, we turn to the *innovation* phase. Surely, even in the socialist system, many individuals had entrepreneurial talent, but it was lying dormant. Perhaps a large project's leader could, to a certain extent, unfold his talent, provided that he was picked for his position because of his abilities and not his party connections. Still, the inherent characteristics of the system did not allow the development of a Schumpeterian-type entrepreneurship.[22] Let us return, one by one, to the conditions reviewed earlier when discussing capitalism, and study the situation under the socialist system.

A. *Centralization, bureaucratic commands, and permissions.*—The plan of technical innovation is one chapter in the state plan. The central planners set key changes to be carried out regarding the composition and the quality, together with the production technology, of the products. What follows is the disaggregation of the central-plan numbers into plans for sectors, for subsectors, and, at the end, to companies. The "command economy" means, among other things, that firms receive detailed orders about when they should replace one product with a new one, and which old machinery or technology should be replaced with a new one. Before the final approval of the plan, company managers are allowed to make suggestions, so, among other things, they can initiate the adaptation of a new product or a new technology; that is to say, they can join in the process of innovation diffusion. However, they must ask for permission for all significant initiatives. If an action happens to be on large scale, even their immediate superiors cannot decide by themselves, but, instead, they must turn to the higher levels of the hierarchy for approval. The more extensive an initiative is, the higher one has to go for the final decision, and the longer the bureaucratic process preceding the actual action.[23]

---

21. Following his retirement, Marcell Jánosi has been living on a very modest pension. He died in 2012. See the story of the floppy in Kovács (1999) and Drávucz (2004).
22. For empirical studies see the references in note 8 of this essay. For a theoretical explanation, see Berliner (1976); Gomulka (1983); Kornai (1980 and 1992).
23. For a powerful theoretical analysis of the relationship between centralization and innovation, see Qian and Xu (1998).

As opposed to the situation just described, if, in capitalism, a very promising innovation is rejected by the first company, another one may be willing to embrace it. This is made possible by decentralization, private property, and the market. In the centralized socialist economies, the innovative idea follows the official pathways, and in the case of a declared negative decision, no appeal can be made.

B. *No (or only insignificant) reward.*—If the higher authority deems a technical innovation in a factory unit successful, the manager and perhaps his immediate colleagues receive a bonus, an amount equal one or two months of salary, at best.

C. *There is no competition between producers and sellers.*[24]—Production is strongly concentrated. Many companies enjoy monopolist positions, or at least a (regional) monopoly in producing an entire group of products. The chronic shortage of products creates monopolistic behavior even when many producers operate in parallel. The shortage economy, one of the strongest system-specific properties of socialism, paralyzes the forceful engine of innovation, the incentive to fight for the favors of the customer (Kornai 1971; 1980; 1992, chapters 11–12). The producer/seller is not compelled to attract the buyer by offering him a new and better product, since the latter is happy to get anything in the shop, even an obsolete and poor-quality product.

There are examples of inventive activities motivated by chronic shortages: ingeniously created substitutes for missing materials or machinery parts (Laki 1984–1985). These results of the inventors' creative mind, however, do not become widespread, commercially successful innovations in the Schumpeterian sense.[25] Table 2.1 features only one revolutionary innovation that did not appear first in a capitalist country but, rather, in the Soviet Union: synthetic rubber. Its inventor had been doing research on the subject for decades; the employment of it in industry was rendered necessary by the shortage of natural rubber.

D. *The tight limits of experimenting.*—Capitalism allows for hundreds or thousands of barren or barely fruitful attempts, so that, afterward, one out of the hundreds or thousands would succeed and bring immense success. In the socialist planned economy, actors are inclined to avoid risks. As a result, the application of revolutionarily significant innovations are more or less excluded, since those always mean a leap into the dark, as success is necessarily unpredictable. As far as followers are concerned, some economies follow up

---

24. As mentioned before, the defense industry was an exception, because in this area the Soviet empire was in a truly fierce competition with the West.

25. Not only did the socialist system suffer from chronic shortages. During wars, shortages occur in capitalist economies as well. During World War II, the shortage of raw materials spurred innovating activities to develop *Ersatz* (substitute) raw materials.

quickly, others slowly. The socialist economies belong to the group characterized by the slowest pace. They prefer to maintain the already known, old production procedures, and produce the old well-tried products; new technologies and new products have too many uncertain characteristics making the planning of the directives difficult.

E. *There is no capital waiting to be utilized; investment allocation is rigid.*—Central planning is not miserly with the resources devoted to capital formation. The share of investment carved out from the total output is typically higher than in the capitalist economies. However, this enormous volume is appropriated ahead of time to the last penny. Moreover, most of the time over-allocation takes place; in other words, the ensemble of all project plans prescribes the requisition of more resources than the required amount to execute the plan. It never happens that unallocated capital is waiting for someone with a good idea. The allocators do not search for an entrepreneur waiting to step forward with a proposal for innovation. Flexible capital markets are unknown. Instead, the rigid and bureaucratic regulation of project activities takes place, and to devote capital resources to activities with possibly uncertain outcomes is unconceivable. No foolish minister of industry or factory manager could be found who would demand money for ventures admitting in advance that the money may be wasted and the innovation may not succeed.[26]

At this point, it is worth running through points A to E again about the description of the mechanisms of innovation, because these points are actually the consequences of the basic characteristics of the capitalist and the socialist systems. The reviewed phenomena are the direct results of private property and market coordination in one system and of public property and bureaucratic coordination in the other.

I do not claim that a country's pace of technical progress solely depends on its being governed by a capitalist or a socialist system. Numerous other factors play significant roles: the country's state of economic development; the level of education, including the training of researchers; the level and the institutional framework of financing academic research and industrial R&D activity; research financed by the military; and so on. Luck undeniably also plays a role. It was a matter of luck that a company like Nokia appeared in Finland, not Denmark or Norway, and, for a certain period, reached unparalleled success in the diffusion of mobile phones. Certainly outstanding personalities had very great influence on the course of events. Who could say how technical progress would have developed in the absence of a Bill Gates,

---

26. For the analysis of the relationship between flexibility of financing, centralization, and innovation, see Huang and Xu (1998).

a Steve Jobs, or a Mark Zuckerberg?[27] Admitting the relevance of all other explanatory factors, I maintain the proposition: The *system-specific effect* is quite strong.[28]

2.5 POLITICAL FACTORS AND TECHNICAL PROGRESS

The decisive factor explaining the nature of the innovative process is the influence of the system-specific features of the economy, which is, of course, ultimately determined by the political structure of the system. There are, however, several direct linkages between the political structure and technical progress. I will briefly touch on a few linkages.

Communist dictatorship aggressively promoted innovations in the information-communication sphere when it provided efficient technology for political propaganda and, more generally, the spreading of the official ideology. Lenin was among the first political leaders to understand the relevance of the cinema for propaganda purposes. Also, the USSR was among the fastest countries to introduce television broadcasting, because it was a highly centralized medium in the first period, concentrated in a single or only a few studios, and subject to the tough political control of the Party. Also, the program of the radio stations could be easily controlled and transmitted through loudspeakers, even to remote villages.

Radio and television were supported by the communist regime as long as tough central control was feasible. Luckily, as the integrated-circuit (IC) technology developed further, complete centralization and censorship became technically impossible. There was a wall in Berlin that stopped people from crossing the border of the two worlds, but no wall could be built to stop radio and TV waves from moving through the Iron Curtain from West Germany to East Germany, from Munich to the whole of Eastern Europe, and jamming was a poor device to stop the destabilizing impact of Western broadcasts and

---

27. Following the pioneering work by Zvi Griliches (1957), there is rich recent literature discussing the problems of diffusion, leaders, and followers in the innovation process (see, for example, Davila, Epstein, and Shelton, 2006; Freeman and Soate, 2003; Rogers 1995). Rogers' book (1995) is perhaps the most quoted work in the literature written for businessmen and managers interested in the practical issues of innovation. In this otherwise excellent and very carefully written book, the name Schumpeter is not even mentioned, nor is any other *economic* theory of innovation.

28. The experience of the divided Germany is especially instructive. East Germany, beside Czechoslovakia, was the most developed country in the socialist region. It started with an excellent research infrastructure and devoted resources generously to higher education, academic and industrial research. Yet it was not able to step forward with even one breakthrough revolutionary innovation. In spite of having first-rate, highly skilled experts at disposal, the rate of following the pioneering innovations was in most sectors slower than in West Germany (Bauer 1999; Stokes 2000).

TV stations. Among the certainly numerous factors leading to the collapse of the socialist system, one was the technical impossibility of airtight isolation of the Soviet Union and other socialist countries from the voice coming from the rest of the world.

The final turmoil in the socialist block occurred in the period when copying machines, e-mail, and the Internet became available even in this area. Gorbachev called for *glasnost* (openness), and through the open doors of the Internet, e-mail, radio, and TV waves information flowed from abroad, and later also from open-minded awakening domestic citizens in ever larger volume. It had a devastating effect on old dogmas, frozen beliefs, misleading party propaganda, liberating the minds of more and more people (Shane 1994; Kedzie 1997a and 1997b; Stolyarov 2008). Let me come back to the relationship between political structure and technical progress at a later point.

2.6 FIRST SUMMARY: SYSTEMS AND TECHNICAL PROGRESS

Assume for a moment that the vision of Marx, Lenin, and Trotsky had been materialized, and the world-revolution was victorious all over the globe, without a spot of capitalism left. In such a case, we would never have gotten the computer and the transistor radio, the refrigerator and the supermarket, the Internet and the escalator, CD and DVD, digital photography, the mobile phone, and all the other revolutionary technical changes. Our way of life, at least with respect to the use of various devices and equipment, would have more or less stagnated at the standard taken over from the last spots of capitalism before its final defeat.

Therefore, we arrive at fundamental issues of explaining and understanding the long-lasting trends of human history. The technologies (instruments, devices, equipments, and so on) utilized in all activities (not only in production of goods, but in all other individual and social activities) are developed in a complex social process. That complex process is what we call concisely "technical progress." The speed and other properties of technical progress are determined by several factors. The general philosophy underlying this essay (and my other writings) is the following: One of the strongest explanatory factors is the system. A strong causal relationship is working between the type of system (capitalism or socialism) as one of the *causes*, and the speed and other properties of technical progress as the *effect*.

I am using the concept of technical progress as generally accepted by the whole economics profession. We must be aware that the second word, *progress*, has an appreciative or even laudatory sound, as it reflects a value judgment: it is better to live in a world with automatic dishwashers, mobile phones, and CDs than in a world without those products. But is it really better? Nobody, even the most enthusiastic fans of modern technology would reply with a simple yes without qualifications and reservations. Since the invention of fire and the knife all new instruments and technologies have been used for both good and evil purposes. It is a trivial, but still extremely important, fact of life that the latest great wave of technical progress, namely the headlong development in the sphere of computers, electronics, digital instruments, and modern technologies of information and communication can serve criminals, sex offenders, terrorists, and extremist political movements, also opening new technology for tricky advertising to mislead or, at least, to bother people. The substitution of the work of human beings by robots can lead to the dehumanization of various activities and contacts. Sitting in front of the screen of the computer or TV day and night can distract children and adults from more worthy studies and entertainment. Technical progress has been and will be used not only for peaceful, but also for military activities, and not only for defense of the homeland but for aggression as well. Yet, the majority of people, myself included, call the direction of technical changes *progress*, because it brings many more benefits than drawbacks or dangers (see the survey results that prove this to be the majority opinion, later).

Based on this value judgment, I regard the promoting impact of capitalism on technical progress as one of the greatest virtues of that system, and the retarding impact of socialism on technical progress as one of the greatest vices of that other system.

SECTION 3

Transformation and the Acceleration of Technical Progress

Entering the world of capitalism, all postsocialist countries have opened the door for entrepreneurship, pathbreaking innovations, the fast diffusion of new products and new technologies. The change of the basic features of the economy has created the conditions for the acceleration of technical progress in this part of the world.

When formulating the above sentences I tried to be cautious. Capitalism has a built-in propensity for entrepreneurship, innovation, and dynamism. However, this is just a propensity, an inclination, a disposition—not more than that. It is not like a law of physics, which *must* materialize. Subsection 2.3 of this essay, discussing innovation under capitalism, underlines that beside the decisive impact of system-specific factors, other circumstances also exert a significant influence. The diversity of these other, non-system-specific factors explains the differences in the speed of the innovative process between various transition economies. As entrepreneurship, innovation, and dynamism come to life through human action, it is the social, political, and legal environment created by human beings that influence how far and how quickly the propensity is breaking through. It depends on the business climate, and it depends, to a large extent, on the courage, inspiration, and competence of individuals who might become entrepreneurs.

3.1 NEW INNOVATOR ENTREPRENEURS

Let us start with innovations introducing revolutionary new products. The first example is Skype, listed among the great revolutionary innovations in Table 2.1. The core of the invention, the software, was developed in Estonia, the programmers Ahti Heinla, Priit Kasesalu, and Jaan Tallinn are celebrated people in their home country. Although the leading innovators, Niklas Zennström and Janus Friis, are Swedish and Danish, respectively, the company launching the worldwide distribution was registered originally in Estonia. The software team of the company is still working there. Following the criteria applied in this essay, it might be regarded as an Estonian innovation. It was so successful that, first, the USA-based eBay paid a huge price for the pioneering company when it took Skype over. Later Microsoft bought the company.

Let me bring a second example from the success stories of the fast developing Chinese automobile industry. Cars using alternative energy sources instead of petroleum products are attracting ever-increasing attention, and the Chinese BYD automobile giant is more and more successful in this market. Although other companies have tried to construct electric or hybrid buses and cars, BYD is regarded by many as the company reaching a real breakthrough in introducing these environment-friendly vehicles into public transport. The Chinese firm is listed among the 50 most innovative companies in the FAST world list.

The third, less spectacular, but still remarkable example is the story of the Hungarian high-tech company Graphisoft. The inventor-innovator, Gábor Bojár, a former senior fellow in an academic research institute, created a program for three-dimensional design targeted for utilization mainly by architects (Bojár 2007). Although not unique in the field, compared with other products, his software is elegant, efficient, and, therefore, commercially successful in several countries. Bojár's company is marketing the product worldwide. This is a classical example of a Schumpeterian entrepreneurial career. What a difference there is between the stories of the two Hungarians: floppy disc inventor Jánosi not succeeding in the pre-1989 era, remaining poor and virtually unknown, and Graphisoft creator Bojár reaching fame, reputation, and a big fortune.

The fourth story is about data-recovery from damaged hard disks. It starts also in Kádár-era Hungary, characterized by halfway market reforms. At the time, there were already quite a few computers around, but they were rather expensive in the Hungarian environment. If a computer breaks down, the most valuable part, the hard drive, should not be dumped. It is worthwhile to restore it and make it ready for use in another computer, put together from used parts. Two brothers, János and Sándor Kürti acquire special skills in the restoration of hard drives. Then came the creative idea: the same skill could be used if the data stored on the hard disk got lost. Everybody knows the traumatic feeling of losing a large amount of data on their computer. The Kürtis learned the technique, or more precisely the art, of conjuring data believed to be lost forever from the damaged disk. After 1989, this very special knowledge became a marketable service, and the Kürti brothers founded a company and trained several experts in their art. They now have customers all over the world (Kürti and Fabiány 2008; Laki 2009), making theirs another story of highly successful Schumpeterian innovators.

My fifth example is about Prezi, a new Hungarian company. Oral presentations of all kinds were illustrated for their audiences with texts, formulae, and simple figures drawn on boards in "ancient times." As technology was developing, that was replaced by slides, later by texts and pictures projected with a mechanical projector, and recently by the computer-controlled Powerpoint slides. Prezi is a rival of Powerpoint, but with Prezi we can zoom in and out on texts and pictures, according to the structure of our presentation, on the basis of the Internet-downloadable program. The innovation was developed by Hungarian researchers, and an originally Hungarian firm, which is now international, distributes it widely, winning several high-status international awards.

Although three of the five examples come from Hungary, due to my personal connections with people familiar with those cases, I am convinced that there are many similar stories in other postsocialist countries.

3.2 THE ACCELERATION OF FOLLOW-UP AND DIFFUSION

As postsocialist economies were moving forward in enlarging the private sector and creating the institutions of market co-ordination, technical progress accelerated in many ways, including the faster follow-up of innovations introduced elsewhere. The increasing openness of formerly isolationist national markets and the competition of imported goods create a pressure on producers and service providers. This influence is one of the important forces encouraging innovation.[1]

The need for access to a telephone line has been self-evident to everyone in the West in the last decades, and not the least so for citizens of socialist countries, where telephone service has always been in very short supply, reserved for the privileged and provided for others only after a waiting period of several years. There were not enough lines, because planners assigned it a low priority and allocated resources to other sectors. As long as socialism prevailed, it seemed to be hopeless to change the relationship of supply and demand in the telephone service. Then followed the shift from the socialist to the capitalist system and together with it the situation completely reversed in the telephone sector. Table 3.1 shows that, in a relatively short time, old-style land line phone service became accessible to everyone. In addition, a revolutionary new product, the mobile phone conquered the phone market[2] (see Tables 3.2–3.4).

---

1. This cause–effect relationship between import competition and innovation is confirmed by a convincing econometric study by Gorodnichenko, Svejnar, and Terrel (2010).
2. In some countries, for example, in Hungary, it has not only stopped the further increase of cable-connected phone service, but has actually started to replace it in many households.

Table 3.1. TELEPHONE LINES: COMPARATIVE DATA (NUMBER OF LINES PER 1,000 PEOPLE)

Year	Bulgaria	Hungary	Poland	Romania	Soviet Union (Russia)	Greece	Italy
1979	91	52	53	67	67	226	217
1980	102	58	55	73	70	235	232
1985	167	70	67	86	102	314	306
1990	247	96	87	102	140	389	393
1995	307	209	149	131	168	484	436
2000	360	372	286	176	219	515	476
2005	322	339	310	201	279	564	427
2010	297	298	200	209	314	517	355

Sources: United Nations Statistics Division (2009b) for data before 2005, and the World Bank (2012) for data related to 2010.

Table 3.2. PENETRATION OF MODERN COMMUNICATION TECHNOLOGY IN EU COUNTRIES: 15 OLD EU MEMBER STATES (EU15) VERSUS 10 NEW POSTSOCIALIST MEMBER STATES (EU10)

Indicator	Unit of measurement	Group	1995	2001	2007
GDP	per capita, constant 2000 USD	EU15	19,706	23,747	26,781
		EU10	3,469	4,425	6,295
GDP	per capita, PPP, constant 2005 USD	EU15	25,831	31,134	35,058
		EU10	9,758	12,286	17,570
Personal computers	per 100 people	EU15	16	35	37
		EU10	3	12	33
Internet users	per 100 people	EU15	3	32	64
		EU10	1	14	48
Broadband subscribers	per 100 people	EU15	NA	2	24
		EU10	NA	0	12
Mobile phone subscriptions	per 100 people	EU15	7	77	116
		EU10	1	40	118

Note: Figures are simple means for each country group. For missing data (NA), see source.
Source: World Bank (2008).

Table 3.3. PENETRATION OF MODERN COMMUNICATION TECHNOLOGY IN EU COUNTRIES: FIVE VISEGRÁD COUNTRIES (V5) VERSUS THREE SOUTH EUROPEAN COUNTRIES (S3)

Indicator	Unit of measurement	Group	1995	1997	1999	2001	2003	2005	2007	2009	2011
GDP	per capita, constant 2000 USD	S3	10 475	11 105	11 959	12 745	13 164	13 649	14 349	13 743	13 241
		V5	5 029	5 439	5 800	6 205	6 660	7 318	8 231	8 044	8 379
GDP	per capita, PPP, constant 2005 USD	S3	18 716	19 845	21 371	22 772	23 510	24 370	25 618	24 540	23 646
		V5	12 646	13 630	14 495	15 524	16 665	18 335	20 570	20 134	21 015
Personal computers	per 100 people	S3	5	7	9	14	15	17	28		
		V5	4	6	9	12	18	23	39		
Internet users	per 100 people	S3	1	3	10	16	29	36	44	50	59
		V5	1	3	7	16	31	43	55	58	66
Broadband subscribers	per 100 people	S3	NA	NA	0	1	3	8	14	16	22
		V5	NA	NA	0	0	1	6	13	16	15
Mobile phone subscriptions	per 100 people	S3	3	12	40	74	88	100	115	113	112
		V5	1	5	18	51	75	91	111	115	117

Note: Figures are simple averages for each country group. Visegrád countries (V5): the Czech Republic, Hungary, Poland, Slovakia, and Slovenia; South European countries (S3): Greece, Portugal, and Spain.
Source: World Bank (2012).

Table 3.4. PENETRATION OF MODERN COMMUNICATION TECHNOLOGY IN RUSSIA AND SOME OTHER COUNTRIES

Indicator	Unit of measurement	Country	1995	2001	2007
GDP	per capita, USD	Russia	1,618	1,870	2,858
		Brazil	3,611	3,696	4,222
		Mexico	4,892	5,864	6,543
GDP	per capita PPP	Russia	7,853	9,076	13,873
		Brazil	7,727	7,910	9,034
		Mexico	9 949	11 927	13 307
Personal computers	per 100 people	Russia	2	8	NA
		Brazil	2	6	NA
		Mexico	3	7	NA
Internet users	per 100 people	Russia	0	3	21
		Brazil	0	5	35
		Mexico	0	7	23
Broadband subscribers	per 100 people	Russia	NA	0	3
		Brazil	NA	0	4
		Mexico	NA	0	4
Mobile phone subscriptions	per 100 people	Russia	0	5	115
		Brazil	1	16	63
		Mexico	1	22	63

Source: World Bank (2008).

The penetration of these services occurred at great speed (Cooper 2009). Because the use of the phone has become unconstrained on the supply side, nowadays only the demand constraint is effective.

The clear causal relationship between capitalism and the abundant supply of the phone service is present on several levels. The transition to private ownership based on the liberalized market economy put an end to the shortage economy. Phone service is supplied because domestic or foreign entrepreneurs profit from this business. Because of the close substitutability of the cable-connected telephone by mobile phones, the cable-connected phones cannot remain a monopoly. On the contrary, we witness a fierce rivalry among phone companies. Thirty years ago in the Soviet Union or in Eastern Europe the would-be customer begged the bureaucracy for the great favor of getting a phone line. Nowadays phone companies are bidding for the favor of the customer.

I, for one, remember well my own troubles due to the lack of a phone line in my home, and I am grateful to postsocialist transition and to capitalism for the fact that I now have a phone at home, and all members of my family have their own phones. I am grateful for the improved chances of technical progress due to the change of the system. I know that *gratitude* is a word missing from the vocabulary of economics and political science. Yet, I want to use exactly that term because it clearly reflects not only my rational understanding of a positive causal relationship between capitalism and innovation in general, and the shift toward capitalism and the availability of phone services in particular, but also a strong emotion toward the post-1989 changes. In spite of all shortcomings and lost battles, the advent of capitalism made possible all the products of technical progress that are finally available to us, the citizens of the postsocialist region.

Tables 3.2–3.4 show similar results for several other, and no less important, diffusion processes: the use of computers, access to the Internet, and so on. The speed of following the pioneering countries has accelerated quite spectacularly.

Numerous entrepreneurs have taken the role of the pioneer—the first person on a world-wide scale to introduce a revolutionary innovation and adapt an idea to the actual local circumstances and achieve great successes. The followers may be regarded as Schumpeterian innovators as well. One of them is the Chinese businessman Ma Yun, the founder and leader of the Alibaba Group. The main activity of the companies belonging to his group is business-to-business trade over the Internet, especially trading between small companies. The Alibaba Group is now the largest company of that sector in China, and one of the largest in the world. Ma Yun started as a high school teacher and became a multi-billionaire.[3] The story of Alibaba is a spectacular success story, but hundreds of other impressive innovation stories have evolved in China, Russia, and in other countries of the postsocialist world.

To sum up, the time gap between the most developed countries and the postsocialist countries has not disappeared, but is narrower now than it was in the socialist era when the gap typically increased over time.[4]

3.3 CREATIVE DESTRUCTION

The process of innovation and the dynamics of firms' entry into and exit are closely associated. Schumpeter coined the name "creative destruction" for the latter, describing concisely and precisely the two inseparable sides of

---

3. See http://www.alibaba.com (company information).
4. According to the Information Society Index, reflecting the development of various aspects of "information society" in a synthetic way, several postsocialist countries (for example, the Czech Republic, Hungary, and Slovenia) have achieved a decent position in the ranking (Karvalics 2009). The whole group of countries observed is moving ahead, and it is getting higher values each year, though it takes strong efforts just to hold the rank achieved today.

fast technical progress. It is easy to appreciate happy arrivals to the business world, especially if they appear in the form of successful innovations. But there is no fast progress without the sad events of bankruptcies, business failure, exits from the field, and the accompanying bitter phenomena of lay-offs and unemployment.

Transition economies have had the bad fortune of experiencing two big waves of creative destruction. I called the first one, occurring in the early 1990s, "transformational recession" in an earlier article (Kornai 1993). It caused trauma in all postsocialist countries, leading to a huge number of exits and creating the first shock of mass unemployment after decades of overemployment and job security. The present recession (2009–) is not yet over, but—looking with some degree of optimism into the near future—it will probably lead to a smaller fall of production than the decline of output under the transformational recession. That was probably one of the deepest recessions in economic history, but the world paid less attention to it than to the present crisis because we, the citizens of the former communist region, were the only victims of the transformational recession, and the rest of the world did not share the painful experience.

The transformational recession carried a dreadfully high price tag of suffering, but it created benefits as well. It compelled quick adjustments to a radical shift in the composition of the internal and external market, and also cleared the way for more dynamism, more innovation, and higher productivity. Many obsolete production lines, smoky and rusty factories, and poorly supplied shops disappeared, and brand new production units, located in modern buildings equipped with the latest technology, and new supermarkets and shopping centers appeared. Well-organized data are available on business entry and exit in the postsocialist area. The article by Bartelsman, Haltiwanger, and Scarpetta (2004) provides a careful report and analysis, based on firm-level data, of the process of creative destruction across 24 countries, including several transition countries: Estonia, Hungary, Latvia, Romania, and Slovenia. We present here only one diagram for the sake of illustration (see Figure 3.1), covering firms with at least 20 employees in the 1990s.

In the first years of transition, the number of entries was much larger than the number of exits, which was different from more mature market economies in which the difference of these two flows is usually smaller or negative. Many large (formerly state-owned) companies went out of business, and small business entered in huge numbers. Total firm turnover (the ratio of exit and entry) was between 3 and 8 percent in most industrial countries, and more than 10 percent in some of the transition economies in the 1990s.

The turbulence caused by the fast turnover and short lifespan of newly created firms later calmed down. By the end of the 1990s, the characteristic demographical data of the firm population came fairly close to those observed in other countries. Figure 3.2 shows the trend toward a more balanced ratio

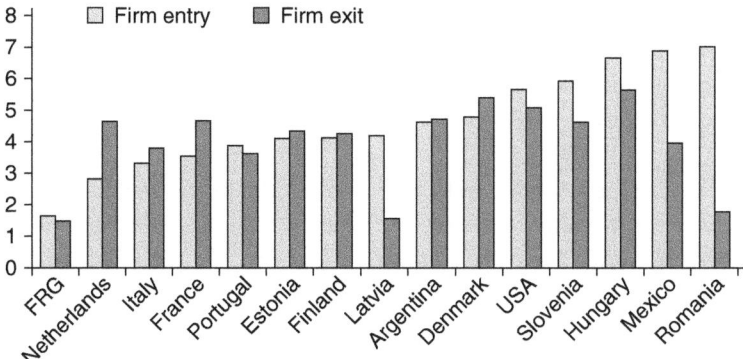

Figure 3.1.
Firms' entry and exit rates in the 1990s
Note: Columns in light gray show the entry rates, defined as the number of new firms divided by the total number of incumbent and entrant firms in a given year. Columns in dark gray show the exit rates, defined as the number of firms exiting the market in a given year divided by the population of origin, that is, the incumbents in the previous year.
Source: Bartelsman et al. (2004, 16: Figure 1, Panel C).

between entry and exit. The gray line is approaching the zero position, where the numbers of employee-weighted entry and exit rates cancel each other out. It took several years to get over the worst phase of the destructive side of the Schumpeterian process. Postsocialist economies started to grow with increased efficiency, producing a much more up-to-date output mix, when

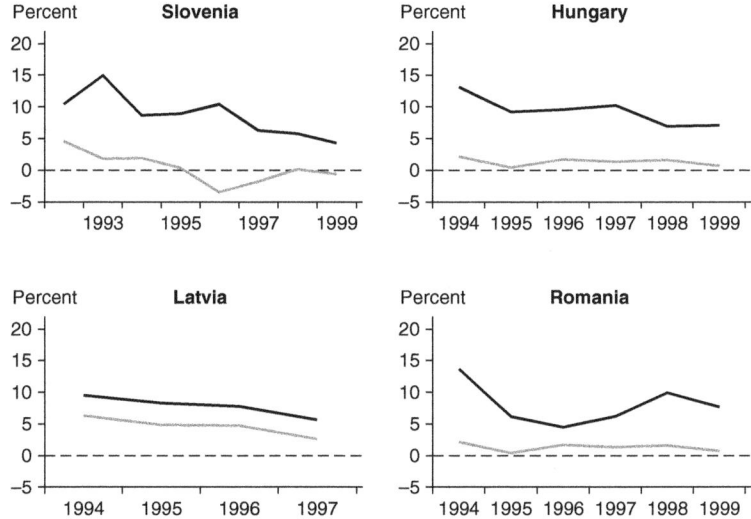

Figure 3.2.
The evolution of gross and net firm flows in transition economies
Note: The calculations cover the whole business sector. The black line shows the total turnover (entry rate plus exit rate), the gray line the net flow (entry rate minus exit rate).
Source: Bartelsman et al. (2004, 17: Figure 2, Panel B).

suddenly a new external shock, the impact of the global recession, shook the economy. The people of the postsocialist region are going through a second painful recession. It is quite understandable that nowadays the word "capitalism" does not resonate pleasantly in the ears of the citizens of postsocialist countries.

It is too early to ask the question of whether the present recession—beside causing disturbance and suffering—will have a cleansing effect in the Schumpeterian sense. Will the destruction clear the way for more construction in the postsocialist region? Ten or more years from now will provide sufficient evidence to answer that question. It would require a separate long study to discuss the policy implications of the positive description provided earlier. What I can do here is just offer a few hints at policy options and the dilemmas associated with the choice between the options.

1. Accepting the basic Schumpeterian idea of creative destruction does not imply an automatic approval of all specific manifestations of destruction. If the blind market forces lead to the exit of a firm, some organizations (the central or local government, the financial sector, or some other entities) might consider a bailout. Here, we are in the middle of a huge area of theoretical and practical problems discussed in the literature on the soft budget constraint and moral hazard. I have discussed this issue in several articles (Kornai, Maskin, and Roland 2003; Kornai 2009b). At this point, I want to add only one remark: the Schumpeterian process of innovation is accompanied by the spectacularly rapid growth of exactly the sectors and subsectors that are the most promising and most "fashionable" (remember the mass entry and tumultuous growth of dot-com firms). This process has inevitably two sides: Many projects are needed for the few great successes, and, at the same time, we may get too many of them. If that occurs, "natural selection" follows, and we must not fight for the survival of each species destined for extinction. Policymakers might posit strong arguments in favor of certain bailouts, for example, to protect the economy as a whole from far-reaching serious macroeconomic damage caused by excessive numbers of exits. However, the counterarguments must be also carefully considered.

2. The debate about the causes of the recent recession is ongoing. A well-known train of thought refers to the easy-going lending policy of the financial sector and is calling for much more rigorous, more conservative lending rules in the future. I do not reject this line of thinking, but I must add a warning. The Schumpeterian process of innovation requires relatively easy access to capital for risky projects that might fail or might lead to the fantastic achievements of technical progress (see points D and E in the earlier survey of circumstances, presented in subsection 2.3, necessary to the Schumpeterian process of innovation). The general mood calls for

caution and stronger risk-aversion than before the recession. I agree that more caution is needed than before but it would be a fatal mistake to apply a very conservative attitude blindly. Lending criteria should be carefully differentiated so as to leave the chances for financing risky but promising innovative projects open.

3. We hear loud calls for regulation and warnings against the unfettered rule of market forces. These calls and warnings are legitimate, up to a certain limit. Beyond that, we might enter the area of overregulation, the bureaucratic obstacles of starting businesses, which can dampen the vigor of the entrepreneurial spirit. Moreover, in quite a few postsocialist countries, it is still a difficult obstacle race to start a business (see the 2009 report of the World Bank and the International Finance Corporation, *Doing Business*). Policymakers should avoid both types of mistake; going too far in deregulation, or introducing too much (and/or ill-targeted) regulation.

4. The public mood is upset because of skyrocketing earnings of many business people and top managers. We hear calls for practical measures against this phenomenon. Although the anger is morally justified and psychologically understandable, nevertheless an (unpopular) caveat is needed. One of the conditions of the Schumpeterian process (condition B in the listing in subsection 2.3) is the gigantic reward in the case of success. Not simply a large, but a huge, reward. Only that encourages the would-be innovators to take the large risk of failure. Let us remember that, in this context, not only the first pioneers of introducing the great breakthrough inventions deserve the name "innovators"; the entrepreneurs who are quick to follow the (domestic or foreign) pioneers also do. On the other hand, how difficult it is to imagine the work of an honest and competent jury that is able to draw the line between a well-deserved and an undeservedly high reward. I am not prepared to propose a practical decision, but just want to draw the attention to the two (mutually contradictory) aspects of very high business income.

SECTION 4

Reflection of Historical Reality in People's Minds

4.1 THE BASIC PHENOMENON: LACK OF UNDERSTANDING

In the preceding Section 3, I described the historical reality of the interaction between the Great Transformation, that is, the change of the system, and technical progress. Allowing for errors in the description, I am convinced about its basic accuracy, supported by sufficient evidence. We have to separate the description of historical reality and the reflection of that reality in people's minds. The reflexive process works differently in different people. The reality described in the earlier sections is perceived, understood, and evaluated differently by each individual, depending on his/her social status, education, personal history and character.

The first question we must raise is about the evaluation of technical progress. Do people regard the past and future appearance of inventions and innovations, new products, and new technologies as advancement or are they afraid of the process and regard it as harmful or dangerous? The question has been asked in some international surveys; Tables 4.1 and 4.2 give us interesting insights. Considering benefits and harms caused by technical progress, two thirds of Polish and Hungarian respondents find the positive effect stronger than the negative. In that respect, a larger proportion of citizens of these two postsocialist countries are in favor of technical progress than in Austria, Finland, Italy, and Spain, and in the postsocialist Czech Republic. The proportion of respondents approving technical progress is much higher when the question is about the future impact (see the fifth column of Table 4.1 and the first column of Table 4.2).

The second question aims not at the evaluation but at causality. I take the risk and start with a bold general conjecture. The majority of citizens in the

Table 4.1. EVALUATION OF TECHNICAL PROGRESS

	Scientific and technological progress will help to cure diseases such as AIDS, cancer, etc.	Thanks to science and technology, there will be greater opportunities for future generations	Science and technology make our lives healthier, easier and more comfortable	Science and technology will help eliminate poverty and hunger around the world	The benefits of science are greater than the harmful effects it could have
AT	82	71	71	33	48
FIN	89	77	77	21	50
IT	82	73	76	50	57
SP	79	66	73	37	57
CZ	85	74	70	35	44
HU	94	81	79	34	63
PL	89	93	83	45	65

Note: The following question was asked: "Do you agree with the following statements?" The table shows the proportions of positive answers in percent of the total number of respondents. AT = Austria, FIN = Finland, IT = Italy, SP = Spain, PL = Poland, HU = Hungary, CZ = Czech Republic.
Source: Eurobarometer (2005).

Table 4.2. EXPECTATIONS CONCERNING THE IMPACT OF NEW TECHNOLOGIES (PERCENT)

Country	Solar energy	Computers and information technology	Biotechnology and genetic engineering	The Internet	Mobile phones	New energy sources to power cars	Air transport
EU15	90	85	63	77	67	90	79
EU10	84	87	64	81	70	86	79
Germany	95	89	65	75	57	92	72
UK	91	92	65	81	61	90	80
Hungary	87	87	74	78	67	81	75
Poland	89	92	63	86	80	88	88
Romania	78	86	65	82	75	84	85

Note: The following question was asked: "Do you think the following new technologies will have positive, negative, or neutral effects?" Only the proportions of positive answers are shown.
Source: Eurobarometer (2005).

postsocialist region do not understand the basic causal relationship between capitalism and technological progress. Although the innovations of the last 50–100 years, and, in particular, the revolutionary change of information and communication technology, has dramatically changed everyone's life, and most people enjoy the advantages of fast technological change, they do not attribute this great change to capitalism.[1]

On the contrary, a large part of the population has moderate or even vehement anti-capitalist feelings. Although they take advantage of the mobile phone, the Internet, the bar code in the supermarket, plastic materials and synthetic fibers, modern household appliances, the Xerox copier, and so on, they do not acknowledge that almost all of them are creations of the despised or hated capitalist system. That is conjecture, and, to my regret, I cannot refer to one single survey, public opinion pole, or value survey supporting, correcting, or refuting that conjecture.[2] Among the hundreds of more or less relevant questions asked of the informants, nobody ever asked in any form the question formulated here: What do you think and how do you feel about the interaction between the overall system (capitalism, socialism, transition from socialism to capitalism) on the one hand, and technical progress, on the other?

Let me maintain the conjecture until we get the first survey data providing a reliable insight into people's minds concerning these questions and the results call for the modification of the conjecture. The lack of surveys seems, in some strange way, an indirect support of my conjecture. If professional researchers studying social change and people's sentiments vis-á-vis the changes completely ignore this set of questions, then what can we expect from the average citizen? The complete lack of surveys related to these vital issues is a clear indication of intellectual indifference toward the understanding of the relationship between the political and economic sphere and the acceleration of technical progress. Public opinion is shaped by a complex social process. Everyone takes part in it—the parents and the teachers in the kindergarten and the primary school, our neighbors at home, and our colleague at the workplace. I would make a few remarks about professional groups carrying special responsibility for shaping public opinion.

---

1. In subsection 3.2, I spoke about the shortage of telephone lines under socialism and the abundant supply after 1989, and I made a subjective remark: I am *grateful* to capitalism for this change of my life. Perhaps I am not the only one who has this feeling, but I am afraid, we are a small minority.

2. With the help of my assistant Dániel Róna, we tried to review the most respected surveys carefully. We checked the four best-known transnational surveys looking for the question formulated in the text and did not find anything resembling the content of that question. The results of these surveys are on record and available from the author.

4.2 THE RESPONSIBILITY OF THE ECONOMIC PROFESSION

What do we teach students? The exciting and important new current of growth theory, inspired to a large extent by Schumpeter (Aghion and Howitt 1998; Grossman and Helpman 1991), is acknowledged to be worth studying by the rest of the profession, and respect for the theory is usually expressed in a polite footnote but without profoundly penetrating the thinking of mainstream economics. Highly distinguished economists put a heavy emphasis on entrepreneurship in explaining the virtues of capitalism (Baumol 2002; Baumol, Litan, and Schramm 2007; Phelps 2008). The recent representatives of the Austrian school (see, for example, Kirzner 1985, 119–149) never tire of drawing attention to the innovative nature of spontaneous market forces. Economists specializing in comparative economics and the study of socialist and postsocialist economies draw attention to the strong causal relationship between the specific properties of a system and the characteristics of technical progress; an excellent example is given by Balcerowicz (1995, chapter 6). Nevertheless, these valuable ideas do not penetrate, via courses on microeconomics, to the routine education of young economists.

There is a simple but decisive test for what we should teach students: let us check the most influential introductory textbooks. Consider Gregory Mankiw's (2009) textbook, which is one of the most widely used texts in the United States, and it is also translated into several languages. It is used as a textbook in my country, Hungary, as well. It is a masterpiece in didactics, well written, full of interesting illustrations of the main propositions. Yet, not a single sentence on the Schumpeterian innovative process can be found! There are several dozen names in the index, but Schumpeter's name does not appear. There are a few pallid paragraphs about the increase of factor productivity and technical progress, but that does not compensate for the lack of the vivid description of the innovative process and the profound explanation of the dynamism of capitalism.

With the help of my research assistant, Judit Hürkecz, we checked seven other popular introductory textbooks, widely used in teaching in the United States and Europe, including Hungary and other postsocialist countries.[3] Every remark made on Mankiw's book applies exactly to almost all other books as well. Out of the small sample of eight books, there is only one exception.[4]

3. The list of these textbooks is on record, and available upon request from the author.
4. Small wonder that the exception in our sample is the work of Baumol and Blinder (2009). William Baumol is one of the intellectual leaders advocating a Schumpeterian approach in understanding capitalism. At the beginning of this subsection I have cited names of distinguished economists who are perfectly aware of the role of entrepreneurship and the Schumpeterian approach. If these scholars (and a few others accepting a similar view of the capitalist economy) are teaching microeconomics, they certainly do not ignore the explanation of the innovative process and the role of the capitalist system in generating breakthrough innovations.

Let me add a reservation. I focus here only on *introductory texts,* because they play a crucial role in the formation of the thinking of students; they do the "imprinting" of the conditional reflexes and automatisms of the thought process.

Our small sample is, of course, not representative. It is beyond the limits of my present research and this First Essay to analyze a large and representative sample of textbooks and draw the appropriate conclusions. Until I do not meet well-substantiated refusal, I maintain the hypothesis claiming that a large (probably dominant) part of the higher education introducing students to the principles of economics does not explain this highly important system-specific property of capitalism sufficiently.

Mainstream economics is often accused of advertising the favorable properties of capitalism. If so, it is doing a rather poor job in teaching by failing to mention that one of the main virtues of the system is its inclination toward unstoppable innovation.

The gross domestic product (GDP) has become the dominant indicator when it comes to the measurement of growth. It is a great achievement of economists and statisticians to have an operational definition and methodology for measuring GDP, uniformly accepted all over the world. However, the success of this measure has generated some kind of laziness in evaluating the successes and failures of the development process. Attention is focused on GDP growth rates to an exaggerated extent. Perhaps, a few other indicators also get attention: inflation, fiscal balance, the current account, measures of inequality, and a few more, but there are no widely accepted and regularly observed indicators of measuring success or failure, acceleration or deceleration of technical progress—understanding the term *technical progress* in the spirit of this study. Postsocialist economies in Eastern Central Europe reached the pre-1990 level of GDP around 1994–2000, and the successor states of the Soviet Union even later; some are still below that level. In the meantime, the way of life has completely changed for a large part of the population. Here, in the context of this essay, I do not refer to the changes in the political environment, income distribution, and social mobility. Besides all these very important changes, I refer to the accelerated use of new products and new technologies in people's everyday lives that are created by the capitalist innovative process. We lament problems with the level of the GDP, but a large part of the population is now connected to the rest of the society by phone and the Internet, a much larger number of people have cars and modern household appliances. and use several other new products formerly available to people in the West only. We should elaborate appropriate indicators and measurement methods to reach a more correct observation and demonstration of the effects of technical progress on everyday life.

The need to complement the measurement of GDP with other indicators to reflect other aspects of welfare and development is well known to every economist and economic statistician. Important new initiatives are emerging to improve the measurement of growth, and are complementing the data on aggregate output with various indicators of health, education, income distribution, and so on.[5] I am worried that the aspect highlighted in this essay—the impact of technical progress on the way of life—may still not receive sufficient attention in the course of reforming statistics.

4.3 THE RESPONSIBILITY OF POLITICIANS

Politicians are, self-evidently, in charge of governmental policy. Everything mentioned earlier with respect to the policy implications of the analysis belongs to the competence of political decision makers. Right now, however, I will make a few remarks about another aspect of political activity. Political leaders are also educators of their nations.

With the help of Tibor Meszmann and a few colleagues, we read some public speeches of political leaders of Bulgaria, Croatia, the Czech Republic, Hungary, Poland, Serbia, Slovakia, and Slovenia. In each country, we chose the speeches or writings of the head of state and/or the prime minister, and the leader(s) of the most influential opposition party (or parties). We tried to select speeches or written statements offering a general overview of the country's successes and failures (like the State of the Union address in the United States), mostly delivered at the occasions of national holidays and events. Most of the texts we analyzed were delivered during the first eight months of 2009. In some cases, we were able to find speeches celebrating the 20th anniversary of the 1989 events, and providing an overall evaluation of the postsocialist transition.[6]

The general finding is easy to summarize. Of the 53 speeches and political statements, there was not a single one explaining the *causal linkage* between capitalism and technical progress and the impact of this progress on people's lives. This virtue of capitalism was not spelled out in order to convince people that moving from socialism to capitalism meant a shift to the world of innovation, modernization, and dynamism.

Some political leaders say a few words about technical progress. The same politicians or some others speak favorably about the capitalist system. However, we did not find the argument just explained in their speeches. The sample of 53 statements is large enough to spell out loudly that this is a shocking and disappointing observation. We observe, here, not the conduct of radical

---

5. A group of economists and statisticians, headed by Joseph Stiglitz, Amartya Sen, and Jean-Paul Fitoussi worked on new proposals for improving the measurement of growth and development (see the report Stiglitz, Sen, and Fitoussi 2009).

6. The list of documents studied is on record and available from the author.

anticapitalist political figures from the extreme right or the extreme left, but of leaders of the political "establishment" in Eastern Europe. They are either in the government or the opposition, but they are certainly friends and not enemies of capitalism, and yet, they miss one of the best arguments in favor of the system. Let us add immediately, very few are ready to take a stand for capitalism. It is becoming quite common among politicians (both on the left and on the right) to emphasize the dark side of the system, and speak out against it.

Certainly, more political speeches and written statements should be checked. I would welcome any counterexamples, that is, speeches by politicians emphasizing the role of capitalism in generating innovation and adding the acceleration of technical progress to the list of successes achieved in the era of transition. However, as long as it is not refuted, I maintain the proposition: Politicians at all points of the political spectrum carry heavy responsibility for neglecting the explanation of the causal relationship "capitalism → innovation → changes in the way of life." Understanding this crucial linkage would be an effective antidote to anticapitalist sentiments—and our political leaders do not provide that antidote.

Neglect is, of course, the milder sin. What I find most irritating is populist demagoguery against capitalism, by those who make practical use of all the discoveries and innovations generated by capitalism. It is morally repulsive to see political activists mobilizing people for an extremist anticapitalist meeting or demonstration using a personal computer, mobile phones, and communication channels provided by satellites and optic fiber. That is happening in the postsocialist region. Political activists, denying even the simple fact that the change of system has already happened, put their populist anticapitalist slogans on a blog or website, give inflammatory speeches to a mob through electronic loudspeakers, and communicate with each other via mobile phones, thus exploiting the technique generated by capitalism.

4.4 INTERCONNECTIVITY AND DEMOCRACY

Although we know practically nothing about the comprehension and evaluation of the "capitalism → innovation → changes in the way of life" causal linkage in people's minds, we have some insights into the opposite direction of interaction, namely, the effect of technical progress (or more precisely, of progress in the information and communication technology sector) on the political views of people in postsocialist countries. Tables 4.3–4.5 summarize survey data on postsocialist area respondents' attitudes toward democracy, capitalism, and the former socialist system. In the tabulations presented here, the population was divided into two classes: people using and not using the

Table 4.3. SATISFACTION WITH THE CURRENT SYSTEM: POPULATION DIVIDED INTO USERS AND NONUSERS OF THE INTERNET

Country	Internet users		Nonusers	
	Mean	%	Mean	%
Central and Eastern Europe	2.6	30	2.8	70
Czech Republic	2.5	42	2.8	57
Hungary*	2.2	23	2.4	77
Poland	2.7	34	2.9	66
Russia	3.0	14	3.1	86
Slovenia	2.2	57	2.1	43

Note: The second and fourth columns contain the percentage of users and nonusers of the Internet, respectively. The following question was asked: "How satisfied are you with the way democracy works?" Answers were expected on a four-degree scale: 1 = completely satisfied; 2 = somewhat satisfied; 3 = not very satisfied; 4 = completely dissatisfied. The table shows the mean (not weighted).
* I have reservations concerning the Hungarian data on Internet users. The figure seems to be too low compared with other statistics.
Source: Rose (2004).

Table 4.4. EVALUATION OF THE PRE-1989 ECONOMIC SYSTEM: POPULATION DIVIDED INTO USERS AND NONUSERS OF THE INTERNET

Country	Internet users		Nonusers	
	Mean	%	Mean	%
Central and Eastern Europe	1.9	30	0.4	70
Czech Republic	2.5	42	0.7	58
Hungary*	0.7	23	−0.5	77
Poland	1.1	34	−0.9	66
Russia	0.9	14	−0.8	86
Slovenia	1.6	57	0.7	43

Note: The second and fourth columns contain the percentage of users and nonusers of the Internet, respectively. The following question was asked: "How satisfied are you with the capitalist system?" Answers were expected on a 21-degree scale: −10 = worst, 0 = neutral, +10 = best. The table shows the mean (not weighted).
* The Hungarian figure of Internet users seems to be too low compared with other statistics. According to another source (Median 2007), 31 percent of the population in the 14–70 age bracket had access to a computer at home, at the workplace, or in school.
Source: Rose (2004).

Table 4.5. EVALUATION OF THE SOCIALIST ECONOMIC SYSTEM: POPULATION DIVIDED INTO USERS AND NONUSERS OF THE INTERNET

Country	Internet users		Nonusers	
	Mean	%	Mean	%
Central and Eastern Europe	1.1	30	3.7	70
Czech Republic	−2.6	42	0.6	58
Hungary*	0.2	23	3.0	77
Poland	−0.4	34	3.4	66
Russia	1.6	14	4.4	86
Slovenia	3.0	57	4.0	43

Note: The second and fourth columns contain the percentage of users and nonusers of the Internet, respectively. The following question was asked: "How satisfied were you with the former socialist system?" Answers were expected on a 21-degree scale: −10 = worst, 0 = neutral, +10 = best. The table shows the mean (not weighted).
* The Hungarian figure of Internet users seems to be too low compared with other statistics. According to another source (Median 2007), 31 percent of the population in the 14–70 age bracket had access to a computer at home, at the workplace, or in school.
Source: Rose (2004).

Internet frequently. The difference is quite impressive.[7] Those connected to the world of modern information technology hold more favorable views about democracy and capitalism, and are more critical of the past regime, which is an encouraging sign. The users of the Internet are more immune to the sentiments of nostalgia for the old socialist order—a feeling strengthened in many, especially since the recent economic crisis.

The empirical results reported earlier fit well into the findings of another line of studies: the research on *interconnectivity*. The intuitive meaning of the term is clearly indicated by the name: Individuals are connected to each other by various technical instruments and procedures. E-mail plays a particularly important role in this respect. The more that people are technically able to send e-mail to others, the tighter the network of connections becomes. That phenomenon is certainly observable and measurable.

I rely here on an exciting study by Christopher R. Kedzie (1997a), who refers to a metric measuring "interconnectivity." Not being an expert in that field, I cannot judge whether the metric used in Kedzie's study is the best available for the purpose he is using it. Conditionally accepting his choice, the basic results of his study are certainly worth mentioning. Besides other calculations that he considered, he looked at the correlation between "democracy" (measured by various indicators) and "interconnectivity." This correlation

---

7. We touch here upon a highly relevant question about whether the appearance of high-tech communication expands social inequality. The search for an answer reaches beyond the limits of this essay.

turns out to be 0.73, stronger than the correlation of democracy with per capita GDP (0.57). I report the proposition with some reservation, due to my lack of knowledge in the area utilized by the interconnectivity index. A more recent study by Frisch (2003), however, supports Kedzie's findings. Hopefully, research in that direction will continue.

At this point, let me recall my earlier remark on the role of modern information and communication technology in dismantling the monolithic power of the communist party and the official Marxist-Leninist ideology. There, I looked at events that happened 20 years ago in the former Soviet Union and in the socialist countries of East Central Europe. The problem is not outdated at all. There are two small countries, Cuba and North Korea, where not much has changed in the economy, and heavy-handed communist dictatorship still prevails. Then, there are two large countries, China and Vietnam, where far-reaching reforms have been introduced and have moved the economy close to capitalism, although the political structure has changed very little, remaining a single-party dictatorship. How will modern infocommunication technology influence those countries? China and Vietnam eagerly utilize all advantages provided by the revolutionary achievements of technical progress, and at the same time, they are scared of the consequences. These two objectives of the leadership—maximum gain from technical progress and maximum protection of the monopoly of power—diametrically contradict each other, resulting in hesitation, steps forward and backward, and ambivalence.

Another major problem to analyze is the prospects: What is the future of the interaction between the forthcoming waves of innovation and the way of life? On my pessimistic days I foresee various evil scenarios. Even without a special talent for prophecy, we can easily predict the misuse of technical achievements. I read several reports about efforts of the Chinese government to apply political censorship of the Internet, block the transmission of certain TV channels, or shut down outspoken blogs.[8] Since an ever-growing share of all computers used in China is produced domestically, it is easy to enforce the incorporation of a centrally controlled censorship software into the operation system. Sadly, large Western corporations, scared of losing the huge Chinese market, are willing to cooperate with the officials in their efforts to introduce political censorship.

When Orwell wrote his book *Nineteen Eighty-Four* sixty years ago (Orwell 1949–1950), Big Brother did not have the equipment envisaged in the novel. Nowadays, however, there would be no technical difficulty involved in the

---

8. See Chao (2009) and Timmer (2009) on Chinese efforts to apply political censorship. For a general overview, see the entry on Internet censorship in Wikipedia (2009b).

installation of cameras and eavesdropping devices in every flat and office. Imagine a future Stalin with the latest gadgets of monitoring and telecommunication, resolved to use it to watch all citizens.

On my more optimistic days, however, I escape these nightmarish visions and hope that modern technology gives birth time and again to decentralization, whatever efforts dictatorships devote to assure or even further strengthen centralization. If the centralizer invents a new way of blocking information, there will be hundreds and thousands of decentralizers, inventive computer users who break through the blockades and barriers.[9]

---

9. In note 8 of this section, I referred to an article by Timmer (2009) published on the Internet. The editor asked for comments. Here is the first comment: "So what is there to keep Chinese citizens from reformatting their hard drives and installing pirated copies of Windows?"

SECTION 5

Concluding Remarks

My essay has covered a vast array of topics. I did not intend to limit the study to one or two issues. We are looking at a huge white area on the otherwise colorful map of research in comparative economics and postsocialist "transitology." The purpose of my essay was to give a general overview of this area.

Among the great number of valuable studies on several topics, some are mentioned in my essay. Unfortunately, each topic has its own large body of literature, but they are sharply separated from each other and lack cross-references. The emphasis here was not on the detailed description and analysis of one or another linkage, but to give an impression of the totality of connections. There are also dozens of themes deserving penetrating research, empirical observation, and theoretical analysis, barely touched upon or not even mentioned in my essay. The study of technical progress and its relationship to society is going on in a multidimensional space. The points discussed in my essay are located in a subspace, and I am aware that there are relevant dimensions outside this subspace. What an exciting and intellectually challenging subject for research! I hope that my essay will encourage further studies in this largely underresearched field.

Let me mention a few dimensions not appearing in my essay:

- What is the effect of the new technology of information and communication on the relationship between individuals, social groups, settlements, countries, and states? What can be expected concerning the relationship between high-tech information and communication, on the one hand, and the nation-state and globalization, on the other? (Castells 1996–1998; Nyíri 2004; Webster et al. 2004).
- The future of capitalism. Does the new age of information lead to a radical change of the basic properties of capitalism? Or does it create a new system that cannot be called capitalism any more? Two Hungarian economists, Katalin Szabó and Balázs Hámori wrote an interesting book with the

following subtitle "Digital Capitalism or a New Economic System?" (2006). See also Haug (2003).
- How does the revolutionary change of information and communication technology affect the practical mode of running a business, especially in the financial sector?
- What are the implications of the new information age concerning property rights, especially with respect to intellectual property?
- A quite different direction of thought is to reconsider at a more abstract philosophical level our general understanding of human history. What is the role of the changes in the technology of production and human interaction on the institutions of society and on the functions of the government?

SECOND ESSAY

Shortage Economy—Surplus Economy

SECTION 1

Introduction[1]

1.1 IMPRESSIONS

The English Wikipedia page entitled "Shortage economy" reveals a photograph of people waiting in line at a shopping-street food store in Poland in the 1980s.[2] Anyone shopping in Poland today will find well-stocked shelves and a rich variety of goods from home and abroad.

In 1999, I visited China on the occasion of the second edition of my study *Economics of Shortage*. Those who took me around—the editors of the book and some students who knew the book well—took me into department stores and to food markets, and one of them remarked, "It's time you wrote a new book, on the economics of surplus instead of the economics of shortage."

I will not write such a book, but I would like, within the bounds of an essay, to outline some basic ideas for the economics of the surplus economy. The central idea can be put like this: Just as the shortage economy is a characteristic attribute of the socialist system, so is the surplus economy of the capitalist system.[3]

Research, according to Schumpeter, begins with a "pre-analytical cognitive act" that delivers the raw material for the analytical efforts. This he calls *vision*.

---

1. I am grateful for help from several colleagues in the research on which it is based and in formulating the text. I would like to single out Attila Chikán and Zsolt Mátyusz for their manifold assistance in collecting the data and clarifying the problems. I have also had much useful advice from the following colleagues: Daniel Brooks, János Gács, Dóra Győrffy, Mária Lackó, Aladár Madarász, Ildikó Magyar, Ágnes Nagy, Éva Palócz, András Prékopa, András Simonovits, Domokos Szász, and István János Tóth.

An earlier and shorter version of the essay was published in Kornai (2010) in Hungarian.

2. See Wikipedia (2012a).

3. I hesitated over the expression. I considered, apart from *surplus*, the words *plenty*, *glut*, and *slack*. *Surplus* seemed the most appropriate for the phenomenon described here.

The vision sheds new light on matters (Schumpeter 1954, 41–42). I am convinced that such pre-analytical vision is contained in the wonder with which an economist of the socialist shortage economy looks upon the ample supply of the capitalist market. This impression I see as important. Perhaps comparing capitalism with another system—with its opposite, in a sense—allows me to see in it something not noticed by fellow economists living within it who are unable to free themselves of their accustomed outlook.

Mainstream economists with whom I discuss the matter usually agree with me only in part. They are easily convinced that the socialist system is a shortage economy, but why should the capitalist system be called a surplus economy? There are certainly large stocks in the stores and factory warehouses, there is usually spare capacity in production—but only as much as required. Producers produce that much and no less, and traders hold that much stock and no less because that is what is needed for market equilibrium. The socialist economy is not in equilibrium, but the capitalist economy is. Equilibrium is the long-term trend, even though there are fluctuations around the equilibrium (a big one at present).

Is the argument just over names? Is what the mainstreamers call market equilibrium what I call a surplus economy, with no real difference between the two states of the economy? If that were the case, I would stop writing at once because names are not worth arguing about.

Though the phenomena before their eyes and mine are identical, we read different things into them because our outlooks differ. I give the facts (large reserves of capacity, amply filled warehouses, labor seeking jobs) an essentially different interpretation. Each producer or trader may arrive individually, by weighing his or her own interests, at the precise stocks and reserve capacities that need to be kept, and yet it may still be that all the salable products in the warehouses and all the products available after a slight delay by drawing on reserve capacity together exceed (substantially exceed) the amount the entirety of buyers could possibly buy. Macroeconomists may conclude that aggregate employment matches the natural rate. Yet many people still feel that they are excluded from employment, and society's performance would be greater if they too were drawn into work.

If I am right and the capitalist system is, indeed, a surplus economy, that has important consequences. It has an effect on the behavior of the actors in the system. It sheds a different light on many features of capitalism. To that extent, this analysis may assist in a fuller *positive* understanding of capitalism.[4]

---

4. The attribute *positive* can have several senses. It can signify a favorable assessment of something. This study uses it not in that sense, but as a concept from the philosophy of science meaning the opposite of *normative*, an approach to describing and explaining reality that is as value-free as possible.

Furthermore, there are some normative conclusions worth noting. Mainstream economists are ill at ease if excess capacity, inflated stocks, or excess supply appear in a capitalist economy. They see such resources as waste, but I see the surplus economy as one of capitalism's great virtues, albeit one with several detrimental side effects.

1.2 A FIRST APPROACH TO CLARIFICATION OF CONCEPTS

Capitalism comes in many varieties. Clearly, there are essential differences among the institutions and modes of operation found in the United States and in Sweden, Brazil, or Japan. The seminal work of Hall and Soskice (2001, 2003) led to a wide-ranging debate on classification of the varieties of capitalism and development of typologies for it. The same can be said of the socialist system. In a particular period, for instance, the 1970s, there were essential divergences between the institutions and operative forms of the Soviet, Chinese, Czechoslovak, and Hungarian economies. I am aware how important it is to grasp the differences among systemic variants, and yet I will be ignoring them in what follows. The *capitalist system* and the *socialist system* are interpreted in this essay as two theoretical models, or "ideal types," to use Max Weber's expression. I am talking throughout in a general, abstract sense about these two great systems. Numerous though the variants are, all have many important common attributes, and it is precisely the influence of these that I have placed in the foreground of my investigations in this essay, as I did earlier when I was examining the socialist system.

The vast majority of economists have no problem with basic concepts such as *supply* and *demand*. Early editions of Samuelson's famous textbook had, as a motto of one of the chapters, "You can make even a parrot into a learned political economist—all it must learn are the two words 'supply' and 'demand'" (Samuelson 1980[1948], 52). These two concepts, unfortunately, cause several problems for me, as do several other standard concepts in microeconomics, but they can only be subjected to critical analysis and the conceptual apparatus presented more thoroughly after outlining the phenomena that I wish to use in the examination. This I will do in two stages. I present the proposed concepts loosely in the introduction. I accept that most of my readers use the customary vocabulary, not the one I would try to introduce. So let me offer the following conceptual explanations in advance.

What I call *surplus* corresponds more or less to what standard economics calls *excess supply*. In other words, it refers to cases in which supply exceeds demand.

The *surplus economy*, if, for want of better understanding, I had to use the standard terminology, I would call an *economy of excess supply*, and the *shortage economy* an *economy of excess demand*. The former is a market state in which phenomena of excess supply are common, the latter is a market state in which phenomena of excess demand are common.

Having said so much in advance, I hope I have produced the right associations in my economist readers, so that they can follow my argument without difficulty. Later, as I proceed with explaining my ideas, I will return to provide in detail more accurate definitions of my concepts and the problems of measurement they present.

1.3 THE PLACE THAT THE APPROACH TAKEN IN THE ESSAY OCCUPIES IN ECONOMIC DISCOURSE

There is hardly a sentence in the essay that has no antecedent in the literature. All schools of economics have much to say on the market. Those in the most comfortable position are the mainstream economists: they have little trouble with their conceptual framework or with grounding in theory their analyses of partial aspects they examine, as they can find them ready-made in textbooks and literature on the subject.

This study can also be seen as a debate contribution: I take issue with the mainstream on some important questions and propose another approach to them. I cannot, sad to say, make my task easier by joining one of the "heterodox" schools wholly or partly opposed to the mainstream, and just add a layer to their intellectual structure or use their terminology.

Yet I do not feel alone. Though not the whole structure of my thoughts, I have taken over many important elements in my line of thought from predecessors. On some questions, my propositions show resemblance or correspondence with certain mainstream precepts, and at several important points they tie in with one or other of the heterodox schools. I will gladly point to these adoptions and overlaps in due course.

There were several inducements to write this study. All conscientious economists have been prompted to examine themselves by the still-current economic crisis. We have to think whether the tools we use to analyze the processes in the economy are the right ones. In my case, there are also additional motivations. I came to realize over 50 years ago, in the years 1955–1956, when working on the dissertation for my candidacy degree, *Overcentralization in Economic Administration* (Kornai 1994 [1959]), that chronic shortage is one of the basic problems with the socialist economy. The questions of shortage, surplus, equilibrium, and disequilibrium recurred frequently in my later works, *Anti-Equilibrium*, *Economics of Shortage*, and *The Socialist System* (Kornai 1971, 1980, and 1992). This is a recurrent theme that seems to dog me through a lifetime. However, what I offer in this study is not just a return to my old concerns. The theme may continue, but my theoretical knowledge and practical experience have grown over the period. I hope that my analytical apparatus, repeatedly revived and honed, has developed step by step. I would like to think that this study reshapes my earlier analyses, so that it is more subtly conceived, in some points corrected, and in many details thoroughly reworked.

My earlier researches focused on processes in the socialist economy, with capitalism appearing mainly for comparison's sake, as a contrasting case. Now I shift the center of gravity and concentrate on examining capitalism. The study not only seeks to develop the analytical apparatus further, but also to go beyond my earlier works in the *subject* of the analysis.[5] What I am attempting is to complete a semicircle, to fit some missing pieces into a jigsaw.[6] I would like to prove to myself (and perhaps to my readers) that the methods and approaches of my works can be applied to the capitalist market as well.

1.4 AN ADVANCE LOOK AT THE BOUNDARIES AND STRUCTURE OF THE SUBJECT MATTER

Basically what is covered in the Second Essay is the capitalist system. Only for the sake of comparison are some aspects of socialism also discussed.[7]

Modern capitalism typically contains a mixed economy: Private ownership and the sphere coordinated by the market mechanism are joined by a substantial amount of public ownership and activity coordinated by bureaucratic mechanisms.

Sections 1-5 deal exclusively with the market sphere. Section 6 considers the nonmarket sphere as well.

The study examines only the market for goods and services and the labor market, that is, the *real* sphere of the economy. I do not deal in detail with the *monetary sphere*; the financial sector; the market transactions in money, credit, or investments in financial assets; nor with the fiscal and monetary policy of the state. The essay will only tangentially touch on this large set of issues.

I recognize that it is almost impossible to discuss the markets for goods, services, and labor and ignore the financial sector—in other words money,

---

5. Although the study joins with the works just listed and rests on research findings they contain, readers cannot be expected to know them in advance. I have tried to phrase myself so that those who have not read any of my earlier works can follow my argument. I must add that knowledge of *The Socialist System* (Kornai 1993) will be a help in understanding the study; the present research can be considered a continuation of it.

6. Unfortunately, there are still some elements, some essential jigsaw pieces missing. As stressed also in the next section, the study does not deal with the monetary sphere, although no comprehensive explanation of the operation of the market can do without it.

7. All I wish to say on socialism in terms of this study appears in my book *The Socialist System* (Kornai 1992).

credit, interest, and monetary and fiscal policy—or the interaction of the two spheres. It is almost impossible, but I have decided to make the distinction nonetheless. I am embarking here on a study of no great length, that is, not on a fat book to cover the entire capitalist system.

I have excluded some very important segments of the system, but the subject-matter still remains very broad. I must be very brief in touching on some great and difficult questions, each with its own vast literature and each deserving a study in itself.

Let me outline the structure of the essay for readers' convenience.

Sections 2–6 cover the *basic case*, with Sections 2–5 describing the *phenomenon* and the *causal relations* that engender and reproduce it. Section 6 deals with the *consequences* and an evaluation of them. Section 7 discusses *special cases* beyond the basic case. By the end of the essay it will become clear to readers what I call the basic case and what I consider to be special cases.

SECTION 2

The Market for Goods and Services: The Mechanism for the Reproduction of Surplus

2.1 AN EXAMPLE FROM ECONOMIC HISTORY: THE U.S. TELEPHONE SYSTEM

Let me give an example from economic history of the phenomena that will be discussed later in general terms: What happened with telephone services in the United States (Grover and Lebeau 1996; Atkin, Lau, and Lin 2006). Let us begin with the early 1980s, when almost all calls were made by fixed land lines and the huge AT&T concern held a near-monopoly.

First came radical changes in *technology*, as cell phones began to spread fast in the late 1980s (King and West 2002).[1] More will be said of technology changes in a moment.

There was a change in *market structure* in 1984, when the AT&T divestiture took place in line with a federal antitrust settlement. The structure of market participants has changed several times since, through mergers and demergers, and market entries and exits, but the basic structure of the market form remains. There is neither a monopoly nor perfect competition, but *monopolistic competition* among a small number of very powerful rival concerns.

This characteristic market structure caused, and was caused by, the dynamism of the sector. Successive innovations were made. The cell phone could forward not only sound, but also written messages, and later, pictures. Cell phones, small enough for the pocket, added to their functions the

---

[1]. In an exception to the rule that the United States leads in technology and Europe follows, the order was reversed with the spread of cell phone networks.

transmission of written texts and later pictures and videos, photography, photograph storage, a calculator, and so on.

The other direction of innovation has led away from the traditional telephone set, toward software such as Skype and other similar networks, which allow computers to be used as phones and even as video phones.

The fusion of the functions of computers and telephones has also taken other forms: the pocket iPhone, then the iPad, and their many portable small rivals perform many other information transmitting and entertainment functions besides those of a mobile phone.

Each new surge of innovation brings new producers and service providers into the sector, while older companies disappear or become marginal. However, the main characteristic of the market remains: a few huge firms dominate the market, competing with, complementing, cooperating with, or supplanting each other.

There is no way of defining clear bounds for the sector on the supply side. It includes the whole supply network, the research firms developing the innovations, the manufacturers of technical equipment, the providers of telecom services, the sellers of equipment and programs, the developers of software, and so on. The bounds are blurred, as the telecom sector merges into the computer sector, the entertainment industry, photography, and other sectors.

The bounds are equally permeable on the demand side. Once upon a time, there were clear distinctions among the demands of individuals relating to telephony, correspondence, telegraphy, photography, learning, ad hoc information, and so on. Now, each technological line satisfies several of these. The permeability of the bounds makes it impossible to state clearly what "supply cluster" faces what "demand cluster."

The phenomenon of increasing return to scale applies to most firms in this segment of the economy. The initial investment required for entry is substantial, as are the fixed costs of operation. The greater the volume of sales, the more widely these fixed costs are spread. Each firm is interested in persuading as many buyers as possible to use its equipment and its services, rather than its rivals'. The limits of volume growth are not set by cost considerations but by constraints on sales.

The Schumpeterian process of creative destruction rolls on, with the creation going faster than the destruction. The forces that prompt entry and expansion are extremely strong, but there are strong brakes on exit and exclusion. Those who have once entered the sector fight tooth and nail to stay as participants, even if they take losses. As cell phones proliferate, fixed-line services lose ground (Figure 2.1), but the loss is quite a slow one, far from being proportionate to the expansion in cell phones. One more cell phone user does not result in one fewer landline phone user. The two networks have existed side by side for a long time, and the technical conditions for linking them are being explored. The various telephone technologies and the ramifications of

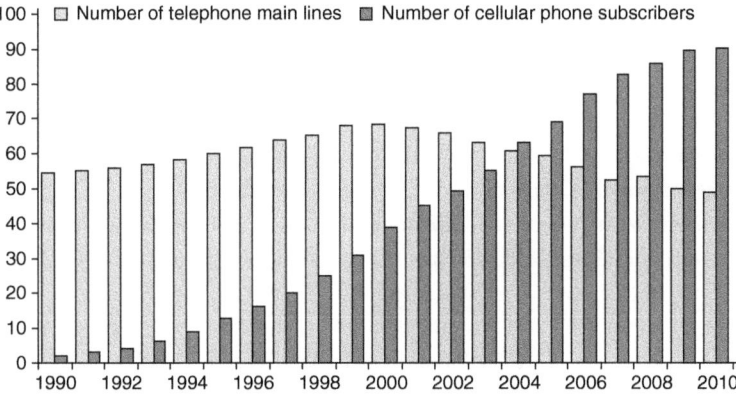

Figure 2.1.
Telephone main lines and cellular phone subscribers per 100 inhabitants in the United States, 1990–2010
Source: World Bank (2012).

them contain very large amounts of excess capacity. In other words, there is large excess supply apparent in telephonic services.

This is little more than a telegraphic account of a process lasting several decades. If market researchers had attempted to interview heads of production firms and service providers at any point in that long period, and asked if they were capable of serving many more users of telephone services than they actually were, the answer would probably have been a hearty yes. This is a characteristic excess-supply symptom, and, in that sense, the telephone-sector market is in a state of chronic excess supply.

Now let us compare this for a moment with conditions in the Soviet Union and East European socialist countries in the 1980s (Table 2.1). There, many households were unable to get a telephone for years, or they spent years on the waiting list for one, or they had to use connections to get one out of turn. Those who managed to get one found that phoning was a wearing business because

Table 2.1. FIXED TELEPHONE LINES PER 100 INHABITANTS IN SOME SOCIALIST COUNTRIES AND IN THE UNITED STATES, 1980–1988

Country	1980	1984	1988
Bulgaria	10.2	15.6	21.3
Hungary	5.8	6.6	8.2
Poland	5.5	6.4	7.8
Romania	7.3	8.4	9.8
Soviet Union	7.0	9.6	12.3
United States	40.8	46.8	50.8

Source: United Nations Statistics Division (2009a).

the system was overloaded and there were long waits for a connection. If the same question had been put to the heads of the state telephone enterprise—would they be capable of serving many more telephone users than they actually were?—the answer would have been a resounding no. They would have pointed emphatically at the long queues for telephone lines. The telephone sector under that system was in a state of chronic excess demand.

That is how the surplus economy operates on the telephone sector under one system and the shortage economy works under the other.[2]

2.2 SUPPLY-RELATED PROCESSES

The historical example presents features that characterize the operation of capitalist markets in general. The task now is to outline a theoretical generalization.

The words *operation of the market* cause a well-known graph of every introductory textbook to flash before all economists. The graph shows the marginal cost curve of a one-product, profit-maximizing firm, the demand curve, and the equilibrium price and optimum volume at the intersection between them. Let us break with this diagram (not to mention other abstractions), which offers a *static*, momentary picture of the firm's decision making. We pass beyond the most disturbing shortcoming of such textbook models, their static character, and focus on the *dynamics* of the market, even if we have to do that in a less elegant verbal form.

To start with supply, its path is a dynamic process whose changes occur in several dimensions:

- There is continual variation in the set of suppliers whose elements consist of units, firms, and individual producers and providers of a good or service: continual entries, mergers formed among the existing members, splits of other members, and, finally, exits. The demography of the set shows constant variation.[3]
- There is continual variation in the specific assortment of goods and services available to buyers. The selection increases over the long term as production differentiates. New products continually appear and old ones vanish. This unceasing change in the assortment can be found among individual

---

2. Objectivity requires me to add that the change of system coincided with a technical leap: the introduction of cell phones. The change of system would probably have sped up the expansion of the telephone network in any case, without the leap, but to what extent cannot be determined.

3. See the study by Bartelsman et al. (2004), cited in the First Essay of this volume. Figure 3.2 in the First Essay presents the corporate demography of the OECD countries in detail.

producers and providers, but it becomes more apparent if a group of firms, a whole sector, or the whole economy of a country is observed.
- Aggregating the data at sector or macro level reveals recurrent short- and long-term fluctuation, and, measured historically, continual growth in the long term.

Because the assortment continually changes, continual surplus also appears: product volume not bought by the aggregate of buyers or capacity not utilized by the aggregate of users. The formation of unsold stock and idle capacity is also a dynamic process.

How does this surplus form? Why do phenomena of excess supply appear commonly? There are at least four kinds of motive force to explain this.

1. *Monopolistic competition.*—After the pioneering works by Chamberlin (1962 [1933]) and Robinson (1969 [1933]), the theory of monopolistic competition and imperfect competition was incorporated into mainstream economics. These important theories give backing to my ideas by confirming that excess capacity appears in firms engaged in monopolistic competition. When setting volume, they do not voluntarily go so far as firms engaging in perfect competition would. Voluntarily, in maximizing their profits, they use their capacity to a smaller extent.[4]

Our attention here is directed at markets exhibiting an imperfect market structure, in the form normally known as monopolistic competition. ("Oligopolistic" would be more apposite, but "monopolistic" is more widespread in the literature.[5])

Firms in monopolistic competition can win customers from rivals, not only with more favorable price offers, but also with non-price-related inducements: better quality, politer service, extra services such as home delivery, and so on. Most importantly of all, it can introduce new products, but that will be examined separately.[6]

---

4. This aspect of monopolistic competition is presented graphically in a superb article by Evsey D. Domar, in connection with the subject with which this study is concerned: why phenomena of excess supply appear systematically in the capitalist market economy (Domar 1989). I have found many works that show kinship in one respect or another with my own line of thought and from which I have been able to use one argument or another, but Domar's is the only one to pass through my hands where I can sense such an intellectual kinship in full, not just in detail.

5. I do not know any statistics to show what proportion of total goods and services turnover in a given country over a given period took place under a market structure of perfect competition. I can only chance a guess that it is relatively small. Monopolistic competition is the dominant market form.

6. In Weitzman's model (2000) for comparing the socialist and capitalist economies, variable E, "selling effort" plays the central role. Weitzman shows monopolistic competition demands a high E of producers and sellers, whereas in a centrally planned economy the value of E is low.

2. *Uncertainty of demand.*—Consider a retail outlet. The store sells goods in a defined range, say electrical household appliances and electronic goods ranging from refrigerators to laptop computers, TV sets to printer cables (a common retail profile). The example covers retail trading, so that the surplus appears in the form of product stocks. My point here is more general than that. It concerns not only retail trading, but also the production of all goods and services. The analysis covers not only stocks of products, but also unutilized capacity for production or service provision available immediately or with a very short delay. In other words, retail trading is used only for the sake of illustration.

To return to the retail example, the seller cannot predict accurately how many buyers will walk in or exactly what products they will be seeking. He would like customers to leave the store empty-handed as rarely as possible. Let us call the proportion of satisfied buyers to all visitors to the store the *safety level*.[7] Let us assume that the range of products that conceivably may interest visitors to the store is known, but the actual composition and aggregate volume of demand is uncertain. It is clear that the higher the safety level at which sellers wish to run the store, the bigger the stock they must hold.

Literature on operations research offers several models for handling the problem numerically.[8] The requisite size of stock is influenced by several factors, exemplified by the following:

- Although the demand is uncertain, a good seller approximately knows the composition of its demand and the extent and spread of demand fluctuations (Ramey and West 1999).
- Stock is usually replaced in bursts or batches, not continually. Requisite stock levels are usually set in cooperation with suppliers.
- Each visitor leaving empty-handed is a loss, but so is stock that hangs about too long. The two types of loss must be weighed soberly.

This essay is intended to contribute to the theory of economics, not to the literature of operations research on inventory policy.[9] It can be observed in

---

7. The safety level may be expressed in another form, depending on the purpose of calculation, for instance, as the volume of satisfied buying intentions to the total of buying intentions, instead of as the proportion of satisfied buyers to all buyers.

8. There is extensive literature on inventories and capacity reserves, examined in several disciplines, notably microeconomics, operations research, and management science (e.g., Chopra and Meindl 2003, Chapters 11 and 12; Toomey 2000). The mathematical models use various methodologies, such as the theory of stochastic processes and stochastic programming (Prékopa 1995).

9. Relations of uncertain demand, of supply, and of inventories touch another problem sphere at several points, dealt with in a new, highly influential research program in economics: *search theory* and *matching theory*. Both buyers and sellers are seeking each other, and when they succeed, there is "matching." It is clear that the more efficient the search on both sides, the smaller the inventories required to be sure of meeting buyer demand. The theories of search and matching are treated in the labor market section of my essay.

actual retail practice that some stores manage their reordering and stocking policies more efficiently than others. Many producers or sellers lack any well-elaborated stocking policy at all, relying simply on instinct borne of experience. Nonetheless, it remains true that one of the main weapons for maintaining and improving the market position of a seller operating under strong monopolistic competition is a high safety level in meeting buyer demands. This can be obtained by keeping a high, well-chosen stock.

Satisfying demand at a high safety level is one of the main features of a surplus economy. Although sellers set the size of their stocks according to their own *individual* interests, the sum total of individual stocks held in this segment of turnover on an aggregate level of the sellers as a whole will produce surplus supply. If each store belonged to a single chain with one large common warehouse, this *centralized* system could guarantee a given level of security for buyers with far smaller aggregate stocks than those required under a *decentralized* system of stores all competing with each other. Decentralization and competition tie down extra capital. As compensation for this, decentralization brings many other big advantages, which have already been discussed and will be referred to again many times in the rest of this book.

Beyond the retail sector, the same line of argument can be applied to the problems of stocks and capacity reserves in producer firms.

A prescriptive operations-research modeler seeking to develop a practical business policy may take the safety level as given and seek the requisite size and content of stocks and capacity reserves to meet it. However, the descriptive–positive analysis in this study calls for a reversal of this approach. The stocks and the capacity reserves are given. So at what safety level will they meet the demand? It is a shame that such observations and calculations have never been made under the capitalist or the socialist system. I am convinced that the safety level is high in a surplus economy and low in a shortage economy.[10]

3. *Innovation and creative destruction.*—The forces inducing the accumulation of surplus would still apply if technical development stagnated, but it does not stagnate, it surges irrevocably forward.[11] A producer or seller in imperfect, monopolistic competition gains a big advantage by offering buyers something new, a good or service not offered by competitors. This applies all the more to innovators bringing in a revolutionary product that is new in global terms, but the statement can be extended to those in the wake of such a pioneer, those who are fast followers in introducing the innovation into their own or another country.

---

10. The difference is reduced by a general acceptance by buyers in a shortage economy that it will be impossible to find certain desired products in the stores. The phenomenon resembles that of the "discouraged worker" who ceases to seek a job on the capitalist labor market.

11. The First Essay of this volume reviews the literature of the problem and formulates my conclusions on it. The arguments in the two essays are closely connected.

How does this affect the surplus appearing in the economy? Just because something new appears in some place, and is beginning to attract demand, it does not mean that all previous products disappear quickly. There are many forces tending to promote its survival.

Some of the tools and expertise in the factories making them are product specific. The innovation may call for capital investment and retraining, or it may require hiring new labor. If there is no chance of adapting, all previous investment will be lost—not only the plant, but the effort and intellectual input that went into introducing and promoting products. A lot of capital and labor have been put into the factory making the previous product. Naturally, its owners are keen to get a return and their employees are keen to keep their jobs. Often the state will assist in keeping alive a firm threatened with exit. (This phenomenon I have called a soft budget constraint, and I will return to it later.)

This means, ultimately, that the capacity to produce or provide a new product or service is additional to existing capacity. Though the share of the old capacity slowly falls, the new and the surviving old capacity together make an excess over demand. This is one of the main mechanisms behind the state of constant excess supply.

To use the oft-quoted words of Schumpeter (2010 [1942]), the rate of creation—seemingly—is greater than that of destruction.[12] Incidentally, the reproduction of surplus may occur even without this difference of rate. If there were surplus initially, the initial proportion (between excess capacity to total capacity, for instance) will remain if the rates of creation and destruction are identical. It seems quite unlikely that the shift should occur in the opposite direction, that is, that the destruction, the running down of capacity, should be faster than the creation over any long period. I see no examples of old products vanishing faster than new products gained ground.

What I have outlined could be expressed in formalized theoretical models. The process of "creation" and "destruction" can hopefully be expressed in statistically observed indicators or indices. Either way, these are testable conjectures susceptible to proof or disproof.

Let me note here what motive forces 1–3 have in common: the relation between *competition among sellers* and *phenomena of surplus*. Surplus is at once the cause and the effect of competition. In a market situation in which demand ubiquitously equaled supply, what would induce sellers to compete? It would be a numb state of rest. Competition is intensified by the presence of surplus (buyers have more chances to choose) and induces rivalry (sellers want to get rid of surplus). Conversely, competition and rivalry continually reproduce the surplus.

4. *Economies of scale.*—The simplest models of standard microeconomics (and those imbedded most deeply in the minds of young economists) assume

---

12. For a more extended discussion of "destructive coordination," see Vahabi (2004).

that the curve of a producer firm's average expenditure is U-shaped in the short run. If the volume falls to the right of the minimum, on the upward line of the U, marginal costs *rise*. So there is a volume of production that the firm does not want to exceed. This is not an external constraint but, rather, it is a point at which it ceases voluntarily to raise production volume, in order to maximize its profits.

The situation is different if marginal costs *fall* as a function of volume, or to put it another way, there is an *increasing return to scale*. The later is very frequent in real economic activity. It occurs whenever the fixed costs of a producer, service provider, or retail unit represent a high proportion of its total costs. The higher the production volume, the lower the unit cost. This clears away the internal constraint on increasing volume, so that only external constrains may impede it, primarily the fact that there will be no demand for more than a certain quantity of the product. It is not the firm's own interest that prompts it to cease to increase its production volume.

This influences the appearance of excess capacity in two dimensions of time: the long and the short run. Large firms facing monopolistic competition invest boldly (even overboldly) in new capacity, prompted strongly by the idea that the bigger the factory, the greater the scope for economies of scale. Although the industry as a whole may be suffering from idle capacity, a succession of new, large plants are built. A typical example of this is the automotive industry, which will be considered later.

In the short run, most producer firms experiencing an increasing return to scale do not increase their production to full capacity, even though this would be the most beneficial course for them. Normally, the demand constraint keeps production at a much smaller volume. Then decision makers tend to sense that the remainder is indeed *excess* capacity, because the firm has every interest in producing more than its actual output and it has the capacity to do so. Where there is a decreasing return to scale, decision makers rate the situation differently. Although they might, in physical or technical terms, produce more, doing so would reduce their profits, and so they can stop without hesitation at the level that maximizes profits.[13]

Four separate motive forces have been mentioned for clarity's sake. What they have in common, in the context of this essay, is their contribution to the surplus economy, the reproduction of phenomena of chronic excess supply. Often two, three, or even all four motive forces appear together, affecting and

---

13. The great significance of increasing return as a function of scale is underlined by many economists, notably Kaldor (1981) and Arthur (1994). Increasing return affects the economy in several ways, of which I have mentioned one—the inducement to create surplus capacity. A well-known book by Helpman and Krugman (1985) examines the effect of the phenomenon of increasing return on the international division of labor and international trade.

reinforcing each other in influences on the supply-related processes and the development of excess supply.

Most authors, in examining one of the four, assume the objective of the firm is to maximize profits. This is convenient in terms of mathematical modeling, and mainstream economists have been passing that idea round, but more thorough sociological and social psychological researchers show that "profit maximization," as the main characteristic feature of the firm's behavior, is not a universally valid description. The "company" is not an impersonal, intangible entity; its decision making is done by people. There are roles in the decision making of a modern large company for owners (including the main shareholders with a stronger say) and for leading managers. Often their interests fail to coincide, and which prevails depends on their relative strengths or on what compromise is reached. The time horizon is also a problem, that is, the extent to which they seek immediate profits or how much they heed the company's long-term interests.

The motivation of the decision makers cannot be described in the single word *profit*. They are also driven by desire for power and prestige, and to improve their public images. Especially important are vanity and the desire for respect they may gain by being the top competitor with the largest share of the market.[14] These motives often coincide, but they may also conflict. All four processes described earlier still apply if the corporate decision makers are not out to maximize profits or if that is only one of their motivations, but they are driven also by one of the other influences just mentioned. What the innovating entrepreneur sees before him is not necessarily the way to maximize profits. There is a huge driving force produced by the spirit of competition, by the desire to be the first to introduce an innovation.[15] Also very strong is the urge to expand in pursuit of increased power: "Let us be the biggest and most powerful! Let us rule the market!" Among the other motives driving entrepreneurs is an instinctive vitality and urge for action, the *animal spirits* described by Keynes (1967 [1936], 161–162) and Akerlof and Shiller (2009). I termed this kind of motivation an *expansion drive* in my book *Economics of Shortage* (Kornai 1980).

---

14. Motivations behind managerial behavior are dealt with in many works by members of the school known as behavioral economics. Apart from various researches into economic psychology, there is a big literature in psychology covering various (often conflicting) motivation theories. Economists have by no means exhausted the potential for utilizing these up-to-date psychological findings.

15. Steve Jobs, whose name is associated with Apple Corporation and such products of revolutionary importance as the iPhone, iPod, and iPad, is certainly one of the great innovators of our time. His biography by Isaacson (2011) shows convincingly that Jobs was motivated strongly by a desire that his products should be "perfect" and should work to strengthen his own charismatic reputation, on occasions to the detriment of his company's profits. Nonetheless, the profit motive also influenced his decisions strongly.

There is a very wide range of behavior patterns for corporate decision makers, and they combine in each decision maker in different proportions.[16] The four motive forces of generating surplus, described here, apply even if the corporate decision maker is driven not (only) by a desire to maximize profit but also by any of the other driving forces outlined.

2.3 DEMAND-RELATED PROCESSES

The formation of demand is also a dynamic process, affected not just by buyers' tastes, incomes, or wealth, but by such factors as the supply at any particular point in time (especially important to the subject here). For instance, the arrival of new products awakens new demands, and older products go out of style. Despite the view deeply imbedded in mainstream economists, there are not two separate curves intersecting somewhere, because supply is one of the main explanatory variables of demand at any time, and *vice versa*.

The processes of supply and demand influence each other mutually. This interaction would still be conceivable if the processes went ahead more or less in parallel, growing at more or less the same rate. The aim here, however, is to explain why demand falls behind supply in a surplus economy—why phenomena of excess supply appear even while the demand is basically satisfied.

The previous subsection introduced some forces that *drive up* the supply-related processes. Let us now look at some forces that dampen the demand-related processes and prevent demand running away.

The most important is the conflict of interest between employers and employees. The employees would like to get higher wages. The interest of the employers is ambivalent. Each one, individually, as the owner of its company has an interest in resisting employees' efforts to get a pay rise. It is worth paying up to the marginal product of labor, which is included in the calculation.[17] If he succeeds in pushing pay below that (helped perhaps by chronic unemployment), he can save further costs. If the employees can win their pay demands, that will bite into the individual company's profits. However, the group of all employers has a collective interest in higher income of all employees because that would raise macro demand and widen the market. That is some kind of

---

16. It is hard to find an "average" representative for a group of people, because this blurs the *heterogeneity* of those composing it. This is trivial to psychologists or even writers, but it took economists a good while to start dealing seriously with this self-evident fact and scrutinizing models that ignore the heterogeneity of decision-making groups. (See Kirman 1992.)

17. It may be worth paying more than that—the so-called efficiency wage of the preferred groups of workers whose expertise and loyalty are especially needed by their employers. The study returns to this in the section describing labor market aspects. Suffice it to say here that employers cannot go too far even with the efficiency wage before it ceases to be worthwhile.

noncooperative game in which the individual interest of the employers gets through with a greater force than their collective interest.

Whichever way the battle goes, any running away of wages is blocked in the capitalist system by the dominant *individual* interests of employers. Ultimately the employees' income constrains the expansion of production.

As production and productivity rise in the long term, so do employee incomes. But wages are sticky, failing to track the production and productivity rise closely. So the disposition is for demand to fall behind a vigorous expansion of production.[18]

The argument following here clearly lies close to the Marxist point of view. (See Marx, 1978 [1967–1994], notably Chapters 23 and 25.) I acknowledge the kinship, though I dissociate myself from Marxist political economy in many important respects.[19] Under capitalism, the basic inducement to expand the supply is not fiscal or monetary policy, though these may strengthen or weaken the basic force. The main incentive is the *intrinsic interest* of firms' owners and managers. Intrinsic interest sets limits to the growth of demand as well. The driving forces for the formation of surplus are found on the micro level.[20]

This mechanism, driven by the conflict of interest just described, operates strongly if household and corporate spending is curbed by a hard budget constraint. This sets limits to excess spending and loosening of wage constraints.

Softness and hardness of the budget constraint affect the creation of surplus in contradictory ways. On the one hand, the budget constraint on firms and on households has to be hard to restrain demand and prevent it from running away. On the other, surplus capacity is increased if lame-duck firms are kept going artificially, hat is, if the budget constraint is soft. It is not the *logic* of the description and interpretation that has gone wrong and produced contradictory effects but, rather, the *reality* of two opposite effects.

2.4 THE PRICING PROCESS

Prices, according to the dogmatic neoclassical scheme, are the means by which supply–demand disequilibria have to be righted. Where there is excess supply, the price falls and induces the decrease of supply and the increase of demand. Price movements do indeed perform this task in part, but only in part, not because of random errors, but through systematic distortions.

---

18. For the explanation of sticky wages by the "implicit contract theory" see Azariadis, 1975.

19. I have stated in detail in several articles (including Kornai 2009a) the questions on which I accept the Marxist approach, to what extent I apply it in explaining some phenomena, and the subjects on which I decidedly oppose Marx's views.

20. Several similar elements appear in the line of argument advanced by Bhaduri (2007).

Pricing, too, is a dynamic process. It cannot be seen as one of approximating to the equilibrium price in continual steps, as Walrasian theories of *tâtonnement* describe. Before the price reaches the point of equilibrium, both supply and demand will have changed, which they do continually, as I have tried to show. There is no convergence on a specific target as the target keeps moving.

It is now generally accepted that prices on a capitalist market are sticky. This is something on which the more enlightened mainstream economists (Mankiw 1985; Ball and Mankiw 1995; Blinder et al. 1998; Bils and Klenow 2004) agree, as do some of the heterodox schools, such as the post-Keynesians (Lee 1998). Many reasons are given for the stickiness of prices: for example, delay in sensing change in supply–demand relations or reluctance of firms to incur the extra costs of repricing (menu costs).

Market prices subject to monopolistic competition are set by sellers; buyers accept them or seek other sellers.[21] The price stickiness is asymmetric—stronger downward. Even if excess supply is perceived, sellers fear for their profits and remain reluctant to cut prices permanently.[22] Firms collectively (and makers of monetary policy) quail at the sight of deflation and its macroeconomic destructiveness. I would like to stress this asymmetry of price stickiness because it is one of the main explanations for the general asymmetry in a capitalist market economy: it inclines toward the dominance of phenomena of excess supply.

Prices, within the joint supply–demand price movement, do not eliminate the general state of excess supply; they reproduce it. Price fluctuations remain within the band typical of a surplus economy.

---

21. Tibor Scitovsky (1985) introduced the distinction between price makers and price takers. He stressed that sellers in monopolistic competition set the prices and pointed to various effects of this, including the appearance of idle capacity and the swelling of inventories. Several empirical studies demonstrate that firms' actual routine in determining the volume and the price differs significantly from the rules assumed in standard textbook economics (see Blinder et al., 1998; Keen 2002).

22. They are more likely to try temporary price cuts or bargain sales to dispose of unsold stocks.

SECTION 3

The Market for Goods and Services: The Conceptual Apparatus and Measurement Methods

Let me now fulfill my initial promise and set about presenting the conceptual apparatus and examining observations of the phenomena and ways to measure them.

What exactly are *supply* and *demand*? It would do no harm if those who had accepted the expressions unhesitatingly began to feel a little less certain.[1] The word *excess* has appeared several times, but I have yet to state its meaning clearly: in excess of what, excess supply by comparison with what?

3.1 "PURE," EASILY HANDLED CASES

1. *A service firm in a state of excess supply.*—Let us imagine as a thought experiment an interview with a service firm executive, for instance, a hotel manager.[2] The hotel operates in a surplus economy. The customary indices in the hotel industry are the *occupancy rate* or its complement, the *vacancy rate*, each in percentage terms. Let us put it to the manager: "What occupancy rate

---

1. In my book *Anti-Equilibrium* (Kornai 1971), I tried to clarify what lies behind these generally accepted and applied expressions and pointed out how murky their definitions are. There was little reaction to my considerations. Looking back on what I wrote, 40 years later, I can see that my concerns and objections have been justified. Relying on knowledge obtained since then, I try here to re-express my criticisms and my terminological and methodological recommendations, hoping that they will have more effect this time.

2. Throughout this account of the supply side, I talk about firms, but my arguments apply equally to individual producers, service providers, and traders.

would you be able and willing to attain next week?" Append to the question the following conditions and riders:

- The prices set by the hotel itself will apply next week.
- The question covers a very short period. The hotel's capacity is finite in the short term, being set ultimately by the number of rooms available. Consideration of this physical constraint alone yields the *theoretical capacity*, but there are often likely to be obstacles (such as maintenance or other technical problems) that prevent some rooms being taken. Bearing these in mind, the manager can arrive at the *practical capacity*.[3] One hundred percent utilization of the *practical* capacity will be taken in the example and later in the essay as *full occupancy*.[4] The respondent may answer only with a realistic, sober estimate of practical capacity. We are interested in the realistic willingness to provide the service, not with dreams or aspirations.
- The respondent is not being asked to forecast likely performance or the number of guests expected. Let the respondent assume that guests seeking accommodation may appear any day at any time. In other words, he or she should consider, if it depended on the hotel alone, how many guests it would willingly accommodate, that is, what is the occupancy rate he or she would like to achieve.

It would be surprising if the respondent did not say, "I would like the hotel to be full, in other words I would prefer to see full occupancy of the practical capacity." During the week in question, it will turn out what the actual occupancy was. Let us assume it averages 75 percent. Clearly the difference, 25 percentage points, is a numerical statement of the excess supply.

Let us suppose the original question has been posed and the actual measurement made in every hotel in the city, and they all show excess supply. This yields after the event an accurate picture of supply and demand in this partial market. The *ex ante* responses of the hotel managers add up to the supply in the given week, and the *ex post* figures to the demand. Total supply

---

3. Capacity utilization indices are published regularly by the U.S. Federal Reserve Board. The definition used by the FED is as follows: "The capacity indexes produced by the Federal Reserve Board are designed to capture the concept of *sustainable maximum output*, the greatest level of output a plant can maintain within the framework of a realistic work schedule after factoring in normal downtime and assuming sufficient availability of labor and material inputs to operate the capital in place. The concept roughly corresponds to the full-input point on a production function, with the qualification that capacity represents a sustainable maximum rather than some higher unsustainable short-term maximum. For example, a firm may postpone routine maintenance or temporarily boost overtime to produce above capacity. In the long run, these actions are not sustainable." (Morin and Stevens 2004, 3–4).

4. Though practical capacity is normally less than 100 percent, it is possible to imagine capacity of more than 100 percent. To stay with the example: the hotel has so many guests that it has to postpone regular maintenance.

exceeds total demand in the example. There is no need to ask guests about their demand because the pervading excess supply means that the demand equals the actual volume of transactions (purchases and sales).

This is called the "rule of the shorter side." If there is excess supply, the demand is on the shorter side and the supply on the longer. The volume of actual transactions is always equal to the shorter side.

The rule has important consequences for the methods of observation and measurement. Only the size of the shorter side can be gauged from the statistics of actual purchases and sales. Estimating the longer side calls for other methods. In the imaginary example, the one chosen was the simplest method of gauging the longer side: to question those responsible about their willingness to sell. Had it been assumed that the hotel would willingly let all its rooms, the questioning might have been replaced by measuring its practical capacity in advance.

To return to the initial question, talking of excess entails knowing in excess in relation to something else. The example yielded a clear answer: supply was greater than actual transaction volume, which coincided with demand.

2. *A trading firm selling stored products in a state of excess supply.*[5]—Although there are capacity limits to retail activity (physical capacity of the unit, productivity of the staff, etc.), the fundamental constraint on supply is the stock available. To gauge the supply over a short period (say a week), not at a moment in time, as with the service company discussed, the question to ask the manager of the trading company is how much the firm is able and willing to sell to buyers at the prevalent price, including the initial stock and the extra stock added during the week. The presumable reply will be the whole quantity.[6] This quantity—the ability and willingness of the seller to sell—can be taken as trader's supply.

Two conditions should be added to bring this line of thought to a clear conclusion.

- The restocking quantities have been ordered before the interview is made. We ask the respondent to assume he or she cannot adjust the order in the coming week. We stick to our original "short-term" ex ante interpretation of the problem.
- The other condition applies to ourselves, the framers of the thought experiment. Let us assume that some closing stock of all products remains at the end of the week. No product in the store has sold out. In other words, the demand side is shorter for all products.

---

5. A trading company may act as an intermediary in the market of services, but I do not examine this special case.

6. It would probably be going too far for the store to be quite empty at the end of the week, like the Warsaw store mentioned at the beginning of the study, because it would put buyers off from returning. There is no danger of this case occurring in a market economy and it can safely be ignored.

If the two conditions are met, it can be established exactly at the end of the week how much the excess supply was, because it is identical with the closing stock. The result takes the form of simple identities.

> Supply = opening stock plus additions to stock during the week
>
> Demand = actual purchases and sales (the shorter side)
>
> Excess supply = closing stock

The closing stock is the quantity of stock that the seller would have liked to sell ex ante, but failed to do so, as established ex post.

3. *A manufacturing firm in a state of excess supply.*—Consider another situation. The subject this time is a manager at a manufacturing firm (say a vehicle factory) producing physically tangible, durable goods. The interview with him is known to be taking place in a situation of excess supply.

It is less self-evident than in the first two cases how to frame the question that will reveal the supply.

As in the two previous interviews, let us first put the question in a very short-term sense, covering the coming week. Here we are addressing the manufacturing firm in its role as the *seller* (perhaps the manager will even call in the sales manager when responding). Thenceforth the question and assumptions and conditions coincide with what has been said in relation to the trading company. The vehicle company is able and willing to sell as many automobiles as it currently has in its yard, plus the number completed in the coming week. (The rhythm of completion of the finished product can no longer be influenced.) So that is the supply for sale in the coming week. The excess supply (the quantity that cannot be sold) will equal the closing stock.

Quite another question with quite different assumptions is called for if the manager is addressed as the one directing *production*. With as complex a product as an automobile, it is not useful or customary to gauge a term as short as a week. Let us ask for his ideas about the next quarter.

This part of the interview (and its terms and conditions) resembles that of case 1, the service firm. The respondent will be asked to assume that there are sufficient orders. So if it depends on him or her alone, what will the preferred number of units be? The response will be a desire to approach the factory's practical capacity as closely as possible. This is more likely to be the answer if volume is subject to a *constant* return to scale as it approaches practical capacity, and even more likely if an increasing return to scale applies in production (which is the likely case in a vehicle factory).

The subsequent line of thought also coincides with the service-firm case. If production turned out to be less than practical capacity, because too few orders were received, or if the sales position could not be expected to improve sooner or later, an interim reduction in the production targets would be made.

It could be seen after the quarter was up that the firm had not managed to utilize its practical production capacity. Ex post the idle capacity can be classed as excess supply.

Notice that two types of excess supply appear in the production firm: stock unsold despite willingness to sell, and capacity unused despite willingness to produce. Both consist of cars, but the two clearly defined numbers cannot be added together. The former is visible in the yard, in tangible automobiles, the latter only in imagination, as the quantitative description of an unfulfilled production desire. Both the unsold stock readily available for sale and the idle capacity expressible as potential surplus can actually be classed as excess supply, from different angles, but the sum of the data cannot be interpreted.

Although I have performed the conceptual clarification as imaginary interview questions, there luckily exist real surveys based on similar questions.

Table 3.1 makes an international comparison of industrial-capacity-utilization data. The researchers analyzed data for 34 countries over a long timeline, from 1978 to 2008. This table covers 13 countries, for which over 100 observations are available! It presents the mean over the period for each country.

Figure 3.1 presents the time series of utilization for the United States. The report's authors stress that the capacity to which actual utilization is

Table 3.1. RATIO OF CAPACITY UTILIZATION: INTERNATIONAL COMPARISON, 1978–2008

Country	Mean	Number of observations	Standard deviation
Belgium	79.0	121	2.89
Canada	81.3	152	4.11
France	84.4	130	2.02
Germany	83.6	154	3.51
Italy	75.7	154	2.70
Japan	79.0	153	8.11
Netherlands	82.5	147	2.58
New Zealand	89.2	153	2.13
Norway	82.4	138	2.70
Portugal	78.9	126	2.49
Spain	79.8	154	3.03
Switzerland	83.8	154	3.33
United States	80.4	145	3.91

Note: Data show the capacity utilization in manufacturing. "Mean" is the average value for capacity utilization reported for the given countries across all available observations of this country. "Number of observations" relates to the length of the time series for a county available in the official statistics when the paper was written. The data on capacity utilization are quarterly, thus $N = 40$ would imply that the series goes so far back to cover 10 years.
Source: Etter, Graff, and Müller (2008, 8).

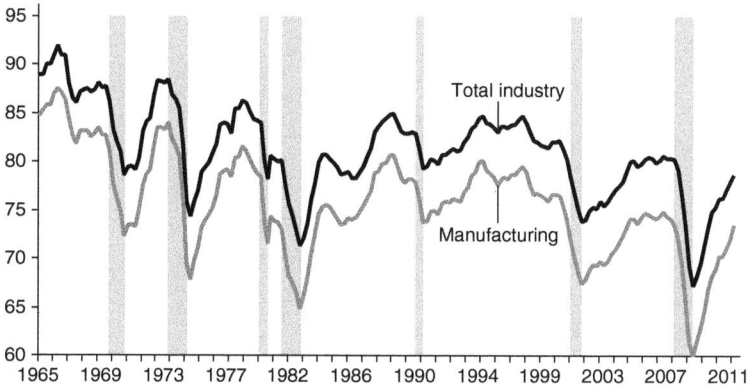

Figure 3.1.
Rate of capacity utilization, United States, 1965–2011
Note: The gray vertical areas represent periods of recession. The recession areas were determined according to the definitions of the National Bureau of Economic Research (NBER).
Source: Federal Reserve Statistical Release (2010).

compared shows long-term sustainable production level, i.e., the practical capacity (see also Corrado and Mattey 1997). As another example, the time-series for France appears in Figure 3.2.

The table and graphs clearly prompt the following conclusions:

The capacity utilization rate differs by country. Annual rates fluctuate, but it is usually below 90 percent.[7] This backs the assertion that substantial idle capacity is ubiquitous, a chronic phenomenon, in a capitalist economy.

Figure 3.2.
Rate of capacity utilization, France, 1965–2005
Source: Allain and Canry (2008). The authors, Olivier Allain and Nicolas Canry made available the numerical data. I am grateful for their help.

7. The exception is shown in Figure 3.1, where the utilization of capacity in the United States exceeds 90 percent in the first two years of the time series.

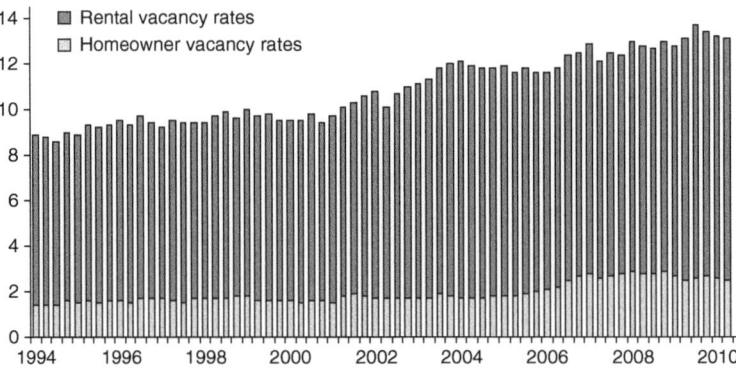

Figure 3.3.
Rental and homeowner vacancy rates, United States, 1994–2011 (percent)
Source: U. S. Census Bureau (2012).

Table 3.1 and Figures 3.1 and 3.2 show utilization of industrial capacities. Similar surveys are being made of utilization of housing stock. For the purposes of this study, the figures for owner-occupied housing and rented housing units for sale and for rent can be added together: the sum can be taken as the housing sector's unused capacity. Figure 3.3 shows clearly that the combined proportion never sank below 8 percent in the United States in any one year, and it reached 12 percent in 2004. This marks a substantial proportion of excess supply.[8]

3.2 THE FIRST DIFFICULTY: CONTINUAL MUTUAL ADJUSTMENT OF SUPPLY AND DEMAND

The three "pure cases" discussed have yielded a definition of the concept of "excess supply" and a method of measuring it, except that I have intentionally facilitated the matter with various abstractions in order to arrive at clear definitions and measurement methods for a first look at measurement. I would now like to address and introduce readers to what happens in practice, to the events of real business activity, which differ from the idealized and simplified world of the three introductory examples.

I am not thinking of how observers of the events or statisticians measuring them may make mistakes, for these will cause random errors. The frequent

---

8. For comparison's sake, let me mention the housing shortage, one of the most depressing features of the socialist economy. The related Wikipedia article (2012b) gives the following figures for the extent of the shortage in 1986 as a proportion of the total housing stock: 30.2 percent in the Soviet Union, 27.4 percent in Bulgaria, 23.9 percent in Poland, and 17.1 percent in East Germany.

problem is that the situation precludes applying such pure definitions and measurement methods consistently.

The first difficult problem has been touched upon in Section 2 of this essay, in describing the process of demand formation. Now, let us look, from the measurement point of view, at the supply and demand sides concurrently.

The events in both supply and demand form a dynamic process for every seller and every buyer. The producers' or sellers' propensity to sell varies continually, as adjustments are made under the pressure to conform to the prevailing situation. Which moment in the process of their maturation marks the "true" supply? Market researchers regularly ask the executives of production companies what they plan to produce or sell. Then, they compare the plan with actual production or sales. The "true" figure may depart from the plan either way.[9] The problem is to know at what stage the intention-forming process was when the executives were asked. How did the information that was gained on demand affect the formation of supply? The closer a manager gets to the end of the adjustment of supply to demand, the more closely plan and realization coincide.

The same can be said about buyers' desire to buy. At which moment does it translate into "true" demand? When do they set out to buy? When do they enter the store? When do they fail to find the item and buy something else instead? Or, a while later, when do they buy something else in a second or third store?

I am not tackling the question of *notional* versus *actual* demand and supply. These terms are widely used in the theoretical literature by the "disequilibrium school" (see Benassy 1982). Notional demand is a fictional static snapshot, and actual demand is another fictional static snapshot. The same applies to the terms *notional supply* and *actual supply*. I suggest instead that demand-formation is not composed of two still photographs but it is a movie; a continuous interaction between buying intention (which may or may not be well defined at the beginning) and adjustment to the available supply and *vice versa*. Instead of two static numbers (notional and actual), we see an adjustment *process*. In a surplus economy this process does not run against supply constraints very often, but, even when it does, we witness a certain adjustment of demand to supply.

We can trace the process with each seller and each buyer, but if we seek to total a multitude of buyers' intentions and willingness to sell or a multitude of sellers' intentions and willingness to buy at a given moment or over a short period, we are adding up elements of heterogeneous quality.[10] As a result, the interpretation of the total is unclear (or, without further questioning in each case, impossible.)

---

9. See, for instance, the widely applied measurements of the Business Tendency Survey (OECD 2003).

10. I have already mentioned the problem of heterogeneity: the difficulties arising if the behavior of a group is to be described by the behavior of a representative, "average" individual within it. Heterogeneity poses especially great difficulties in recording supply and demand.

To illustrate this, let us return to the hotel trade. If there are 20 guests in a city, 10 seeking 4-star and 10 seeking 2-star accommodations, and they find what they want, then everyone is satisfied. But if all 20 sought 4-star accommodation and 10 had to make do with 2-star, then 10 are satisfied, and the other 10 are disappointed, even though the factual statistical record of hotel occupancy will be the same in both cases. So if everybody found a room, one way or another, according to the "shorter side rule" the actual total of rooms occupied can be called the guests' demand. However, the aggregation disguises the fact that some disappointed guests did not get exactly what they wanted, and, because of forced substitution, they felt less satisfied.

3.3 THE SECOND DIFFICULTY: PARALLEL OCCURRENCES OF EXCESS SUPPLY AND EXCESS DEMAND

In the experimental lines of thinking described early in this section, I made my task easier by assuming that, for each transaction, the demand was the shorter side, and I thereby ruled out the possibility of excess demand. Keeping the shorter-side rule in mind, it is clear that, in such cases, what the descriptive, factual, statistical record reflects is the demand, because we were obviously dealing with a market with excess supply.

However, we cannot be so certain of that in practice. Phenomena of excess supply and excess demand may occur simultaneously. There may be few guests in some hotels, yet other guests may not find the accommodation they would like. Finally, there is some rearrangement every day. Let us say that the daily comprehensive statistics are compiled for the occupancy of all the hotels in the city. This report alone will not reveal whether this reflects the demand or the supply.

Phenomena of excess supply and excess demand do not just coexist; there may be interaction between them. Sellers with excess, unsold supply may, as buyers, lack the money to purchase what they intended. The fall in their demand causes excess supply in other sellers, and so on (Clower 1965 and 1967; Leijonhufvud 1968). The excess-supply phenomena have spillover, multiplier effects.

It would be good if such statistics for micro excess demand and excess supply were recorded separately. Then, significant statements could be made on their distribution, and the stochastic characteristics of the microphenomena determined.

3.4 DIVERSION: OBSERVING THE OBSTACLES TO AND MICRO CONSTRAINTS OF PRODUCTION

The last subsection tackled the problem of coexisting phenomena of excess supply and excess demand. Great help in understanding and observing them could be given by a regular international survey I will describe, but care must be taken to interpret the methodology of it correctly.

Every quarter for several decades, 26 international business research institutes in 26 European countries have been asking a sample of managers chosen from a multitude of industrial companies the following question:[11]

"What are the main factors that currently restrict your production?

- There are no such factors.
- Shortage of labor.
- Shortage of materials and/or equipment.
- Financial constraints.
- Other factors (please detail)."

As an example, I append the Hungarian time series (see Figure 3.4 and Table A.1 in the Appendix). Before drawing conclusions from this in relation to the present study, it is worth thinking again about what exactly the managers are

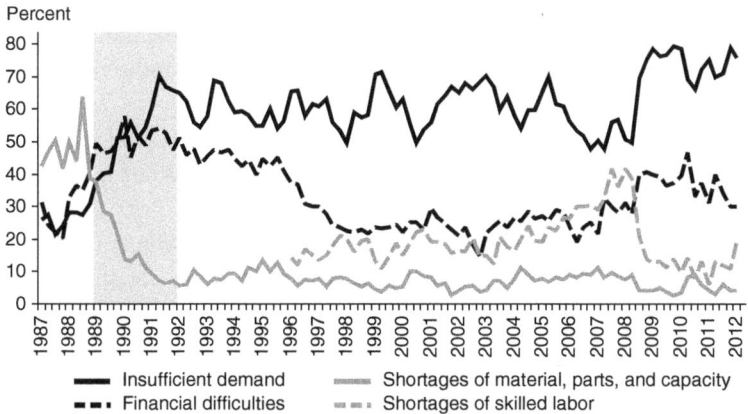

Figure 3.4.
Impediments to manufacturing production, Hungary, 1987–2012 (percent mentioned)
Note: The respondents were asked about the different factors that might hinder production. They could mention more than one impediment in their answers. The chart illustrates, for the sake of a better overview, only a few time series, that is, not all columns of the numerical table are illustrated. The vertical axis represents the relative frequency of mentions in percentage. The interpretation of the continuous gray line on the lower half of the graph, that is, the curve of shortages of material, parts, and capacity, is based on the following logic. For each survey period, we choose the highest number of the five variables (concerning material, spare part, and capacity shortage), that is, the highest relative frequency. In other words, the highest number means the proportion of respondents who mentioned at least one of the five types of impediments. The continuous gray curve illustrates the series of these highest numbers. The gray area is covering the years following the collapse of the Berlin Wall, that is, the first period of moving from the socialist to the capitalist system. The data refer to the first quarter of the year.
Source: Direct communication of Kopint-Tárki (Institute for Economic and Market Research, Budapest). The graph is based on the data of Table A.1 in the Appendix.

---

11. For the methodology of the survey see OECD (2003) and Nilsson (2001).

being asked by the researchers. For comparison's sake, look at the virtual question put in point 3 of subsection 3.1, discussing the "pure" cases. There the question was different—essentially different! The researchers are not asking these managers in 26 countries what they think of their production ex ante, what volume they would produce *if there were demand*, calculating in advance with the customary impediments to production on the input side. The question now is *not* about supply, but the ex ante volume. Nor have the researchers asked whether, provided the production company would be capable of producing 500 units and there were a realistic possibility of doing so on the output side, they would like to produce those 500 units. In other words, they were not asked how big the supply *would be* irrespective of the demand.

Instead the researchers' questions assume tacitly that the production manager considers the various obstacles, when drawing up the production targets, and arrives at a realistic, feasible plan. This can be done (according to the line of thinking in this study) with a snapshot of the supply-formation process at a fairly advanced stage. Now, they ask, in the midst of that advanced process of supply formation, what factors customarily impede production, that is, "If you forecast the likely events well, what obstacles do you usually take into account?" These are not exactly the words of the question raised in the survey. I revealed here the implicit assumptions that underlie the framing of the question.

This sensible and revealing question yields sensible and revealing responses,[12] but it does not reveal what demand constraints at the micro level confront the original supply, which would go up to the barrier of practical capacity. Hence, the survey data do not allow us to deduce *directly* the size of the micro-level excess demand or excess supply, and so it does not and cannot give a clear, *direct* answer to the principal question in this study (surplus economy? shortage economy?).

Nonetheless, it is possible (with due caution) to gain *indirect* guidance from these data for my research questions. Note how the proportions of responses mentioning input troubles and insufficient demand vary in Hungary's figures. The gray vertical band in Figure 3.4 marks the change-of-system period. The timeline shows clearly that up to the change of system, corporate efforts at continuity and growth of production under the socialist shortage economy encountered obstacles mainly on the resources side: shortage of labor, especially skilled labor, and shortages of materials and components were the commonest problems. Two-thirds of the respondents cited at least one of those troubles on the input side. Nor was insufficient demand rare, but that kind of obstacle did not feature in more than one-third of the responses before 1989.

---

12. The survey, carried out in 26 countries, was not meant to measure the scale or dispersion of phenomena of excess supply and excess demand, but to offer practical assistance in forecasting fluctuations, which it did to the full.

The proportions more or less reversed after the change of system. About two-thirds of respondents mentioned demand-side obstacles in the 2000s, and mentions of shortages of materials and components were very rare.[13]

3.5 THE THIRD DIFFICULTY: DISTINGUISHING "NECESSARY" FROM "SUPERFLUOUS" STOCKS

Returning to the main line of argument, let us look at problems of conceptualization and measurement.

In the "pure" cases at the beginning of Section 3, the unsold closing stock was classed as excess supply. It may not have struck readers, but it is my duty to point out that this is problematic.

With stationary stocks and stationary replacement, if the unsold stock of a product *rises* over a period, there is clearly excess supply of it. Earlier, however, it was stressed that demand is not stationary, it continually varies, not least in response to changes in supply. Holding stocks is designed to facilitate the mutual adjustment of supply and demand.

When can it be said that stocks are "too big," constituting excess supply? Before addressing the question, let me refer to the security level introduced in subsection 2.2, which is designated B in the discussion that follows. It could be said, for instance, that the stocks were adequate, not too big, if 90 percent of buyers found what they were looking for and only 10 percent had to make a forced substitution or leave the store without making a purchase ($B = 0.9$), but the stocks were superfluously big (constituting excess supply) if they produced a proportion of only 9 percent of disappointed customers instead of 10 ($B = 0.91$). Yet frankly, this starting point is arbitrary. Why should B be exactly 0.9? Why not 0.85 or 0.96? The security level B is not determined, but *necessarily undetermined:* determination of it is effected to some extent by the spontaneous drives and adjustment mechanisms described in Section 2.[14]

So it is *necessarily undetermined* where the "necessary" quantity of stocks ends, and where the "superfluous," "exaggerated" quantity that can be labeled unhesitatingly *excess* supply begins.

Although this quantitative threshold remains undetermined, we might be certain of the existence of certain important relations.

- With customary continuity and organization of restocking, the security level rises along with the appropriately composed stocks. If the

---

13. It is worth noting that shortages of skilled labor cause problems also in an economy that has become capitalist in character.

14. It is consistent with this statement that some firm or other should follow purposeful, sophisticated rules for stocks and repeat orders, and thereby influence the security level B for its own customers.

size and composition of the stocks are taken as given, the security level rises with the flexibility and smoothness of restocking and the speed at which orders are fulfilled.[15] These connections are obvious. Numerous operations-research models have been devised to quantify and analyze these relations.

- If a firm's inventory policy allows a high level of security to be attained, this influences both the seller (e.g., strengthening competitive position) and the buyer (offering greater choice and a greater chance of finding the goods most desired).

So far, there has been discussion only of excess supply, because that is central to this study, but the line of argument can be extended to excess demand as well. If all those willing and financially able to make a purchase leave the store empty-handed ($B = 0$), the stocks are clearly too small. But what if it turns out ex post that the actual size and composition of demand generate a figure of $B = 0.3$ or $B = 0.4$? Are the stocks "too small" then? Let me repeat: the threshold value below which it can be clearly stated that the stocks are lower than "required" is undetermined.

To return to the definition problem: the ideas just described suffice in themselves to sow doubts about using the attributes "superfluous" or "excess." For my part, I try to avoid in this study (sometimes unsuccessfully) the problem of whether we face superfluous stocks or superfluous capacity.

In my work, *Economics of Shortage* (Kornai 1980), I used the word *slack* for what is termed here *surplus*. I have spent more time among native English speakers and read more of the English daily press than I had when I wrote *Economics of Shortage*. I now sense the pejorative tinge to the word *slack*, which implies that its appearance points to looseness and that at least part of the stock or the capacity is superfluous. I have been led to seek a more neutral word by a desire to avoid such judgmental overtones. I leave intentionally open the question of whether idle capacity, residual stocks, and slow turnover counted as wastefulness, or clever management of reserves, or special attention to unpredictable buyers.

Although I insist that the threshold value for "exaggeration" and "superfluity" are indeterminable, it does not follow that the size of unsold stocks and unsatisfied customers are indifferent and not worth attention. On the contrary, these are important magnitudes; they are observable and expressible numerically by suitable methods.

Instructive analysis can be made of the composition of stocks (see Chikán 1984). Let us look at Table 3.2.

---

15. The just-in-time policy for replenishing stocks appeared and spread in Japan. If necessary inputs are not kept in stock, but always arrive in time, continuity of production can be maintained at lower overall stock levels.

Table 3.2. RATIO OF INPUT AND OUTPUT STOCKS: INTERNATIONAL COMPARISON, 1981–1985

Country	Average input stock per average output stock in manufacturing, 1981–1985
Socialist countries	
Bulgaria	5.07
Czechoslovakia	3.07
Hungary	6.10
Poland	4.49
Soviet Union	3.16
Capitalist countries	
Australia	1.36
Austria	1.06
Canada	0.92
Finland	1.92
Japan	1.09
Norway	1.10
Portugal	1.66
Sweden	0.81
United Kingdom	1.02
United States	1.02
West Germany	0.71

Source: Compiled by A. Chikán. Published in Kornai, *The Socialist System* (1992, 250).

The calculation rests on the following line of argument. Whatever the system may be like, the need for continuity of production and sales and the avoidance of shocks require stocks to be kept of the inputs required for production and of the output of production. However, the proportions between the two are system specific. So on which side is the stronger buffer of stocks required? Table 3.2 supports the assertion that there is a shortage economy under the socialist system, because there was great uncertainty about restocking with inputs, whereas the ubiquitous shortage of the finished product made sales relatively easy, so that the proportion of input stocks to output stocks was very high (Farkas 1980). However, under the capitalist system, the proportion is much lower. This shows that instances of shortage were far less expected in inputs procurement under the capitalist system, whereas the output stocks swelled, because sales were more difficult and because producers want to offer buyers faster service and a greater variety.

3.6 THE FOURTH DIFFICULTY: UNJUSTIFIED AGGREGATION

Let us look at a partial market that is trading mutually related goods or services. It is customary in models of standard microeconomics to list "net excess demand" as the explanatory variables for price change. The price setting rule is this: If net excess demand is positive, the price rises; if negative, the price falls. The famed figure in Walrasian economics, the "auctioneer," and the price office of Oscar Lange (1968 [1936–37]), a follower of Walrasian theory, handles prices according to the rule just outlined, until they arrive at the equilibrium price.

Arriving at "net excess demand" involves a simple addition: It is the sum of the positive excess-demand data and the negative excess-supply data.

This seems logical at first hearing, although there is a grave logical error behind it. Let us say we are examining the load on an airport at a certain level of aggregation: what was the utilization rate of capacity on the planes leaving the airport on a certain day? Excess demand: some passengers could not travel at the desired time. Excess supply: some planes were leaving half full. Net excess demand: the number of rejected passengers minus the number of empty seats over a given period. This is, however, a meaningless sum. Does it console passengers unable to leave on the 9 AM flight from Budapest to Copenhagen that there were empty seats on the 7 PM flight to the same destination? They may have had important appointments for that afternoon.[16]

Altering the excess demand function to "net" values is a methodological move often made in theoretical models and in empirical, econometric examinations.[17] Rethinking the problem suggests strict prohibition on constructing such aggregate figures for "net excess demand" or "net excess supply."

All the measurement difficulties mentioned warn against misleading aggregations. In fact, thorough consideration of some troubles points to the need for a complete ban on them. Let us look again at the problems discussed so far, purely from the aggregation point of view:

1. It is not permissible to add closing stock to the "surplus" appearing in the form of idle capacity; these represent different ranks of "availability." Of the two types of occurrence of surplus, the second, surplus capacity, is more essential, for one thing because it is more persistent and harder to reduce than stocks, whose size are easier to control.

---

16. The flights leaving a given airport to diverse destinations at various times must be regarded as differing, *heterogeneous* goods. Thus, the well-known aggregation problems caused by heterogeneity appear.

17. The problems of aggregation appear strongly with the disequilibrium models employed in the macroeconomic analysis of the socialist countries (see Portes and Winter 1980; Portes et al. 1987). For a review of the debate see Davis and Charemza (1989), and van Brabant (1990).

THE MARKET FOR GOODS AND SERVICES: CONCEPTS (85)

2. Both supply and demand develop as dynamic processes. The propensity of each seller or buyer to sell or buy may alter and mature in the interim. With snapshot cross-section measurements at specific times, it is wrong to add propensities to sell or buy that are heterogeneous in terms of the "maturation" process.
3. The last, perhaps severest problem was just mentioned: it is wrong to "net out," that is, subtract the net sum of excess demand from the net sum of excess supply at any level of aggregation.

These observations certainly apply to aggregation at lower (micro) and medium levels. The line of argument points straight to the need for the greatest caution in interpreting macro-level data. It is *impossible* to establish the macro supply and macro demand for one particular economy at one particular time.

I have to admit I am at a loss to explain where to place in my thinking the indicator for the "gap" between actual and potential GDP that is employed widely in macro-analyses. This, too, is a kind of index of excess supply, similar to excess capacity in a production company or in an industry. It seems likely that this should raise the same concerns and reservations that I mentioned just now in relation to aggregated indicators at lower levels. Certainly the problem awaits further clarification. For my part, I would not dare at present either to accept or reject this indicator, which is widely respected and used.

I could list more statistical and observation difficulties and anomalies, but these objections may suffice to explain why I prefer the "shortage economy–surplus economy" pair of concepts for describing the general market state of a particular country, and shrink from using the "excess-demand economy–excess-supply economy" pair of concepts that many find easier to grasp.

3.7 PRAGMATIC SUGGESTIONS FOR MEASUREMENT AND A CONCEPTUAL APPARATUS

Based on what has been said, I for one am prepared to abandon the idea of working out how much the total supply and total demand at given prices in a given market will be, and establishing quantitatively the size of the excess supply or the excess demand. I will not try to characterize the general state of the market by a cardinal indicator.

However, that does not mean abandoning the task of measurement. Instead of aggregate, cardinal measurement, it is possible to use several partial indicators that shed light on characteristic manifestations of the surplus economy and shortage economy, and on the state and changes of these at a given time.

Let me list some examples of such indicators.

- The capacity of producers and service providers and its utilization of their capacities.
- The stock turnover, as well as the proportions of the constituents of stocks in relation to each other and to the volume of sales.
- Questioning of producers on the obstacles to production.
- Queuing and wait-list times, the buying intention of queuers compared with the actual sale.

Examples of such indicators are to be found in several parts of this essay, demonstrating that they are measurement methods applicable in practice.

There may also be other indicators that reflect some features of instances of surplus and shortage. Inventive economists, market researchers, and statisticians may devise further observation and measurement procedures. Unfortunately, the desirable order of a theoretical idea being based on practical observations and measurements cannot always be achieved. Often, it is reversed; a theory based on suppositions creates the demand for observing and measuring a phenomenon, and only then are the practical arrangements made in order to get the statistical data.

All the measurements mentioned convey more than two discrete states, excess supply, and excess demand. They report on the phenomenon's intensity or "weight." It is not immaterial whether idle capacity amounts to 10 or 30 percentage points, whether stocks in the warehouse suffice for 3 or 20 months, or whether the waiting period for a product or service is 3 months or 3 years.

Based on the indicators presented and other, similar ones, it becomes possible to perform analyses of the distribution and dynamics of instances of surplus and shortage (or classifying them more finely, of those of various intensities or "weights"), and identify the stochastic features of the distributions.

3.8 FORMATION OF SYNTHETIC INDICATORS OR "COMPOSITE INDICES"

It would be worth seeking to calculate "composite indices" covering a broader sphere or a country's whole economy in order to show the frequency and intensity of shortage and surplus phenomena. Such summary indicators are being used for various purposes. Let me list a couple of well-known examples:

- A "freedom index" is designed to reflect the state of freedom of enterprise and individual rights in a country in a given year (Freedom House 2010).
- A "corruption index" presents the spread and severity of instances of corruption in a country in a given year (Transparency International 2010).

- A "business climate index" seeks to reflect the "mood" of decision makers in the business world, the optimism or pessimism in their expectations. (On the French calculations, see Clavel and Minodier 2009; Erkel-Rousse and Minodier 2009.)

The starting point for such calculations is the recognition of the impossibility of measuring the *aggregate* volume or intensity of certain complex phenomena directly. However, it is possible to measure several *partial* phenomena. An example would be to design a function: The explanatory variables are the partial indicators of the partial phenomena, and the variable generated by the function is the "composite index" (e.g., "freedom index," "corruption index," "business climate index").[18]

The "composite index" can be derived from the partial, constituent indicators by various procedures. The simplest (and of course the most perfunctory) is to average the partial indicators to arrive at the synthetic indices. Sometimes factor analysis is employed and the factors with the greatest weight and the strongest explanatory force are classed as synthetic indices.

It is not intended in this essay to devise the methodology for calculating "composite indices" capable of measuring shortage and surplus synthetically. I would not even say it was certain that such indices could be drawn in order to get a concise reflection of the phenomena examined here. It would call for careful study of the behavior of the partial indicators reflecting the state of the market. All I wish to say here is that addition and subtraction are not the only available operations for calculating synthetically complex phenomena that are statistically hard to "grasp." It would be worth reconsidering thoroughly the experience gained in summarizing other complex phenomena not measurable by cardinal indicators.

I would like to underline at the end of this section on concept clarification and measurement methods the "neutrality" of the conceptual and measurement apparatus recommended. It can apply to a market in which phenomena of surplus preponderate and phenomena of shortage are dominant. It is also neutral in being appropriate for observing and evaluating the actual state of the market regardless of one's own set of values or sympathy or antipathy toward one system or another.

---

18. I first advanced this a long time ago in my book *Growth, Shortage and Efficiency* (Kornai 1982). I later began a major research program with several colleagues, to devise partial indicators of shortage. These were designed to lead, ultimately, to the calculation of a synthetic index of shortage. The project ended with the change of system, when the participants, myself included, set themselves other tasks. Luckily, the shortage economy ceased in Hungary, and therefore the subject lost immediacy. Only now it does occur to me again when the problem of synthetic measurement of surplus phenomena arises.

SECTION 4

The Labor Market: The Mechanism for the Reproduction of Surplus

4.1 CONCEPTUAL CLARIFICATION AND MEASUREMENT

Some conceptual clarification and examination of related measurement problems are needed before turning to substantive analysis of the labor market. I would like to use the same approach as I did for discussing the market for products and services. So I have to clarify what relation persists between the conceptual apparatus of my study and the indicators used in labor statistics.[1]

The situation is relatively easy with incidents of shortage. The *number of vacancies* recorded in the statistics is a good reflection of labor shortage. Also recorded is the *number of registered unemployed*, which is clearly a fundamental piece of data for labor surplus, but numerical analysis of surplus on the labor market cannot stop there.

Let us begin, in the spirit of this essay, with what has to be measured and contrast it with the data available. The examination will be of a given economy, one at the national scale and at a given time. Let us call the population of the country Q, within which four groups can be distinguished:

1. Some inhabitants will not take work, due to various circumstances. Children are not permitted to work. Those over 14 years of age are considered statistically as able to work. (However, economic history shows that legislation banning child labor is relatively recent and masses of children still work in economically backward countries.) Some inhabitants are precluded from any work by physical and/or mental disabilities or possibly chronic illness. (We need to be cautious: it is not permissible to list automatically as incapable of work all those officially classified as having physical and/or mental disabilities.

---

1. The international definitions appear in the ILO (2010) publication.

Many of them would indeed be capable of work, but the social and economic conditions allowing them to work are lacking.) They include the old, provided that they are precluded from work by illness or physical or mental weakness. (However, not all elderly people are incapable of work, even though the official labor statistics draw a line, say, at 74, between those capable and incapable of work. The writer of these lines feels capable of work although he is 85 at the time of writing.) The parenthetical remarks after each "incapable of work" category indicate that each criterion is, to some extent, problematic. Let us denote the number of inhabitants *incapable of work* as N.

2. The next group consists of those incapable of work, but discouraged for some reason from entering the labor market and seeking an occupation. Let us call this group the section of the population *capable of work but inactive*, to be denoted M. Here are some circumstances that may discourage persons capable of work from seeking a job.

- They may not need to take a job because they can support themselves from other sources (from private means, the earnings of another family member, state assistance, etc.)
- They are retired and can live on their pensions.
- They are discouraged from work by traditions. This is an especially important factor in female employment.
- Other important factors in female employment are the following. Women keep away from employment if they cannot organize care during working hours for family members in their charge: nurseries, infant schools, after-school care centers, institutional day care for elderly dependents, etc., are not available.
- They have sought jobs for a long time unsuccessfully. They see no chance of finding jobs and have stopped searching. This group is known as *discouraged workers* and appears in Hungarian labor statistics as the *passive unemployed*.

These discouraging factors overlap to some extent. It is hard to say (standing as the question does on the borders of economics, sociology, and social psychology) to what extent the decision of those who have decided not to seek work is voluntary or dictated by circumstances. The compulsion may be a social norm ("a woman's place is in the home") or absence of practical conditions required for work (absence or high cost of nursery or infant school care). Where is the point at which a job-seeker gives up hope, ceases to seek work, and "voluntarily" exits from the labor market?

I recognize that the dividing line between the two groups mentioned, those incapable of work and those capable of it but inactive, is not entirely sharp, but the essential content of the distinction is plain.

3. The official statistics record the registered *unemployed*. Let us call the group U. The official figures use strict criteria for distinguishing the

unemployed actively seeking work from the "passive unemployed" who have given up the search (those who have sought work actively in the four weeks before they are questioned, etc.). Naturally, there is a danger of arbitrariness in the distinction (Why four weeks? Why not three or five?), but that is inescapable in any statistical recording process.

4. Finally, the official statistics record the proportion of the population actually *employed* at a given time. Let us denote this as E.

The official statistics call the sum of those actively employed and the unemployed actually seeking work the *economically active* section of the population. Literature in English refers to this as the *labor force*. Their number will be called A, where $A = E + U$. (The complementary group in the population *out of the labor force* is called B, where $B = Q - A$.)

The spirit of this study suggests that the labor surplus, called T, should consist not only of the officially registered unemployed, but also the inactive section of the population capable of work, where $T = M + U$. This is the reserve force (to use a Marxian expression) from which labor can be recruited if the labor market needs it. When the business cycle is rising, the market draws on some of the surplus, which not only reduces unemployment, but draws into the active sphere some of the hitherto inactive, non-job-seeking section of the population too. This occurrence is especially perceptible in time of war, when "the reserves are mobilized" in a literal sense and people are drawn into productive work by government order.

The official statistics draw the boundary differently when distinguishing the economically active from the economically inactive. The conceptual differences are indicated more clearly in Table 4.1.

The conceptual framework in this study fails to coincide with official statistical definitions at a critical point: the latter does not regularly survey the inactive section of the population capable of work. There occurs in some studies a category of "age groups capable of work," usually consisting of the 14–64 age groups, but this distinction is not the same, as there are (as I have mentioned), within the age groups, a number of individuals who will not take work under any circumstances, and there are some over the age of 64 who would be capable of work but are inactive.

I assume in what follows that the statistically observed indicator b, the rate of the economically inactive section of the population, provides an acceptable proxy for the indicator m, the rate of those capable of work but economically inactive, which features in the line of argument in this essay but is not recorded statistically. It is an indicator to suit my purpose in the analyses that follow, in which I present comparisons over time for a specific country and the "broad" system-specific differences. My assumptions are based primarily on logical reconsideration of the problem. My guess is that the figure for the section of the population incapable of work is rather rigid and directly depends mainly on demographic and health-care factors. On the other hand,

Table 4.1. LINKAGES BETWEEN CONCEPTS USED IN THIS BOOK AND THOSE USED IN LABOR MARKET STATISTICS

Concepts used in this book		Concepts used in labor market statistics
	Population capable of work (N)	
		Economically inactive population (B)
Labor force surplus ($T = M + U$)	Population capable of work, but inactive (M)	
	Unemployed (U)	
		Economically active population ($A = U + E$)
	Employed (E)	
Labor force shortage	Job vacancies (V)	Job vacancies (V)
Total population ($Q = N + M + U + E$)		Total population (Q) ($Q = B + A$)
Indicator in relative terms (%)		*Indicator in relative terms (%)*
The rate of surplus ($t = T/Q$)		The rate of the economically inactive population ($b = B/Q$)
The rate of population capable of work but economically inactive ($m = M/Q$)		
		Activity rate (or the rate of the economically active population) ($a = A/Q'$)
Unemployment rate ($u = U/Q$)		Unemployment rate ($u = U/Q$) or ($u' = U/Q'$)
The rate of shortage ($v = V/Q$)		Job vacancies to unemployment ratio $v = V/Q$, or $v' = V/W$, where W is the total number of open positions

Note: The official labor-market statistics usually reports the indicators denoted by apostrophes, as u' and v' rates. However, the u and v rates can be easily reproduced from the official labor-market statistics. In order to compute the activity rate, the official labor-market statistics does not apply the total number of the population, Q in the denominator. Instead it applies a subgroup of the total population, Q', the population capable of work aged between 14 and 64.

the selection made *within* the section of the population capable of work about whether to place individuals in the economically active or the inactive sections depends on social and economic factors. The effect of this selection is reflected quite clearly in the variable M that I recommend (which is not measured at present), whereas the official statistics add to this variable a relatively constant figure (the proportion of those incapable of work, N) and observe only the total, $B = N + M$.

It is a task for future research to distinguish empirically between the section of the population incapable of work and that capable of work but inactive, and to measure them. These are observable data—there is no obstacle to measuring them.

4.2 THE SHOCK TO THE LABOR MARKET CAUSED BY THE CHANGE OF SYSTEM

I referred at the beginning of the essay to a Polish photograph of a long queue in front of a food shop during the period of the shortage economy. These days, the shelves are overflowing in Poland and the other postsocialist countries. Customers have become accustomed to the sight and consider it self-evident.

There has been a concurrent change on the labor market. The economically more-developed socialist countries of Central and Eastern Europe and the Soviet Union suffered from intense labor shortage before 1989. The change of system sent a shock through the labor market: massive elimination of jobs, leading to lasting unemployment. Within a few years, there was a marked reduction in the economically active population (those actually at work and those unemployed but actively seeking jobs). On the goods market, it is easy to get used to the surplus economy, but on the labor market it is impossible to get used to it, and it remains constantly oppressive.

For an East European economist like myself, the experience of this turn of events prompted a rethinking of the relation between the state of the labor market and the system—socialist or capitalist—under which it operates. It is depressing to notice the indifference with which this question is treated by Western social scientists. I think I am right in saying that no Western researcher in the field of labor-market economics has taken the trouble to compare experience under capitalism with experience under socialism when seeking the causes of unemployment.

Western participants in economic discourse treat it as self-evident that there is unemployment even under conditions of ostensible full employment. To this day, I cannot read without irritation (even outrage) that oft-repeated, canonized expression the *natural* rate of unemployment.[2] Natural? Did the green Nature of forests and hares, rocks and earthquakes decree at the same time that there should be unemployment? I have been for decades a sharp

---

2. To avoid misunderstandings, this remark does not refer to the *content* of the theory of the "natural rate of unemployment," which is widely debated among macroeconomists with a genuine concern for unemployment. I am irritated not by my colleagues' researches, but by the *word usage*.

critic of the socialist system, but friends and enemies alike of it should realize that it was marked by a chronic shortage of labor, not by chronic unemployment and a sizable surplus of labor.

Let me convey with some figures how dramatic a change the labor market in the postsocialist region underwent. Unfortunately, there are no time series to present the state of the labor market in the period before the change of system, coupled with figures arrived at by the same methods for the period of more than two decades since. Still, it is apparent from the diagrams and tables how traumatic the change was. (Figure 4.1 is from Kornai 1992, 209.)

Figure 4.2 presents data for 2009 in the same way that Figure 4.1 does for 1980.

Note in Figure 4.1 that the activity rate is higher in every socialist country (indicated by the area surrounded by the dashed line) than the capitalist countries of a similar level of development.

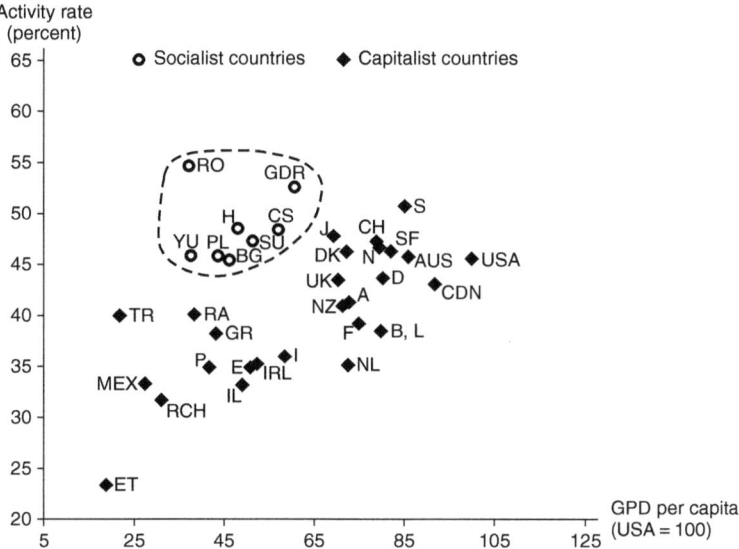

Figure 4.1.
Activity rate and the degree of economic development, 1980
Note: The following countries are included in the sample (in ascending order with respect to the level of GDP per capita): Egypt (ET), Turkey (TR), Mexico (MEX), Chile (RCH), Romania (RO), Yugoslavia (YU), Argentina (RA), Portugal (P), Greece (GR), Poland (PL), Bulgaria (BG), Hungary (H), Israel (IL), USSR (SU), Spain (E), Ireland (IRL), Czechoslovakia (CS), Italy (I), East Germany (GDR), Japan (J), United Kingdom (UK), New Zealand (NZ), Denmark (DK), Austria (A), the Netherlands (NL), France (F), Switzerland (CH), Norway (N), Belgium (B), Luxembourg (L), West Germany (D), Finland (SF), Sweden (S), Australia (AUS), Canada (CDN), and the United States of America (USA). The socialist countries are represented by circles, the capitalist countries by trapezoids. The activity rate presented on the vertical axis of the graph is computed as the ratio between the economically active population and the population capable of work, aged between 14 and 64.
Sources: The figure is from Kornai (1993, 209). János Köllő collected the data and prepared the figure. The GDP per capita data are from a paper by Éva Ehrlich (1985, 100). In the case of the capitalist countries, the GDP per capita and labor-market statistics are taken from a yearbook edited by the United Nations, and those in the case of socialist countries are from a statistical yearbook edited by Comecon.

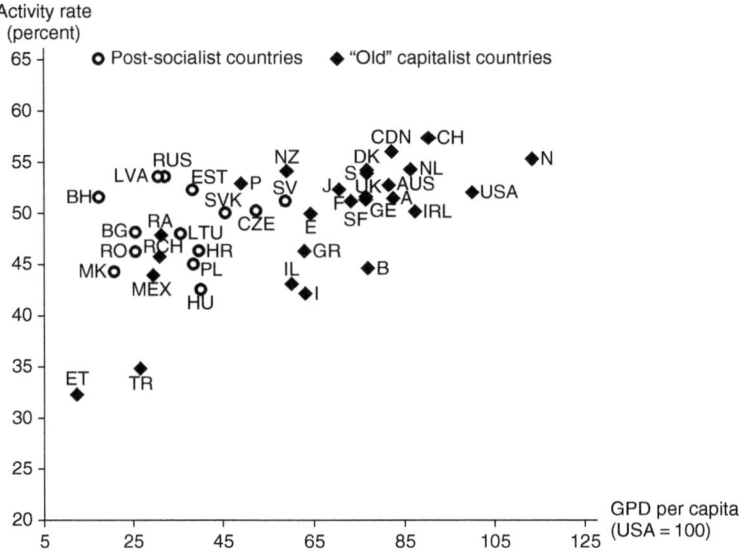

Figure 4.2.
Activity rate and the degree of economic development, 2009
Note: The following countries are included in the sample (in ascending order with respect to the level of GDP per capita): Egypt (ET), Bosnia-Herzegovina (BH), Macedonia (MK), Bulgaria (BG), Romania (RO), Turkey (TR), Mexico (MEX), Latvia (LVA), Chile (RCH), Argentina (RA), Russia (RUS), Lithuania (LTU), Estonia (EST), Croatia (HR), Poland (PL), Hungary (H), Slovakia (SVK), Portugal (P), the Czech Republic (CZE), Slovenia (SV), New Zealand (NZ), Israel (IL), Greece (GR), Italy (I), Spain (E), France (F), Japan (J), Finland (SF), Germany (GE), United Kingdom (UK), Sweden (S), Denmark (DK), Belgium (B), Australia (AUS), Canada (CDN), Austria (A), the Netherlands (NL), Ireland (IRL), Switzerland (CH), United States of America (USA), and Norway (N). The "old" capitalist countries are represented by trapezoids, the postsocialist countries by circles. The activity rate presented on the vertical axes of the graph is computed as the ratio between the economically active population and the population capable of work, aged between 14 and 64. Luxembourg seemed to be an outlier, and, thus, it was omitted from the sample.
Sources: GDP per capita from World Bank (2010); the data used for computing the activity rate are from ILO (2010).

Comparing the two Figures, 4.1 and 4.2, makes the alteration since the change of system apparent: The "sack" surrounded by the dashed line has broken. The countries of the former socialist region no longer tower over the other countries. The positions of the postsocialist countries now are marked with circles. It can be seen how they now mingle with the other circles, largely in line with their developmental ranking within capitalism, or, in one or two cases, lower down.

Unfortunately, no comprehensive surveys covering several countries were made to measure labor shortages at that time. For want of other data, here is a graph based on a survey in Poland from Kornai (1992, 242). The time series of Figure 4.3 ends in 1988. The curve shows the proportion of job vacancies to the unemployed. The logarithmic scale of the vertical axis shows there were no less than 86 unfilled jobs for every job seeker in 1988.

Table 4.2 shows the time series for unemployment and for vacancies, in certain ex-socialist, now postsocialist, countries.

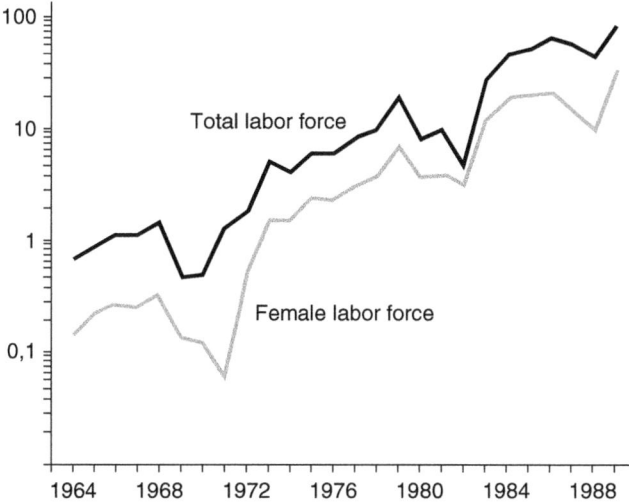

Figure 4.3.
Job vacancies and the number of persons searching for a job in Poland, 1964–1988
Source: The figure is from Kornai (1993, 215). It was prepared by János Köllő and based on data from Fallenbuchl (1982, 33) and Holzmann (1990, 6).

The table reflects the following processes:

- Most countries in the region did not keep unemployment statistics before the change of system, but it is known to have occurred sporadically.[3] However, the figure rose very quickly after 1989–1990 to levels similar to those in the West.
- The single indicator for labor shortage before the change of system that I have been able to obtain has been presented. Even in the toughest years of transformation after the change of system, job vacancies still occurred, but the figures in Table 4.2 are very low: the instances of shortage on the labor market are not intensive.

4.3 "KEYNESIAN" UNEMPLOYMENT

Why did labor shortage appear in the economically more developed socialist countries and why did it continue? It was not because the party-state wanted to follow a policy of "full employment." There was no decision by the ruling political group behind it, or targets drawn up by the central planning bureau. The labor shortage arose out of the system's immanent characteristics and propensities.

---

3. This refers to unemployment "outside of the factory" and not to unemployment "within the factory gates"—to the widespread cases where some employed on a valid employment contract failed to use their working hours properly.

Table 4.2. THE RATE OF UNEMPLOYMENT AND JOB VACANCIES IN EASTERN EUROPE, 1989–2010

Year	Czech Republic		Estonia	Hungary		Latvia		Lithuania		Poland		Slovakia	Slovenia
	u	v	U	u	v	u	u	u	v	u	v	U	u
1989			0.3										
1990		0.4	0.3										
1991	1.2	0.4	0.8		0.2								
1995	2.0	0.9	4.7	4.0	0.3	6.5	6.0	3.5		6.0	3.5	6.0	3.5
2000	4.4	0.5	6.2	2.6	0.5		9.0	3.5		9.0	3.5	9.0	3.5
2005	4.0	0.5	3.9	3.0	0.4	4.4	7.9	3.3	0.2	7.9	3.3	7.9	3.3
2006	3.6	0.8	3.0	3.2	0.4	3.5	6.5	3.0	0.6	6.5	3.0	6.5	3.0
2007	2.7	1.2	2.4	3.1	0.3	3.1	5.4	2.5	0.8	5.4	2.5	5.4	2.5
2008	2.2	1.4	2.9	3.3	0.3	4.0	4.7	2.3	0.7	4.7	2.3	4.7	2.3
2009	3.4	0.4	7.1	4.2	0.2	9.0	6.0	3.0	0.2	6.0	3.0	6.0	3.0
2010	3.7	0.3	8.6	4.8	0.2	9.6	7.1	3.7	0.2	7.1	3.7	7.1	3.7

Note: Both indicators are computed as the ratio between a labor-market indicator and total population. According to the definitions presented in Table 4.1, the columns in this table contain the following indicators for each country: the unemployment rate, $u = U/Q$; the rate of job vacancies: $v = V/Q$. Both labor-market indicators are normalized by total population in order to achieve a better comparability of the three rates. There are no official job-vacancy statistics in the case of Estonia, Slovakia, and Slovenia. Only certain observations of the whole time series are presented.

Sources: Unemployment and total population from ILO (2012); job vacancies from OECD (2012); in the case of Latvia and Lithuania, the time series concerning the number of job vacancies are from Latvijas Statistika (2012) and Statistikos Departamentas (2012).

Let me outline briefly, in a very simplified form, the mechanism described in detail in my earlier works, notably *The Socialist System* (Kornai 1993).

The enterprises are in state ownership. Among other motives, their leaders are motivated by *expansion drive* (one manifestation of Keynesian *animal spirits*), coupled with *investment hunger*, an insatiable appetite for investment: they want to carry out as much real investment as possible irrespective of cost. They are all the more inclined to invest without moderation because there is no hard budget constraint on them. Though the system of bureaucratic allocation of investment resources was some kind of curb, investment overspending was tolerated and bills for loss-making investments were paid.

This investment hunger is an almost sufficient explanation of why the growth (moreover, a rush for growth largely promoted from "above", by the government) should, sooner or later, mop up all the labor reserves. Socialist growth in the early stage could rely on a flood of labor from agriculture into industry, and of women from the household into employment, but these extra sources dried up later and growth met a labor supply constraint.

The classical socialist system exhibits tight state control on prices and wages. So the tension on the labor market does not have the inflationary effects it would in a market economy. But even if there are price and pay rises, firms are far less cost-sensitive than their counterparts under capitalism, due to the soft budget constraint.

Meanwhile the innovation process is far slower than under capitalism. Labor productivity stagnates or grows only by fits and starts. The expansion drive calls mainly for a workforce increase, but the level of workforce economic activity hits a socially tolerable upper limit. Labor shortage becomes a massive, chronic phenomenon.[4]

This is a mirror image or "opposite" case to the unemployment mechanism described by Keynes and Kalecki. (It is not precisely the opposite case, and I will return to that in a moment.) In the socialist case, the animal spirits and with it the macro demand run away as a result of (1) state ownership, (2) a state that picks up every bill and softens the budget constraint, and (3) price and wage controls. If these three key components are changed by history—the dominant role of (1) private ownership, (2) a state that refuses to bail out loss-making projects and hardens the budget constraint, and (3) market prices and wages—the changes reverse the situation. Producers still want to produce more and need more labor to do so, but they run up against demand and financial constraints. These constraints prevent them from going as far in expanding production or hiring labor as the limits of the

---

4. In fact, the attribute "chronic" is problematic as the period of intensive economic growth amid labor shortage did not last long. By the time it deserved the attribute "chronic" the system was collapsing. This, in fact, is where one of the many causes of the collapse can be found: Exhaustion of the labor reserves freely available for production greatly slowed growth under the socialist system, which was incapable of rapid innovation or productivity improvement, and stagnation ensued.

available workforce.[5] Even if the labor surplus increases, the consequences appear in employees' pay only after a delay, if at all. Wages remain sticky. (See Blanchard and Gali 2007.)

In using this "mirror image" metaphor I noted parenthetically that it is not wholly accurate, at least in terms of the history of theory. Keynesian theory sees unemployment as a *cyclical* phenomenon: the fluctuations in the cycle lead to a state in which insufficient demand causes employment to fall. My analysis opposes *chronic* phenomena: the socialist system in a mature stage of economic development displays chronic labor shortage; the capitalist market economy displays chronic labor surplus. Even in times of upswing, there remains a surplus of labor in most countries: labor actively seeking employment but not finding it, and people capable of work who have not registered as unemployed, but whose social and economic circumstances could lead them back to employment. Keynes's theory helps in understanding the causal mechanism behind that lasting, chronic phenomenon, even if my conclusion (by stressing the chronic, lasting nature of the surplus) goes beyond what Keynes stated.

Other mechanisms also contribute to creating and sustaining the capitalist system's labor surplus. Some operate concurrently and some overlap and intertwine.[6] I will return in a moment to cover other explanatory mechanisms. However, a large proportion of the economic profession agrees that one of the mechanisms operating on the labor market is that which gives rise to *Keynesian unemployment*. This has a constant *direction of force*, toward increasing unemployment and decreasing the number of the economically active. Nonetheless, the extent to which this speeds up or slows down depends on other factors, for instance, the economic policy of the state. The effect of increasing the labor surplus is certainly lessened by a loosening of the demand and financial constraints.

4.4 STRUCTURAL UNEMPLOYMENT

The so-called *structural unemployment* is induced by a mechanism deeply imbedded in capitalism.[7] The dynamism and innovation process of the capitalist

---

5. The contrast is presented vividly in the disequilibrium models of Malinvaud (1977) and Benassy (1982).

6. There are hosts of works on the theory of employment, wages, and the labor market. This study does not attempt to sum them up or pick any out. The works mentioned here are exclusively those that bear directly on the subjects of my arguments.

7. There is no consensus on what the attribute *structural* means here. Some see *structural* and *frictional* unemployment as almost identical or largely overlapping terms. No strict demarcation lines can be drawn, of course. In terms of the argument in this study, I reserve the attribute *structural* for the group of phenomena connected with Schumpeterian creative destruction, and the continual reallocation among the products, technologies, branches, regions, and countries of production.

economy—the Schumpeterian creative destruction discussed in detail in Section 2 of this essay—continually creates jobs and at the same time continually eliminates them. These two processes are not in harmony. Those who lose their jobs in one place may not find the jobs being created in another, and they may not be precisely the people required.

Implementation of the *new technologies* introduced into production call for special expertise. This and the skills currently possessed by the workforce will not coincide at many points, so that some employees with the earlier skills become superfluous. Adapting and acquiring the new expertise requires time, during which no work may be found. Furthermore, there are employees who are incapable of adapting to the new technologies and drop out of the workforce altogether.

The dynamism of the economy and the creative destruction are continually compelling *firms* to exit, which again causes job losses. Although new entries, new firms with a demand for new labor, appear continually, that demand may not match the supply of newly redundant labor.

The *rise in labor productivity* has several effects. One common one is for more capital-intensive equipment to replace labor. With the rise in productivity and intensive economic development, production also expands extensively, creating new jobs. But several disproportions arise between the two types of change; the expansion may come late for the redundancies. The two also differ in geographic distribution.

A clear example is the transformation of agriculture within each country. A mass surplus of labor develops in the villages, whereas more urbanized regions cannot absorb the rural labor surplus fast enough.

The restructuring of demand for labor occurs not only within countries but *among countries*. As the development of some more backward countries speeds up (consider, for instance, the breakneck speed of growth in China or India), the cheap exports from such regions squeeze out many producers in more developed countries. As newly urbanized agricultural labor in China or India joins industry, jobs are lost by German or Belgian workers. This is one of the concomitants of globalization.

We have reached one of the most important conclusions to be drawn from this line of argument. The more dynamic a capitalist economy, that is, the more strongly the one, favorable system-specific propensity applies, the more structural unemployment develops, that is, the more strongly the other, unfavorable propensity appears.

Dynamism and innovation are fundamental traits of a capitalist economy, but it must be added that it is not always possible to predict in which direction it will move. Who was aware in the 1930s, as the Western world built up countries of "iron and steel," that a world of information and communication would appear half a century later, for which new expertise would be required. Who could have guessed the rapid reorganization in the geographic distribution of world production we are witnessing now? What is so splendid in capitalism—the new triumphs of human endeavor that it brings, and the fast spread of civilization to which it leads—is accompanied by the loss of millions of jobs and new uncertainty, even in the lives of those who retain their jobs.

4.5 MISMATCHED ADJUSTMENT, FRICTIONAL UNEMPLOYMENT, AND DEMAND

Contributions to the development of labor surplus and unemployment come also from *frictions* in matching labor supply and labor demand. There is commonly a mismatch between the skill supplies of job-seeking workers and the skill demands of vacant jobs. In some cases, this is almost insuperable, and in others, buyers and sellers of labor services match but fail to meet up. This side of the problem is closely tied to the information-flow structure on the labor market. The jobless *are seeking* suitable jobs and employers suitable labor, which is a tiring and time-consuming process, during which the job seekers are out of work. (For the relevant literature on frictional unemployment, search theory, and matching theory see Phelps et al. 1970; Kornai 1971; McCall 1970; Diamond 1982; Roth 1982; Mortensen 1986; Mortensen and Pissarides 1994; Pissarides 2000.)

Mismatches occur under *all* socioeconomic systems, whether the labor market is marked by shortage or surplus. Adaptation friction is a mechanism that is bound to generate some frictional unemployment; to that extent it is *not* system specific. (However, even adaptation friction is influenced by its environment, that is, by the general state of the market. More will be said on that later.)

The structural unemployment covered in the last subsection 4.4 and the frictional unemployment due to information shortcomings and search time discussed in this subsection are closely linked and, in a sense, overlap. If the information were perfect on both sides of the market, including accurate forecasts of future developments, the mismatch caused by structural transformation would be less, and vice versa: if the structure (in terms of technology, sectoral composition, and geographic distribution) were frozen, search and supply–demand matching would be easier. There was trouble with both under the overcentralized, bureaucratically arthritic socialist economy with its sluggish technical development, but the main trouble in that respect was caused by the brakes on technical development. The soaring technical development of capitalism would, in itself, cause marked unemployment even if information on both sides of the market worked well, so I list this among the system-specific attributes of the capitalist system, unlike the frictions due to information shortcomings.[8]

8. Friction due to information shortcomings appears under both systems, but the losses due to error are felt more directly under capitalism than under socialism. A socialist enterprise that employs its labor at low efficiency can survive financial losses

The two partially overlapping phenomena discussed here—continual structural reorganization and friction of matching—lead to coexistence of shortage and surplus on the labor market. This concurrent presence was noted several times in Sections 2 and 3 in connection with the allocation of goods, services, and capacity. At this point, similar phenomena on the labor market can be added to the list. Instructive in this respect are the statistics in Table 4.3,

Table 4.3. THE RATE OF ECONOMICALLY INACTIVE POPULATION, UNEMPLOYMENT, AND JOB VACANCIES: INTERNATIONAL COMPARISON, 1989–2010

	Japan			Spain			Sweden			United Kingdom			USA		
	b	u	v	b	U	v	b	u	v	B	u	V	b	u	v
1980	51.3	1	0.3	63.3	4.1	0.0	47.9	1.2	0.7	53.8	0.0	0.3	53.5	3.3	
1982	50.9	1.1	0.3	63.2	5.7	0.0	47.4	1.9	0.2	53.6	0.0	0.2	53.0	4.6	
1984	50.3	1.3	0.3	62.9	7.3	0.1	47.1	1.9	0.4	51.8	5.7	0.3	52.5	3.6	
1986	50.1	1.4	0.3	62.6	7.7	0.1	46.8	1.5	0.5	51.1	5.5	0.3	51.6	3.4	
1988	49.2	1.3	0.5	60.4	7.5	0.1	46.4	1.0	0.6	50.4	4.4	0.4	51.0	2.7	
1990	47.7	1.1	0.5	60.3	6.5	0.1	45.9	1.0	0.5	59.7	3.4	0.3	50.3	2.8	
1992	46.6	1.2	0.5	59.3	7.4	0.1	47.7	3.0	0.1	50.8	4.8	0.2	50.4	3.7	
1994	46.5	1.6	0.4	58.7	9.9	0.1	49.7	4.8	0.1	51.5	4.6	0.3	50.3	3.0	
1996	46.2	1.8	0.4	57.9	9.3	0.1	49.5	5.0	0.2	51.6	3.9	0.4	50.3	2.7	
1998	45.8	2.2	0.4	57.0	8.0	0.2	50.2	4.2	0.3	51.8	2.9	0.5	50.1	2.3	
2000	46.2	2.6	0.5	55.5	6.2	0.3	49.2	3.0	0.4	51.2	2.7	0.6	49.5	2.0	
2002	47.0	2.9	0.5	55.7	5.0	0.3	48.8	2.7	0.3	51.0	2.5	1.0	49.8	2.9	1.1
2004	47.4	2.5	0.6	52.8	5.2	0.4	48.9	3.3	0.2	51.0	2.3	1.1	49.9	2.8	1.1
2006	47.4	2.2	0.7	51.0	4.2		47.7	3.7	0.4	50.5	2.7	1.0	49.5	2.3	1.3
2008	47.5	2.1	0.5	49.4	5.8		47.1	3.2	0.4	49.2	2.7	1.0	49.4	2.9	1.1
2010	47.7	2.6	0.5	49.9	10.1		47.1	4.4	0.4	49.5	3.9	0.8	50.4	4.8	

Note: All three indicators are computed as the ratio between a labor market indicator and total population. According to the definitions presented in Table 4.1, the three columns in this table contain the following indicators for each country: the rate of economically inactive population, $b = B/Q$; unemployment rate, $u = U/Q$, the rate of job vacancies, $v = V/Q$. All the three labor-market statistics are normalized by total population in order to achieve a better comparability of the three rates. That explains why the figures u are much smaller here than the well-known statistical unemployment rates, where the denominator is not Q, the total population, but the smaller number A, the active population. Only certain observations of the whole time series are presented.
Sources: Economically inactive population, unemployment, total population from ILO (2012); job vacancies from OECD (2012); in the case of the United Kingdom and the United States, the time series concerning the number of job vacancies are from the Office for National Statistics (2012) and the Bureau of Labor Statistics (2012).

(the budget constraint is soft). Employees are less affected by the frictions on the labor market because the wage spread is narrower, and because they can change jobs more easily, if they really want to.

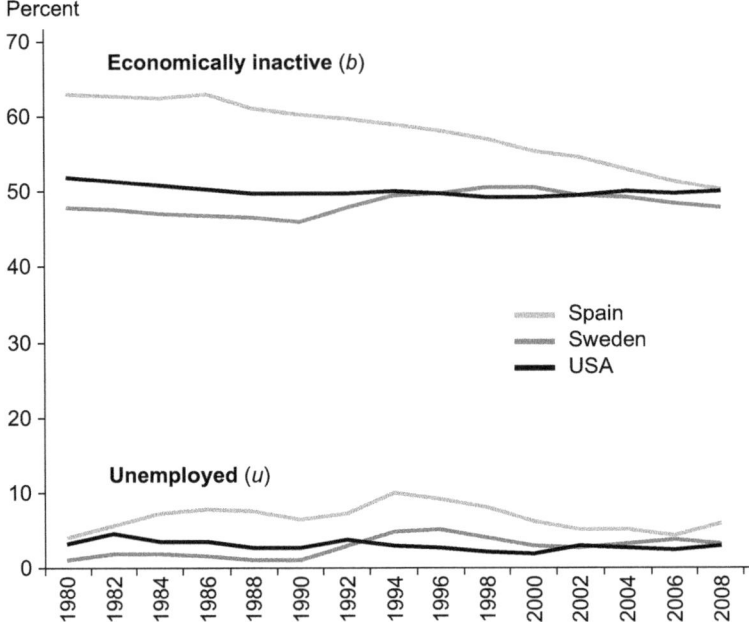

Figure 4.4.
The rate of the economically inactive population and the unemployment rate in three "old" capitalist countries, 1989–2010 (percent)
Note: According to the definitions in Table 4.1, indicators *b* and *u* presented in the case of Spain, Sweden, and the United States are the following: the rate of economically inactive population, $b = B/Q$; the unemployment rate, $u = U/Q$.
Source: See the sources of Table 4.3.

on whose basis time series for three countries have been presented graphically in Figure 4.4.

Both Table 4.3 and Figure 4.4 support the assertions made earlier:

1. Shortage and surplus coexist throughout.
2. In these "old," "traditional" (not ex-socialist) capitalist countries the phenomenon of surplus was far stronger than that of shortage.[9] This also applies to countries (such as Sweden) that led in building up the welfare state, reducing unemployment, and increasing the economically active section of the population.

---

9. Figure 4.1 displays clearly two notably important factors explaining the rate of economically active in the population: development level and the system-specific effect. The time series for each country in Table 4.2 present vividly the effect of economic growth. Other factors also affect the growth rate time series for many countries (the fall in the rate of the economically inactive), above all the change in labor-market institutions. So it is unjustified to compare the data in Figure 4.1 with those in Table 4.2 without performing supplementary analyses.

4.6 THE EFFICIENCY WAGE

The key expression in discussing analytically the other group of phenomena leading to continual reproduction of unemployment is *efficiency wage*. Employers are willing to pay more than a "market-clearing" wage (where labor supply and demand coincide). This efficiency wage is not a manifestation of altruism on the employers' part, but a response to their clear interest, shaped by several factors.

Above all, it is a precaution against *shirking*.[10] It would be very costly if there had to be a supervisor standing behind each worker. It is worth comparing *monitoring* costs with those of paying wages above the market-clearing rate, for the latter is lower in many cases, especially if the performance is difficult to measure numerically, that is, if the quality of output is a real consideration. The greater the intellectual input into a task—the greater the degree to which intellectual performance is expected of the employee—the less apposite it becomes to pay piecework or by the hour, and the harder it is to detect shirking. Instead, internal incentives have to be devised, which is what the *efficiency wage* provides in various ways. When employers appear on the labor market with higher pay offers, they find it easier to pick and choose staff than if they simply are offered the market-clearing rate. And once workers have filled higher-paying jobs, they are all the keener to retain such a pay.

The effect of the efficiency wage is enhanced if employees work harder not only for fear of losing the wage increments, but for fear of losing the jobs themselves. It is in the collective interest of all employers to ensure a chronic surplus of labor, because this becomes a weapon for use in all workplaces. Therefore, even the most enlightened and socially sensitive employers will be, at best, half-hearted supporters of sharply reducing unemployment. They certainly do not want the labor market to tip the other way into labor shortage. So fear of dismissal hangs over all employees. This circumstance is apparent even in the title of a celebrated article by Shapiro and Stiglitz: "Equilibrium unemployment as a worker discipline device" (Shapiro and Stiglitz 1984).[11] This statement may sound very "Marxist," but it is true for all that.

The *macroeconomic* arguments against eliminating unemployment too radically and especially against "overemployment" are well known. If the incentives

---

10. The pioneer paper on the theory of the *efficiency wage* was by Shapiro and Stiglitz (1984). There is an extensive literature of description and causal analysis, including Milgrom and Roberts (1992, 165–195).

11. For the mechanism described to work, it is not necessary for employers to be aware *consciously* of their collective interest in maintaining unemployment. If the labor market became very tense and the employment element neared 100 percent, the requisite efficiency wage for employers would rise unacceptably high. When individual employees raise wages in their own labor-market bargaining, they are, unwittingly even, pushing employment appreciably back down below 100 percent.

to raise wages become too strong, the excess demand for labor will push up costs and prices, initiating an inflationary spiral. This is a justifiable argument.[12] But it does not preclude the other mechanism: employers' collective interest in maintaining unemployment as a way of maintaining discipline.[13]

It should be remembered when discussing the efficiency-wage argument that it will be familiar to all who have read Marx (1978 [1967–1994]) on the "reserve army of industrial workers" (Chapter 25 and in many other parts of the same volume). The presence of that army (or labor surplus, to use the terminology of this study) helps to curb pay and tighten labor discipline, and remains at employers' disposal if they wish to expand production. Nor is there any denying that the theory of the efficiency wage is akin to ideas current in the socialist and anarchist movements that capitalist employers buy the loyalty of a "workers' aristocracy" by giving them higher wages.[14] Intellectual honesty requires that such intellectual kinship, indeed priority, be admitted even by such economists who do not do so willingly or feel ashamed of it.

There is another favorable aspect of the labor surplus: its presence makes adjustment more flexible. It becomes easier to raise or realign production rapidly if the labor needed is easy to mobilize. This, of course, is a technocratic argument. Spare capacity and warehouse stocks are inanimate and do not suffer from being kept in reserve, but labor reserves are human and suffer from waiting on the sidelines.

It is worth stopping for a moment and recalling what was stated in subsection 4.1. Chronic labor shortage appeared in the production sphere in the socialist economies that reached a medium level of development—the Soviet Union and the East European socialist countries. It was generally realized how much this circumstance weakened labor's discipline. Employees justifiably felt they would not be dismissed even if they did not try very hard, or even if they shirked entirely. If they were dismissed, they could easily find other employment. All managers and supervisors continually complained of this. Many of the workers did their work properly out of an underlying sense of honesty and identification with the job, and in some places where it could be done effectively, they might be rewarded for this financially. But they were not haunted by the disciplinary specter of unemployment. The situation, let us admit, had some advantages for the employees. Employment

---

12. This relation is the backbone of the "natural rate of unemployment" theory, on which the pioneer works were Phelps (1968) and Friedman (1968). It can be found in every macroeconomic textbook.

13. Kalecki, describing the attitude of the business leaders, made the following remark: "lasting full employment is not at all to their liking. The workers would 'get out of hand' and the 'captains of industry' would be anxious to 'teach them a lesson.'" (Kalecki 1971, 144)

14. The expression "workers' aristocracy" appeared first in Bakunin's, and later in Kautsky's and Lenin's writings.

gave a reassuring feeling, and all the more if it was secure. The switch from labor shortage to labor surplus had advantages and drawbacks for society as a whole, and those advantages and disadvantages were distributed unevenly among its members.

It is time to sum up. Continual reproduction of labor surplus, chronic unemployment, and underemployment are painful, system-specific features of capitalism that bring suffering, financial loss, and shame to the unemployed, and anxiety to those in work and threatened by unemployment. The choice of whom to hire and whom to leave jobless is often locked in racism and other kinds of discrimination.

It is quite unrealistic to accept and support capitalism while demanding or promising "full employment." It is senseless to conjure with the word "full," though many do, in politics and the social sciences. I can only accept an accurate interpretation: not 97 or 93 percent, but 100 percent. It is not just rigorous researchers who feel that way, but those concerned as well. There is only a 100 percent likelihood of a surgical intervention succeeding if it *always* succeeds. Research physicians or descriptions based on statistical facts may announce that 97 percent can be considered "absolutely certain" and a very good result for medicine. In fact the three percent whose operations did not succeed are left chronically ill, disabled, or dead. For the unemployment rate to be *only* three percent may be an imposing achievement in macroeconomic policy, but those among the three percent are not soothed by the idea that they have been rendered jobless by "structural unemployment." It is possible and imperative to create a macro policy and system of institutions that reduces unemployment and makes it more bearable. This is a realistic task to set, and it is worth doing and striving for. But I see it as misleading to advertise the success of any political regime in "achieving" full employment.

SECTION 5

A Summary of the Positive Description and Causal Analysis

5.1 THE WORKABILITY OF THE CONCEPT OF "EQUILIBRIUM"

Economists reading this study will have realized by this time that I have so far avoided the term "*equilibrium*" where possible. It has arisen here mainly when I refer to some idea of the mainstream.

Few terms have been at the center of so much confusion as *equilibrium*. Various meanings and value judgments have been attached to it by different schools. Some rejoice if an economy or a segment of it is in equilibrium, others do not, or they bewail it. The discourse can crudely be called a "dialog of the deaf," because it proceeds without regard to others' arguments or in misunderstandings over the meanings attached to the terms *equilibrium, disequilibrium, anti-equilibrium*, and *nonequilibrium*.

I have no illusions. I do not think this study and its few observations about equilibrium will restore order to this conceptual chaos. I would be satisfied if readers could understand clearly how I interpret the concept at the time of writing and how I see its workability.[1]

The coinage in Latin was inspired by the balance scale: If each side carries equal weight, the balance may swing, but it will eventually settle into a state of rest, for the two sides balance each other when the weights in each pan are the same. That leads to the colloquial meaning: The opposing forces in a system (e.g., a scale) equal each other and the system is at rest. There is no reason to

---

1. I add "at the time of writing" with a measure of irony at my own expense. I do not deny that my own relations to this important concept have changed several times, and I am sorry that this may confuse my readers. I will not burden this study with a history of how my ideas developed, although I may write one another time. Here I describe only the present state of my ideas.

object to this broad colloquial meaning, which aptly describes a certain state in a range of systems.

The concept of equilibrium *in the realm of mathematical models* can be defined in exact terms. It is not worth seeking a general definition. There are models in which the concept of equilibrium can be interpreted and defined, along with certain attributes of equilibrium. But different exact definitions apply to different models. When analyzing mathematical models of dynamic systems, it may be possible to identify "steady states" or fixed points—these are kindred concepts. (Of course, there are mathematical models within which the concept of equilibrium is not defined.).

Let us turn to the *real world* of practical matters. The concept of equilibrium is employed by physicists, chemists, or biologists, but let us stick within our own social scientific field of economics. There are in real-life economic subsystems that display equilibrium in some sense (where the equilibrium is perfect or approximately so). For instance, the accounts of a country or a company may show exactly the same income as expenditure over a given period. The stocks leaving a warehouse may exactly equal the stocks arriving in it.

Let us now narrow the question down: What is the case with the coordination of production and consumption, sellers and buyers, or the allocation of resources? And what is the situation on the market, with the special mechanisms of coordination and allocation? Does a state of equilibrium exist? My answer is a resounding no. This is not and can never be a steady state on the *real* market, in the operation of real coordination and allocation mechanisms. The forces competing or opposing each other are continually changing. Change, in fact, is the essential event. If there is, by chance, calm for a moment, it is an irrelevant and uninteresting event.

I am not the first or only economist to state this. It is one of the essential propositions of the Austrian school, from Mises and Hayek, through Kirzner, to the adherents to the Austrian school of today.[2] I join them wholeheartedly on this especially important assertion, although there are other important questions where we differ.

The old balance scale used in homes and in markets will tilt back and forth for a while when the foodstuff to be measured is placed on one pan and the weights on the other. If the right weights are chosen, friction will soon reduce the tilt and bring the balance to rest. Equilibrium has been reached in the strict sense, because the cessation of the tilting means the weights in each pan are equal. Be that as it may, the nature of the real economy is essentially different from a balance scale. An attempt was made to show this in Section 2 of this essay. There is continual technical development; this year's

---

2. Here are a few of the seminal works of the Austrian school in which strong attention is paid to the ideas I have just propounded: Hayek (1948), Kirzner (1973), Lachmann (1976), Lavoie (1985), and Cowan and Rizzo (1996).

supply and today's demand differ not only in volume from last year's or that of a decade ago, but also in *quality*. (If I had to choose the name of one scholar to label the sphere of thinking that is needed to complement the Austrian school assertion about the eternal change on the market, it would be Schumpeter's.) The continual innovation process also means that the phrase *market equilibrium* cannot be interpreted. Taking a positive, and not a normative, approach, the question is not the desirability of the "market equilibrium." Whether we wish it or not, there is no equilibrium on a real market and there never can be.[3]

If that argument is right, I am justified in refraining from distinguishing between "necessary" and "excessive" capacity reserves, "necessary" and "excessive" product inventories, or "necessary" and "excessive" labor reserves. I refrain from these distinctions not because of ignorance but, rather, because I am not able to find the right borderlines. I do not use the categories because they do not exist in the real world.

However, it does not follow that the concept of equilibrium has no place in a positive description of the real market. It can be used in thought experiments as a "yardstick" or point of reference. Let me give two examples. In microeconomic theory we can follow Walras, Arrow, and Debreu (or their successors) in determining the Walrasian equilibrium of the market. Walrasian equilibrium develops between sellers and buyers in a world in which all information without exception is available to buyers and sellers, in which the future is predictable, in which every adjustment occurs immediately and without friction, and so on. It can then be asked how far from or near to this imaginary state is the real market before us. Another example is the growth model devised by John von Neumann, in which there is no technical change and each branch advances on an equilibrium path at the same rate. It may be instructive to show how far the real growth path of an economy departs from the von Neumann path; why some branches vanish and why some appear, and why the proportions between the branches keep changing. But an abstract mathematical model is a tool of analysis borrowed from a virtual world, and the von Neumann equilibrium path must not for a moment be viewed as a depiction of real growth.

I see as problematic definitions that derive the concept of equilibrium from a state of "rest" of the actors in the system examined. By this approach, the

---

3. It was obviously *in this sense* that Nicholas Kaldor (I think rightly) called equilibrium economics "irrelevant" (Kaldor 1972). But I must add with today's insight that Kaldor was so irritated by the many theoretical irrelevancies that he ceased to be objective and refused to recognize the usefulness that the mathematical models of equilibrium can display *in the realm of theory*. When Kaldor wrote his angry article, I fell into the same error. I described my views at the time and assessed them self-critically in my autobiography (Kornai 2006a, Chapter 10).

system is in equilibrium if the actors do not wish any longer to move from the point of equilibrium in their own interest. However, it is easy to stray from that into a tautological definition.[4]

The unfortunate buyers in a shortage economy cannot buy goods when they want, where they would originally have bought them, or what they would originally have wanted to buy. Finally, as a result of various forced adjustments, they buy what they manage to find. They have to be content with the bitter knowledge that any further shopping effort could turn out worse still. That might be christened a state of rest, a state of equilibrium, but the term itself would be open to misunderstanding; indeed, it would be downright misleading. By a similar line of thought, I am disturbed also by the concept of "unemployment equilibrium." I acknowledge that within the frames of the model, all participants in the labor market are resigned to the so-called "unemployment equilibrium," but how content can people be if they would gladly have taken work but ran up against one of the barriers to employment (as detailed in the previous section)? Definitions that seek to derive equilibrium or a steady state from a position accepted by participants for fear of something worse rest on shaky psychological and social psychological foundations.

Before the eyes of economists, from Marshall and Walras through to the mainstream of today, who keep a deserved and strictly defined place for the concept of equilibrium is the example of Newtonian *physics*. For my part, if I sought inspiration from the natural sciences, I would prefer to join the economists who have been inspired by Darwin and *evolutionary biology*. There is a thought-provoking similarity between the natural selection and evolution of the living world and the growth and technical development that occur in a decentralized market economy.

Every new business initiative or innovation can be seen as a random mutation. The new product, technology, method of organization, or business association is "struggling for life." Some succeed not only in surviving but in "breeding:" The innovation spreads widely or a high-performing firm grows large. Other mutations are doomed: some innovations disappear, some companies fail. There is natural selection. The live-or-die judgment comes not from a central will possessed of rational foresight and unfailing intelligence, but from the decisive criterion of viability. Chance plays a big part. On the whole, it works well, but not always: Some firms that fail were valuable or, alternatively, some firms survive a long while though better ones could have arisen.

---

4. Great influence has been exerted by theories that define the concept of equilibrium from the point of view of *expectations*: the state of equilibrium is characterized as a fulfillment of rational expectations. This question is not covered in my essay.

Biological and market-economy evolution also bear the resemblance that "equilibrium" is meaningless in them.[5] The change is continual, and propelled by the gap between the drive to survive and proliferate and the opportunities provided by the environment. However, here we must stop for a moment before continuing with the analogy.

Darwin was much influenced by the economist Malthus (Coutts 2010; Jones 1989).[6] In the Darwinian vision, living organisms proliferate but physical resources for their support are in limited supply. The quantity is stagnant or grows more slowly than the combined needs of living organisms. This heightens the struggle, in whose midst there appear successive mutations of evolutionary development. To apply my own vocabulary to this succession of steps over millions of years, the natural world is an anarchic shortage economy, with no planning bureau, food rationing body, police, or KGB. Every individual for himself; those who can, grab more.[7] In standard terms, this is an economy of excess demand, in which natural resources are the shorter side.

The situation in the market economy presented in this study is precisely the opposite. This is a surplus economy, not a shortage one. The weight is on the supply side. However, here, too, evolution is spurred on by two great processes: the differences of and the tensions between the processes on the supply and demand sides.

I am not recommending the mechanical adoption of some evolutionary model, but something less and more. Economics should draw inspiration from the philosophy, outlook and approach of Darwinian theory. Marx and Schumpeter, both great admirers of Darwin, viewed the history of capitalism through Darwinian eyes. I am trying to follow that example in this essay.

Evolutionary economics inspired by the biological theory of Darwinian evolution dates back several decades. It has undergone great development since the pioneering works (Veblen 1898; Nelson and Winter 1982), into a school of thought that has one foot in the mainstream and one out.[8] I feel a close intellectual kinship with their work. I would hope that the practitioners of

---

5. I am talking here of *long-term* evolutionary processes lasting millions of years. Other questions arise in ecology, which can be seen as a branch of biology, in which usually shorter-term processes are examined within the relations between living populations and their environments. Certain systems of the cohabitation of living organisms can be described by a theory in which the analytical instrument of equilibrium is workable. For instance, the animal world of a forest displays cohabitation of predators and prey. Whichever group is removed from the forest by human intervention, the balance of nature will be disturbed. The predators will die out for want of prey, and the prey will proliferate excessively without the predators. (This is described in the Lotka–Voltera model, which is also used to analyze economic phenomena.)

6. I am grateful to András Simonovits for pointing out to me this important fact of intellectual history.

7. See Vahabi (2004) on "destructive power."

8. A good survey can be found in Hodgson (1993).

evolutionary economics will contribute to maturing, mathematically modeling, and broadening the empirical bases of this essay.

5.2 ASYMMETRY

Where the standard economics of the market and its mechanism coordinating production and consumption, sale and purchase sees symmetry between the two sides, I see asymmetry. Nor am I alone in this. There are a number of terms current, and, in Table 5.1, I set out to present the most useful of them.

The first term in Pair 1 (shortage economy) is widespread, and this study seeks to introduce the second (surplus economy). Pairs 2 and 3 are widely current especially among followers of Keynes and Kaldor and in the "post-Keynesian" school.[9] Pair 4 belongs not to theoretical economics, but to business parlance. I sought to introduce Pair 5 in my book *Anti-Equilibrium* (Kornai 1971), but it was not adopted by the economic profession.

It is not especially important which pair of terms finally becomes widespread or whether new ones eventually become widely accepted by economists.

Table 5.1. THE TWO SIDES OF COORDINATION MECHANISM: A SUMMARY OF TERMINOLOGY

Pair of terms	Which features of the mechanism it focuses on
1. Shortage economy *versus* surplus economy	The intention of buying, respectively of producing/selling is not realized. Shortage phenomena, respectively surplus phenomena dominate.
2. Demand-constrained economy *versus* supply-constrained economy (or resource-constrained economy)	Which is the dominant constraint that hinders the expansion of production?
3. Excess supply economy *versus* excess demand economy	In the macroeconomic sense: which aggregated variable is the "longer side"? In the microeconomic sense: which side appears more often and more intensely?
4. Sellers' market *versus* buyers' market	Which side is stronger at the market?
5. Pressure *versus* suction	It refers to the effort made by the market participants: is it the seller who pushes the product on the buyer, or does the buyer intend to "suck" the product to himself?

9. As far as I know, the pair of the opposite terms "demand-constrained" and "resource-constrained systems" were first used by Kornai (1979).

Ultimately, all five pairs reflect the same outlook: there is a lasting and essential divergence between the sides in the buying–selling process: one is "shorter" and one "longer," one stronger, one weaker, one at an advantage over the other, and so on. This I interpret as the *lastingly asymmetric* state of the market.[10]

In this respect I am on the same wavelength as the "disequilibrium" model's creators (Portes and Winter 1980; Benassy 1982; Malinvaud 1977). Although I have been in dispute with them on some important methodological matters (aggregation, etc.), we take the same stand on the essential matter of focusing attention on market states that depart in one direction or the other from the Walrasian equilibrium.

I am also on the same wavelength with the group who talk of *unemployment equilibrium* (Layard, Nickel, and Jackman 1991; Pissarides 2000). Their analysis states that unemployment is lasting, created by continuing mechanisms, not momentary, transitional conditions. Though I have several problems with the term "equilibrium" here, as I mentioned earlier, what is more important is our agreement concerning the permanent presence of surplus labor.

The idea of market symmetry has imbedded itself deeply in economists' thinking. It is much easier to reach agreement with practical capitalist business people in this respect, because life has taught them what rivalry is. They are baffled by an absurdity like "competitive equilibrium." If all goods for sale found buyers, and all buyers found the goods they wished to buy, what incentive would there be to compete? It would be like Olympic Games with as many medals as competitors. Rivalry and the presence of "surplus" are two sides of one and the same thing. It is a matter of taste which aspect one stresses by choosing to call this a *surplus economy* or a *sellers' competition*, or some other expression. The essential point is to convey that the words describe an asymmetric situation, and it does no harm to add that the opposite asymmetric state is also known as the *shortage economy* with *buyers' competition* for the favor of sellers.[11]

---

10. Economists have often met the expression *asymmetric* in recent decades, but usually in the one context of "asymmetric information." Important though this is, it would confuse my line of argument to include it in the analysis here. Doctors are better informed about diagnosis and treatment than patients. Nonetheless, there may develop a "buyers' market" in some segments of medical services under certain economic conditions: if patients pay for the services out of their own pockets, they may choose freely who treats them, and doctors will compete for well-paying private patients. So let us set aside the information problem now and return to it briefly later.

11. Examination of the concept of equilibrium branches in several directions. Here let me mention just one: how *balanced* is growth? Are the economy's proportions not distorted by the growth process? This is an intellectually stimulating and policy-wise relevant question, on which there is a great body of literature. I too have done search into it. But it is not covered in this study.

5.3 A SUMMARY ACCOUNT OF THE TWO DEMAND–SUPPLY REGIMES

I hope readers who have reached this point begin to see an outline of what this essay refers to as the shortage and surplus economies. These are two alternative *demand–supply regimes.*

It is now time to summarize their characteristic features.

To simplify the explanation, let us take an indicator that shows the scale of shortage well in an economy at a given time and another indicator that does the same for surplus. It would be ideal to have the kind of "composite indices" described in subsection 3.8 of this essay, but in their absence, any other indicator that reflects major phenomena of shortage or surplus will suit the purpose, for example, the number of job vacancies as an indicator of shortage and the number of unemployed as one of surplus, or the number on the waiting list for housing as a gauge of shortage and the number of vacant dwellings as a gauge of surplus. Let us denote the shortage indicator as H and the surplus indicator as T, and put aside the question of its specific content or statistical definition.

The rest of what has to be said is depicted in Figure 5.1.

The 45-degree line on the graph shows demand–supply configurations in which $H = T$. The origin ($H = T = 0$) is the point of Walrasian equilibrium.

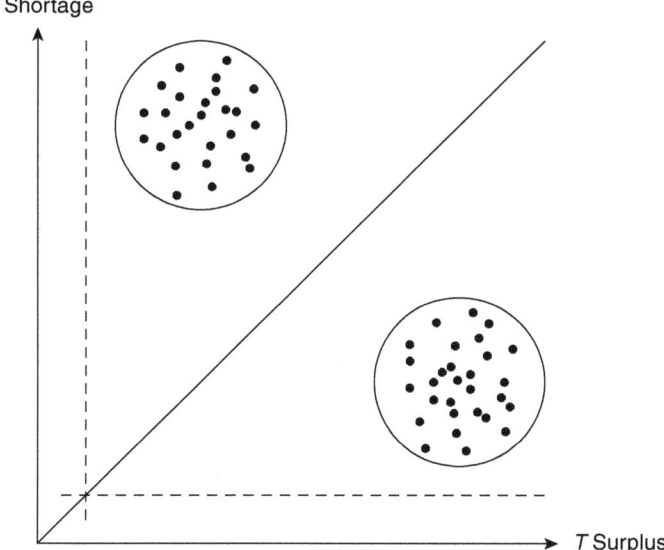

Figure 5.1.
Illustration of the shortage economy and the surplus economy

Above the 45-degree line is the zone of shortage economies, below the line is the zone of surplus economies.

Two thin broken lines appear above the horizontal axis and to the right of the vertical, showing the minima of shortage and surplus. Missing or imperfect information, frictions of adjustments, if nothing else, preclude Walrasian equilibrium on the market. Even in a surplus economy, phenomena of shortage appear, and phenomena of surplus occur in a shortage economy.

Figure 5.1 is usable for two kinds of comparative analysis. The first interpretation is *temporal*: two countries are presented, one a shortage economy, the other a surplus economy. The points show the state of the two economies in various years. The data pairs $H(t)$ and $T(t)$ for any time t are toward the upper left-hand corner for the shortage economy (within the shortage-economy zone) and those for the surplus economy toward the lower right-hand corner (within the surplus-economy zone).

The second interpretation of Figure 5.1 is to present a "cross-section" examination. Each point depicts the state of a single country at the same time. The shortage-economy zone contains the countries in which a state of shortage is typical, the surplus-economy zone contains those in which a state of surplus is typical. Otherwise the explanation of the graph is analogous to the interpretation for plotting one country's changes over time.

The account so far allows essential conclusions to be drawn for defining the concept of the two "regimes." I neither can nor want to give a priori numerical thresholds for the set of values for the data pair H and T that merit each description, "shortage economy" or "surplus economy." As we describe them somewhat loosely on a basis of everyday experience, sober consideration may suggest numerical values as well. If I am seeking a dwelling in a certain neighborhood of a city, it may take me weeks to find the right one, though there are plenty of dwellings for rent, but those weeks do not signify a shortage economy, only the presence of frictional shortage. That H indicator still fits into the lower-right-hand surplus-economy "sack." However, if I have to wait five years for the local authority to allocate me a council dwelling, then I am certainly living in a shortage economy. Then, the value H will be in the upper-left-hand shortage-economy "sack."

Those who live in a shortage economy feel it normal and ordinary if the indicators of the state of the market move around the upper-left-hand zone, whereas those in a surplus economy feel it is normal for them to stay in the bottom-right-hand zone. As in medicine and other sciences dealing with living things, the definition of "normality" (normal level of blood sugar, normal blood pressure) is not a precisely defined number but an interval, and the figure might be anywhere within the normal interval.

The contours of the "sacks" can only be drawn from observations and experiences of real states, with the help of statistical analysis.

Let us sum up the definitions of the two regimes. The shortage economy is a regime in which instances of shortage are general, chronic, and intensive. There may be instances of surplus in it, but they are isolated, transitory, and mostly not intensive.

The surplus economy is a regime in which instances of surplus are general, chronic, and intensive. There may be instances of shortage in it, but they are isolated, transitory, and mostly not intensive.

One underlying idea in this study is that the figures for the state of actual demand–supply configurations, developed historically, are not grouped around the 45-degree line and are not close to the Walrasian point of origin. They are *either* toward the top left *or* toward the bottom right. The points on the 45-degree line symbolize a state of perfect symmetry between the two opposing halves. If the market displayed only symmetrical fluctuation around a point of equilibrium, the points denoting the state of the market would be around the 45-degree line. The location of the two zones on the graph signifies that the real state is *asymmetric*, one "sack" being dominated by the shortage phenomena and the other by those of surplus.

Only single variables H and T appear in Figure 5.1, but, in fact, millions of such variables exist within one country at any moment. This study suggests that there is a strong correlation among the H variables and also strong correlation among the T variables. Again this is primarily an empirical question. The problem calls for extensive research. It is certainly possible to compile intermediate aggregates and/or composite indices, whereby the state of each country can be described by more than 2, but fewer than a million indicators of shortage and surplus—say 5, 10, or 20. Our visual imagination only allows us to conjure up three-dimensional spaces, but readers conversant with mathematics know that even if there can be no visual representation of them, my statements can be generalized for n number of indicators of shortage and surplus. The n number of indicators for a country together forms a point in an n-dimensional space.

1. The demand–supply regime of a given country is a surplus economy if the various points in an n-dimensional space representing the values for the shortage and surplus indicators cluster into a bundle of high values for surplus indicators and low values for shortage ones (in the lower-right-hand corner of the two-dimensional graph).
2. The demand–supply regime of a given country is a shortage economy if the various points in the n-dimensional space representing the values for the shortage and surplus indicators cluster into a bundle of high values for shortage indicators and low values for surplus ones (in the top-left-hand corner of the two-dimensional graph).

It has to be confirmed or rejected empirically that the H and T indicators do not scatter far afield, but group into two clusters, and only disperse within these two zones of *n* dimensions. In a surplus economy shortage is exceptional, and *vice versa*: in a shortage economy surplus is exceptional.

When actual empirical testing is done, the conceptual framework will have to be tightened in many respects. What should be understood by *exceptional*? How literally should it be taken that the value of an indicator must remain within the zone? And so on. I think it would be officious to apply these qualifications now, in this study. The time for that will come when methodical empirical research in this area begins.

Perhaps economists accustomed to mathematical models may expect more rigorous definitions. Unfortunately, I cannot offer them. Perhaps it will become possible to move toward more rigorous definitions through theoretical models and empirical observations. Until then, I would like to avoid pretending precision.

It is worth making a detour here to offer some comments on the relation between the ideas just expressed and *search theory* (ST). (See Mortensen and Pissarides 1994; Pissarides 2000.) My impression is that a significant part of what I have to say could be expressed in the parlance of that theory. Many of the phenomena I have examined can be described using the variables with which ST operates, and some of the connections I have analyzed could be drawn using ST models.[12] Although I do not set about this particular translation task, I hope there will be somebody who does so. It would be good to have it done as soon as possible, as the messages of this book might find easier acceptance in the modern mainstream if they were expressed in ST terms.

However, I must add that, despite some close kinship and large overlaps, there are differences between the puzzles that exponents of ST try to solve and those that concern me. The ST researchers seek to make the search more efficient. The goal before them is for vacancies and job seekers to find each other as soon as possible. They examine with discernment how the dynamics of wages, job creation, job destruction, search, and other factors tie in with unemployment and unfilled jobs; under what conditions the unemployment equilibrium is found. To them it is self-evident that the problems should be examined *within* the capitalist system. I, however, am keen to know why a chronically "tight" labor market is typical of the socialist system and a chronically "loose" one is typical of the capitalist market, how system specific is this chronically asymmetric state of the labor market, skewed toward shortage in

---

12. Well known from labor market literature is the system of coordinates in which horizontal axis shows the rate of unemployment *(u)* and the horizontal axis the rate of job vacancies *(v)*. Figure 5.1 of this essay uses a clearly related mode of depiction, but one that is more general and more comprehensive, because in my arguments I treat surplus labor as one subgroup of the various surplus phenomena and labor shortage as one subgroup of the various shortage phenomena.

one case and surplus in the other.[13] Going beyond the labor market, my essay seeks to convince readers that the *system* has a decisive influence on the general state of the market for products and services and for labor, that is, that buyers and sellers, jobseekers and employers search for each other within a capitalist or socialist environment.

Let me mention here an important branch of mathematics, the offshoot of graph theory known as *matching theory* (Lovász and Plummer 2009).[14] As an illustration, let us consider a situation in which a number of men n match off in pairs with a number of women n. Under what conditions, using what kind of algorithm, will there be "perfect matching," with each finding a pair? This highly promising line in mathematics has aroused great attention among mathematicians and already found a variety of practical applications. Most models of the theory start out from a situation in which there are equal numbers on each side in the matching. To that extent, it is akin to the tradition of the discipline of economics, where the supply and demand sides are likewise symmetrical: there is a chance that each product or service for sale will find a buyer and vice versa.

The situations I examine, however, are marked by asymmetry. To return to the preceding illustration, let us look at the numbers of men and of women. The laws of nature ensure that the numbers will be roughly equal in large communities (e.g., the population of a country). True, but it is not rare for a high proportion of the matching choices to occur predominantly or almost exclusively within a smaller community, for example, with an émigré colony or at a workplace where employees do not have much spare time, so that their acquaintance is limited to their place of work. If the numbers of the sexes differ markedly, the matching chances on the "shorter" side are much better than on the "longer." The former are more able to choose, so that, in a sense, they have the upper hand.

The problem that excites me in my research under what conditions such a situation of unequal chances and the superiority of one side can appear, and how the asymmetry affects the behavior of both sides. My researches would be assisted by a matching theory that offered a mathematical apparatus for analyzing asymmetrical pairing problems.

---

13. I purposely borrow the ST expressions *tight* and *loose* here. In the vocabulary of this essay, a tight market shows frequent shortage and rare surplus phenomena, and a loose market the opposite.

14. I was surprised how little intellectual contact there has been between the exponents of *search theory*, developed within the framework of economics, and of *matching theory*, developed within the framework of mathematics, despite the great overlap in the problems they pose.

5.4 THE GENERATION OF A SURPLUS ECONOMY BY THE CAPITALIST SYSTEM: THE CAUSAL CHAIN

The statements about the two types of demand–supply regime lack more than just empirical support. A reconsideration of the *causal connections* explaining the appearance of instances of shortage and surplus is also needed. Such mechanisms that prompt shortage and surplus have already been mentioned several times in passing. Let me present the propositions in their most general form.

Proposition 1.—Only the capitalist system is capable of producing and reproducing continually a surplus economy encompassing the whole economy. Only capitalism can produce and reproduce continually the mechanisms that generate the chronic symptoms of such a surplus economy.

The direction of the proposition can be reversed.

Proposition 2.—If a given country has a capitalist system, it *necessarily* operates as a surplus economy. A surplus economy is an immanent attribute of capitalism. It does not simply appear because the state has been following one kind of economic policy or another. Fiscal and monetary policy or policy on income distribution and prices may intensify or relieve some phenomena of surplus, but that does not produce a surplus economy. A surplus economy appears because it is one constituent of capitalism, indeed one of its most important characteristic marks.

These are *positive* statements. You may rejoice that capitalism is a surplus economy or condemn it for being so. Normative criteria will be returned to later. All I state here is that wherever capitalism is, there is a surplus economy in the midst of it.

Although these propositions about capitalism and the surplus economy form the central message of this study, let me add some summary propositions about the socialist system elaborated in earlier works of mine.

Proposition 3.—Only the socialist system is capable of producing and reproducing continually a shortage economy encompassing the whole economy. Only socialism can produce and reproduce continually the mechanisms that generate the chronic symptoms of such a shortage economy.

The direction of the proposition can again be reversed:

Proposition 4.—If a given country has a socialist system, it *necessarily* operates as a shortage economy. A shortage economy is an immanent attribute of socialism. It does not simply appear because the state has been following one kind of economic policy or another. The planning process and economic management may intensify or relieve some phenomena of shortage, but that does not produce a shortage economy. A shortage economy appears because it is one constituent of socialism, indeed one of its most important characteristic marks. Wherever socialism is, there is a shortage economy in the midst of it.

I have put my propositions strongly. Later I will reformulate them more subtly, allowing for exceptions, mixed cases, and transitional forms, but initially I want readers to note how these economic systems in their "classic" form do not converge, in this respect, in any "middle road."[15]

I have used the word *proposition* several times here. Perhaps it would be better academic etiquette to term them *conjectures* or *hypotheses*, but I feel it would be hypocritical of me to do so. What I am proposing is backed by a million facts of everyday life. It is almost as an extra that I try to justify them logically as well. Furthermore, 6 of the tables and 10 of the figures in the study support the propositions statistically. I would like to emphasize that these data are intended to form an illustration in support of the propositions, not "evidence" of them.

My propositions are not empty or tautological. They can be refuted. I too have to do further research in the spirit of necessary doubt about my own propositions. The chance of refuting them stays open to my critics.

The four propositions assume the presence of a causal connection. The cause is the capitalist or socialist system and the effect the surplus or shortage economy. Between the cause and the effect are wedged more complex chains of intermediate causes and effects. These I will deal with for the capitalist system when I describe the causal connection in more detail: I try to present this in Figure 5.2. The causal chain for the socialist system has been covered in earlier works of mine.[16]

The figure presents, in symbolic form, only the causal connections that have been discussed in the study so far. These refer in telegraphic style to complicated mechanisms, as a reminder and to provide a concise view of them.

The figure is far from complete: several relations of cause and effect described in the essay are missing. (For example, the effect of international trade.) Even so, it may be too crowded. Also, for the sake of clarity, the arrows of causal effect (with one exception) point in one direction, from left to right. That is the main line of effect, but of course there are counter-effects. For instance, seller rivalry generates excess capacity, whereas excess capacity encourages rivalry. The arrows in the opposite direction have been omitted only for clarity's sake.

---

15. If I were to try to present my line of thought in the mathematical language of equilibrium theories, I would need to devise a model with not one, but two stable points of equilibrium, one "shortage-economy equilibrium" and one "surplus-economy equilibrium." Then in the virtual world of the model, the system would settle around one point of equilibrium or the other. The model would help to show what parameters would have to change for the system to climb out of one equilibrium trap and fall into the other. I note at my own expense that I should perhaps be working toward such an equilibrium-style reformulation. The reformulation would greatly facilitate understanding and acceptance by economists raised on mathematical models of equilibrium who comprehend only that language, all the more because more than one model current in present-day economics displays multiple equilibria, that is, equilibrium points that are markedly different from each other.

16. See, above all, my book *The Socialist System* (Kornai 1992). The causal chain for the shortage economy is described in Chapter 15 there.

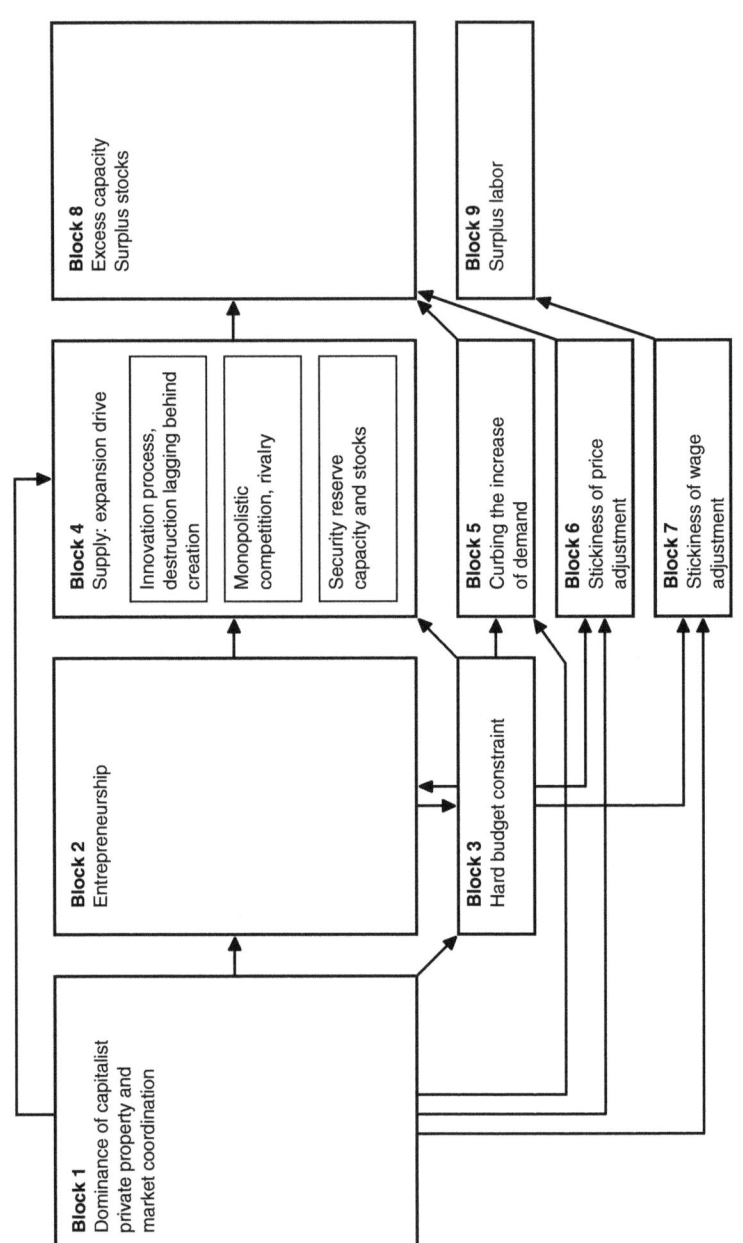

Figure 5.2.
Factors generating surplus economy: the causal chain

Note that the causal chain in Figure 5.2 starts on the left from identical elements and ends on the right in two parallel blocks: the surplus economy on the market for products and services, and the surplus economy on the labor market. In other words, if the capitalist system is examined, it behaves as a surplus economy on both markets of the real sphere. There appear parallel chronic excess capacities and stocks *and* unemployment, incomplete utilization of the potential labor force. Both groups of phenomena can be traced to *common* fundamental causes.[17]

This statement is based principally on the *theoretical* line of argument of the previous sections. Its real existence can be tested empirically. It will be refuted if broad, intensive, continual phenomena of excess supply on the market for goods and services appeared simultaneously with broad, intensive, continual labor shortage. It would not be refuted if it coincided with phenomena of surplus with the opposite sign, so long as they were weak, local, and transitional. (For instance, if there were labor shortages in a few specific trades in a general surplus economy.)

Of the explanatory factors in Figure 5.2 that lie behind the surplus, I stress here only those directly related to the *system*, on whether the country concerned has a capitalist or a socialist system. This is the main subject of this study, to which I want to draw attention, but I am by no means denying that other factors also influence the appearance of instances of surplus and shortage under both systems.

1. One set of factors connects with the frictions, maladjustments, and information gaps. These phenomena can generate either excess supply or excess demand. (I discussed them in the previous section, in the context of the labor market.)
2. Processes of supply, demand, and price-setting are affected in any socio-economic environment by the state's economic policy, notably monetary and fiscal policy. Although this applies under any system, there is an essential difference between the socialist and capitalist systems in how this is done, in the modes of transmission, and in the strength of the effect. As noted in the Introduction, this study touches on this without discussing it thoroughly.

Using the visual idiom of Figure 5.1, factor-group 1 affects the location of the "sack." The less the friction—the smoother the adaptation—the closer comes the whole cluster to the two broken lines marking the minimum of shortage

---

17. This is by no means self-evident. There is debate in macroeconomic discourse, for example, in polemics on the causes of the present crisis, about whether the running away of investment in the upward branch of the cycle leads to the later troubles, or the insufficient demand for labor. Both processes can be fitted into the framework drawn in this study and both were mentioned in Sections 2–4 of my Second Essay.

and surplus in the *real world*. The "zero-shortage, zero-surplus," Walrasian point of equilibrium appears only in the virtual world of theoretical models.

With factor-group 2, the effect of government economic policy can shift the zone in any direction, which is important, of course.[18] (I will return to this in the section on special cases.) For example, they can reinforce the instances of surplus in the surplus economy typical of a capitalist system, while weakening the instances of shortage (shifting the "sack" a little rightward and downward), or *vice versa*. However, governmental economic policy cannot propel the economy into the field above the 45-degree line, that is, turn it into a shortage economy. That would require a change of system on the scale of Tsarist Russia's in 1917 or Eastern Europe's (including East Germany's) after World War II. It would need a radical change in Block 1 of Figure 5.2, with public ownership and bureaucratic coordination seizing dominance from private ownership and market coordination. Similarly, no fiscal or monetary policy is capable of propelling the contents of the "shortage-economy zone" over the 45-degree line. That would call for a radical change in the opposite direction, to create the dominance of private ownership and the market seen in Block 1 of Figure 5.2.

5.5 GENETIC PROPENSITIES

Although I have tried to express myself cautiously, readers may have deduced from the description of the causal chains that I was advancing deterministic relationships. Given the numerical values of the explanatory variables, they would determine the numerical values of the variable to be explained. I need hardly say that no such simplistic explanation occurred to me.

Expressions such as the "attributes" of the socialist or capitalist system occur here and in my earlier works. In fact a system-specific attribute is a *propensity*, rather like an innate, genetic propensity or inclination in a human being. Our blood vessels, for instance, are inclined to harden and calcify with age, but the strength of this inclination varies between individuals. Nor are we at the mercy of fate—eating and drinking habits and other lifestyle factors influence the speed of the process—but the inclination is built into our genetic code.

Not even in the Stalinist or Maoist period was bureaucratic centralization in all countries equally strong. Many variations occurred, but the propensity was coded in. It can be deduced logically and confirmed empirically that the monopoly of power, a one-party system, and the dominance of state ownership lead inevitably to bureaucratic centralization.

18. Leijonhufvud (1973 and 2009) set forth in his articles a similar idea using another metaphor: the macro economy can move within a "corridor," but a macropolicy attempt to cause a big shift would make the economy collide with the corridor wall. Leaving the corridor has serious consequences. Leijonhufvud's ideas are akin to those of this study also in not centering the examination around a special *point* of equilibrium, but acknowledging that market-state attributes may assume *any values within determined bounds* (the walls of the corridor).

The inclination can be combated, but the victory cannot be complete. For the sake of illustration the concept is presented not in terms of tendencies built into every human being, but in the narrower context of family tendencies inherited from forebears. Think of someone whose parents, grandparents and siblings have suffered from heart and circulation complaints. In such cases, it is worth considering whether that person has inherited such an inclination to that disease. This can be seen as a warning of a higher risk of contracting such a disease with age.

If there is such a risk factor, let us not expect to win some kind of *final* victory over it. Those who watch their diet, get some exercise, do not smoke, and are not subject to frequent stress are combating their propensity to heart and other circulatory diseases effectively, but any letup, and the danger reappears.

In this sense (to return to the immediate context of the study) capitalism's system-specific attributes can be seen as propensities that either exert themselves fully or are suppressed by various factors (moderation by decision makers, the moral norms of society, legislation, or other specific state interventions).[19] However, the innate forces still operate and cannot be eliminated by social control or by state regulation. They are present in capitalism's genes.

Let us look at one or two examples.

The genes of capitalism contain a propensity to enterprise. Though it may be suppressed by bureaucratic constraints, a burdensome company tax system, a postrecession credit crunch, and so on, it will emerge repeatedly.

Also in capitalism's genes is the effort of employers to resist the pay claims of their employees. They see it is worth their own while to pay an efficiency wage to some favored group or they may be kind-heartedly inclined to pay more on charitable grounds, for instance, to relieve poverty. However, the spontaneous position for employers as such is to curb wage costs. (This is not self-evident. Socialist factory managers will have this position dictated to them from above.)

The genetically coded propensities mentioned in the earlier line of argument appear mainly on the *micro* level. The propensities of many micro units in the same direction become perceptible on the *macro* level as well, but it is justified to refer to macro-level propensities only if it is possible to discern on the macro level the interests, incentives, signals, and relations that produce the combined effect.

The distinction between a propensity and actual operation of it is an important analytical tool for examining social organizations, systems, and subsystems. I stress this particularly for those who are accustomed to describe the relations of economic organizations and individuals in the mathematical relations between the variables of a conventional mathematical model. For instance, a model of alcoholism might state that the number of beers drunk is the

---

19. Let me mention again here the book by Akerlof and Shiller (2009) in relation to what Keynes called *animal spirits*. As the two authors interpret this psychological phenomenon, it overlaps in several (but not all) respects with what is called here a *system-specific propensity*.

non-negative number X. There is an upper limit imposed by biological factors; there is just no room inside anybody for 20 bottles of beer. For a standard deterministic mathematical model of alcoholism, however, it is immaterial that the variable X increases from 0 to 10, or decreases from 10 to 0. In reality, we are well aware that the processes of becoming dependent and of giving up, of "going" and "coming back," are different. This is not conveyed by standard economic models. Behavioral economics has proved with some noteworthy psychological experiments that people value a $100 gain in their wealth quite differently from a $100 loss. That recognition known to behavioral economists as "aversion to loss" (Kahneman and Tversky 1979 and 1991; McGraw et al. 2010) has not been incorporated into the thinking of a large part of economists.

That recognition plays a key part in the line of argument in this essay. Let me recall in what contexts the phenomenon has appeared.

- Schumpeterian creative destruction.—Creation goes ahead with great verve. Those who are advancing it do so happily and gain material advantage from doing so. Destruction is a bitter pill. The losers resist and show psychological attachment to what has to disappear, and their material interests are also tied up with retaining what should be destroyed, at least temporarily (or they feel that this is in their interest).
- Those who win from rivalry feel joy, or at least gain a better standing, for example by raising their market share. The drive to expand is a strong motivator. For the losers, the loss of position does not occur automatically as it does at a sports event. Those who have performed worse do not withdraw from as much of the field as the victor has won. That is one reason why surplus appears.
- In a capitalist market economy, price-maker firms feel no compunction about raising prices. They do so in the hope of greater profits. But reducing prices is unpleasant and harder to perform. Prices are more resistant downward than upward. This kind of asymmetry is also one explanation for the appearance of surplus.

I stated a few pages ago that the normal state of the demand–supply configuration is marked by asymmetry. That is partly (although not wholly) explained by the aversion to loss just explained. The propensity moves in one direction, though it is not impossible to strive in the opposite direction, but it involves combating strong spontaneous forces and often succeeds only in part.

This argument has important practical implications. There is a need to know which phenomenon or process appears under capitalism as an "immanent," "genetic" propensity, and which one is produced merely by a specific constellation of circumstances. Nor is it immaterial how strong the propensity is.

When the state or some organization tries to combat some strong, spontaneous propensity (as is very justified in many cases), let it do so with open eyes. There is no regulatory barrier or act of state intervention that the possessors of the propensity will not try to combat or evade.

SECTION 6

The Effect and Assessment of the Surplus Economy

6.1 A VIEW OF THE EFFECTS AND THE VALUE JUDGMENTS

Sections 2–5 of this essay took a positive approach to the phenomenon of the surplus economy and its causal factors. Let us now turn to the effects of it. I will still try, as far as possible, to separate objective description of the effects from value judgments about them. The latter are inevitably subjective, because, behind every assessment, there is a system of values. I will append my own evaluation to each item, while occasionally mentioning other assessments different from mine, especially those that feature in public discourse and have a strong influence on public opinion.

Due to the strong causal connections (see Figure 5.2) it is hard to discern what effect can be ascribed to the capitalist system *in general* and what to the *specific* surplus-economy character of the demand–supply regime. I will focus on the latter, eschewing an overall evaluation of capitalism in favor of reviewing and evaluating the narrower field of the effects of a surplus economy (competition among sellers, excess capacities and stocks, excess labor, and the phenomena of surplus discussed so far). This means omitting such fundamentally important questions as democracy, human rights, and constitutionalism, which relate closely to the presence of private ownership and a market economy, but not directly to the subject of the surplus economy (see Kornai 2008).[1]

---

1. A long list could be made of the favorable and unfavorable attributes of capitalism that have been *omitted* from this essay, from its environmental effects through its stimulation or amelioration of international conflicts, to its influence on transformation of family relations. Readers should not expect from this section more than a few isolated (if in themselves noteworthy) extracts from a summary assessment of capitalism.

6.2 INNOVATION

There is an ample and varied literature on the factors that stimulate and impede innovation. My own analysis is presented in the First Essay of this volume.[2]

It is widely agreed that the main spur to such activity is *competition*. Competition among producers (especially in its commonest form of monopolistic competition) creates surplus, as a *cause* and as an *effect* of competition, since producers would like to better their utilization of capacity, and as sellers they would like to dispose of their accumulated inventory, as well as win buyers from rivals with new products and services. It can easily be discerned logically that where there is no surplus there is no competition among sellers—the *drive* deriving from the presence of a salable surplus is absent. Why should the vehicle industry or the telephone service under socialism bother itself with innovation if there are waiting lists for their obsolete models or for telephone lines? The beneficiaries of the rapid modernization that occurs in a surplus economy are all those whose lives are made more comfortable, stimulating, and productive by the technical advances and who experience price reductions as initially expensive new products become steadily cheaper.

These ideas have been detailed in earlier sections. Here, in assessing the surplus economy, I mention them again as this, by my ordering of values, is the *primary, principal economic advantage* of the surplus economy over the shortage economy.

Not everybody agrees with that verdict. For many, the expression *consumer society* has a pejorative ring. They find the succession of new products and services that form one of the main traits of a consumer society excessive and irritating.

There is no denying that the innovation process has its darker sides. It is hard to keep up with it. It is an imposition to keep studying new sets of instructions for use before there has been time to master the old. Let us all decide for ourselves whether the effort is worth the enjoyment of the extra performance offered by the innovation.

Innovation and technical progress in general can, undoubtedly, be dangerous, and technical novelties can be used of harmful effects.[3] This has been a possible fate of every innovation in human history, however, so we must keep that in mind when forming our value judgment.

---

2. The First Essay provides many references to the huge literature on innovation in capitalism. Here I draw special attention to the book of W. Baumol (2002).

3. The First Essay discusses the process of innovation and technical development in detail. It is there where I argue for my own value judgments.

6.3 THE SOVEREIGNTY AND MANIPULATION OF THE CONSUMER

Adequate stocks and reserve capacity that can be started up rapidly allow customers to choose from a range of lines and reject what they do not fancy. This broader selection brought about by a surplus economy is not just a narrowly commercial phenomenon, but more essentially an extension of *human rights of freedom*. Choice is denied in a shortage economy, where forced substitution reduces the satisfaction to be gained from consumption. Apart from the material side, it narrows human rights of freedom along with the smaller range of choice.

Producers or service providers aim to utilize their capacity as fully as possible and pass on their stocks to buyers. The presence of a surplus induces them to adapt to consumer wants. It takes time to make a lasting adjustment of production to consumer needs in the medium or long term, but by holding stocks and spare capacity that can be brought in rapidly, the delay can be lessened. The surplus is the "lubricant" that softens or silences the creaks in the machinery of adaptation.

I do not want to idealize the relation of buyer and seller in a surplus economy. Those who say that consumer sovereignty prevails in a surplus economy (or, more broadly speaking, in a market economy) are exaggerating. A real vassal would submit to a real sovereign in all things.

That is not the case here, mainly because the supply often awakens the demand, especially for new products and services. Secondly, and this also belongs to the full picture, sellers strive actively not only to influence their buyers' tastes (by offering clearly useful information) but to manipulate them (Galbraith 1998 [1958]). Advertising in a shortage economy is a fairly meaningless extravagance, but it is an inevitable side effect of a surplus economy. Those who, for other reasons, see the surplus economy as more advantageous than the shortage economy have to accept the presence of a mass of advertising and promotion, sometimes candid and honest, but sometimes misleading and intended to trick consumers into buying. The costs of advertising are enormous on a society-wide scale, as Table 6.1 shows for several countries.

Advertising costs in the United States ran at 2 percent of GDP in the 2000s. The scale of this becomes clear in comparison with some items of government expenditure. Combined federal and local spending on higher education in 2007 was also 2 percent of GDP, whereas that on family and child assistance programs was 0.6 percent, and on policing and fire fighting 1 percent (Chantrill 2010).

It would not be right to take the argument too far in this direction and claim that producers are really the sovereign ones. However clever they are at manipulating buyers, the latter have a chance to say no to an offered product or service, so long as there is a surplus. In the words of Albert Hirschman

Table 6.1. ADVERTISEMENT EXPENDITURES IN DEVELOPED COUNTRIES, 1975–2007 (ADVERTISEMENT EXPENDITURE TO GDP RATIO, PERCENT)

Year	Argentina	Japan	Italy	New Zealand	USA
1975	na	0.8	na	na	1.7
1985	na	1.1	na	na	2.3
1995	na	1.1	na	na	2.2
2000	1.2	1.2	0.7	1.3	2.5
2005	1.8	1.4	0.6	1.4	2.1
2006	2.0	1.4	0.6	1.3	2.1
2007	2.1	1.4	0.6	1.3	2.0

Note: The advertisement expenditure indicator reflects the total cost of advertisement in newspapers, magazines, radio, plus those made through TV broadcasts, direct mail, billboards, and other forms of advertisement. Based on the definitions provided by these data sources, it was not possible to check whether this indicator covers all the components of the advertisement expenditure.
Sources: GDP data from IMF (2010) and Federal Reserve Bank of St. Louis. (2010); advertisement expenditure from WARC (2007), CS Ad Dataset (2007), and Dentsu (2009).

(1970), there is *exit*: buyers do not need to protest forcefully, simply to depart from the seller. So if the language of political power is to be used, the consumer in a surplus economy is not an absolute, sovereign ruler, but a "strong" president of the republic, who influences decisions and can veto them. In a shortage economy, on the other hand, there is no exit; buyers are vassals, begging goods or services from buyers and providers in a ruling position. The more intensive the shortage, the more subservient they are.

It is clear from the surplus economy–shortage economy pair of opposites how ultimately there are types of *power relations* and subordination-domination at work. This line of argument is usually absent in the teaching of standard mainstream economics.

6.4 PRODUCTIVITY AND COORDINATION

What I said about lubricating the machinery of mutual adaptation between producer and consumer applies also to relations within production. There are problems with supplies of raw materials and components under any system. Some inputs may not arrive from suppliers in time; human errors and lack of discipline may occur. However, the problems are easier to resolve in a surplus economy with inventories and idle capacity that can be mobilized as required. Anyone employed in production (whether a manager or an employee) who has had the chance to compare day-to-day production in the state-owned enterprises of socialism and in the private corporations of capitalism can easily perceive the differences (see Table 3.2 and Figure 3.4 in earlier sections of this essay). The surplus economy is more flexible, works more smoothly and reliably, and is much more robust than the rigid shortage economy troubled by repeated shortages.

The difference certainly contributes to the productivity and growth of the capitalist system, but to be objective, it has to be said that the "lubrication" means that large sums of capital are tied down in large stocks and idle capacity. Many view with antipathy on what they see as "waste" of that huge capital.

The general attributes of economic systems do not rest on exact operations-research calculations. The surplus economy of capitalism has, by nature, a propensity to accumulate large stocks and leave much of the productive capacity idle.

6.5 ADAPTATION

So far, relations of producers and consumers (here individuals or households) and of the interactions between producers has been spoken of separately. Let us look now at the *whole*, the cooperation among all participants in the economy. Cooperation occurs somehow even under the shortage economy, as its persistence for decades went to show.

One of the surplus economy's big advantages is that its coordination, despite frictions, is smoother, faster, and more flexible than the rigid, jerky, belated adaptations of the shortage economy. Many advocates of capitalism—for example, most of the standard mainstream textbooks—see this balancing, coordinating role as the main advantage of the market economy, and some even going so far as to ascribe to it all the market economy's virtues. In my assessment, the number-one position does not go to flexibility of static adaptation, but to the dynamism of the surplus economy and its irresistible propensity for innovation, but I see its favorable adaptive attributes as an important virtue, too.

6.6 DISTRIBUTION OF INCOME AND WEALTH

Inequality of income and wealth appear openly in the surplus economy. Anything can be bought in any quantity if it is paid for. Purchases are only limited by the buyer's purse. Those who can afford less buy less.

The shortage economy, on the other hand, has an equalizing effect, but it is certainly not consistently egalitarian. There are numerous factors that work against full equalization. The distribution of income is unequal. Differentiation of pay is a practical intention in a socialist economy for various reasons: to encourage better performance, to reward political services and loyalty, and so on. So the same rule applies: Those with more money can buy more.

Nor is the inequality confined to buying with money. The allocation system (for instance for housing or for goods in short supply) gives open preference to those close to the ruling party and with influence and connections.

However, the inequalities in wages and in access to goods are normally much smaller than they are in most capitalist countries. This gives the inaccurate, but not wholly erroneous impression that there is little to be had in a shortage economy but we all get some.

The socialist state's paternalist pricing policy and financing of the welfare sectors exert equalizing effects, which ultimately involve a redistribution of incomes. Practically everybody is entitled in a shortage economy to free public education and free health care, including poorer strata that would not be able to pay their cost in a "pure" market economy.[4] Housing rents and staple food prices are kept low with large state subsidies that also benefit those who are low paid.

The consequences appear self-evident in the general state of the demand–supply configuration: grave shortages develop in free or almost-free goods and services. The price of greater equality is intensive shortage. The shortage economy is ultimately more egalitarian than the surplus economy, but the income redistribution that performs the equalization exacerbates the shortage.

6.7 "MATERIALISTIC" AND "SPIRITUAL" VALUES

The surplus economy (the "consumer society") is often blamed for "materializing" people, leading them to think in materialistic terms.[5] Advertising campaigns, shopping malls crammed with goods, and brash new products are accused of developing a distorted set of values and weaning people of respect for spiritual values.

Although I concede the task of examining the issue scientifically to the sociologists, I would like to risk a few comments based on observation of the surplus and shortage economies. Back in the 1970s, I saw women in a Moscow department store fighting and pulling one another's hair over a new consignment of shoes. Were those combatants any less materialistic than the Muscovite women of today who can choose comfortably among the many (superabundant?) shoes in several rival shoe stores?

---

4. The appearance of the welfare state under modern capitalism is discussed in Section 7 of this essay.

5. Historians of economic thinking usually trace this ramified critique of capitalism back to the works of Thorstein Veblen (1975 [1899]) and Galbraith (1998 [1958]). The various critical works have bestowed on the capitalist system or its attitudes a number of epithets: consumerism, consumer capitalism, economic materialism, the affluent society, *Homo consumericus*, commercialism, and so on.

Even sharper historical examples can be given. Did the millions, in Stalin's Ukraine or, several decades later, in Mao's China, who died in the famine, the cruelest stroke of the shortage economy, have less interest in material things—in grain, flour, potatoes, bread—and more in spiritual concerns than their successors who are in a position to buy such goods?[6]

If there is a cause-and-effect relation at all between the general demand–supply regime (surplus economy versus shortage economy) and a "materialistic" view, it may be as follows. The surplus economy, among other factors, contributes to the spread of information and modern means of education. (This was mentioned earlier.) Those who thirst after spiritual and intellectual values or news have far more to choose from than before. The surplus—stocks and idle capacity—extends to the stocks of book publishers and bookstores, to the offerings of radio and TV stations, and to the almost immeasurable quantity of information on the Internet. There is excess supply of these—values and junk alike.

6.8 THE DIRECTION OF CORRUPTION

Corruption is present in every society. Its frequency, severity, and forms are influenced by several factors.[7] I will not even consider here the still unanswerable question of whether corruption is greater or less under capitalism than under socialism, but, instead, confine myself to what is directly connected with the subject of the essay: Does the demand–supply regime have any bearing on corruption?

It does. Who bribes whom? That depends on whether we are in a surplus economy or a shortage economy. To simplify strongly, buyers in a shortage economy try in various ways, some corrupt, to influence sellers. In a surplus economy this is reversed: sellers try in various ways, some corrupt, to influence buyers.

The instances of corruption in a shortage economy are typically minor. Housewives slip money to the butcher to get a good cut of meat. It is more serious if the procurement manager of an enterprise corrupts the representative of a supplier firm to ensure that the enterprise gets some of the scarce

---

6. Chekhov (1973 [1894]: 261) protests against the ideas of the Messianistic prophet Tolstoy this way: "Prudence and justice tell me there is more love for mankind in electricity and steam than in chastity and abstention from meat."

7. Collegium Budapest set up in 2002–2003 an international interdisciplinary research group headed by Susan Rose-Ackerman and myself, entitled *Honesty and Trust in the Light of Post-Socialist Transition*. The findings were incorporated in 40 studies gathered into two volumes (Kornai and Rose-Ackerman 2004; Kornai, Rothstein, and Rose-Ackerman 2004). These contain detailed bibliographies of the literature on the subject.

materials or components in short supply. The petty acts of corruption become serious anomalies because they became prevalent on a mass scale.

The attempts at corruption are very strong in a surplus economy, especially if the seller has a private interest in finding a buyer and the buyer is spending public money. These are not small sums; billions of dollars of taxpayers' money flow into the accounts of private companies. It looks well worthwhile to pay millions to the representative of a purchasing state authority or other state organization, to ensure the seller's company gets the contract and not a rival. To the seller, these millions may be a small percentage of the deal, but to a public servant who is bribed, they are enormous. Corruptible people are ubiquitous. What needs noting here is the *situation* that tempts with great force. I spoke earlier of the great merits of competition among sellers, but the same competition induces attempts at corruption as well.

6.9 THE ADVANTAGES AND DRAWBACKS OF CAPITALIST COMPETITION, THROUGH THE EXAMPLE OF THE AUTOMOTIVE INDUSTRY

I would like to illustrate these ideas about the advantages and drawbacks of the surplus economy and capitalist competition by taking an example from economic history and economic policy: the development of the automotive industry over the last few decades.[8] Very large surplus capacity emerged over a long period in all vehicle-making countries. Figure 6.1 shows that the proportion of idle capacity ranged between 12 and 27 percent and showed a rising tendency in the 1990–2008 period. It is justifiable to talk here of chronic excess capacity.

Enormous reserves of cars have accumulated at the factories and car dealers.[9] Every analyst of the sector knew about the large excess capacity and unsold stocks as the analysts often sounded the alarm. That is clearly demonstrated by Figure 6.2.

Although all the factory managers realized there was very large excess capacity on a global scale, they were unable to control their urge to expand. Ever more capacity appeared, as each firm hoped to win market share from its rivals. As a result, vehicle making became one of the crisis industries when the world recession began in 2008, especially in the United States.

---

8. For an overall account, see, for example, Haugh et al. (2010), OECD (2009), and Orsato and Wells (2006).

9. Although surplus is a main attribute of the vehicle industry, some luxury cars are to be waited for in their market for months. This situation is a vivid example of the description in Section 3, that is, that surplus and shortage may coexist, but one of them is dominant, whereas the other is exceptional.

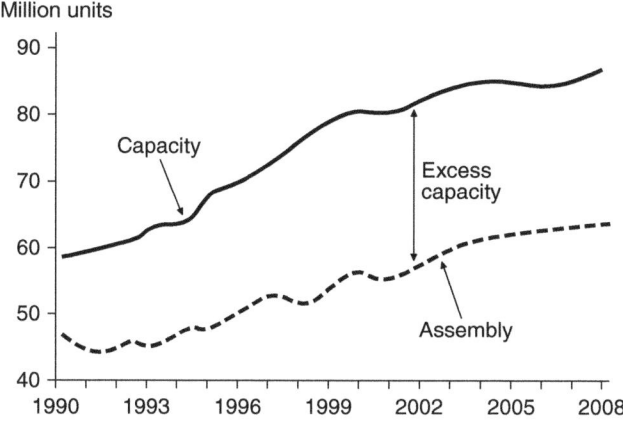

Figure 6.1.
Excess capacity in the automotive industry, 1990–2008
Note: The figure relates to the world automotive industry, specifically to the so-called light vehicles. In Europe, vehicles weighing less than 3.5 tons are classified in this category.
Source: Francas et al. (2009, 248).

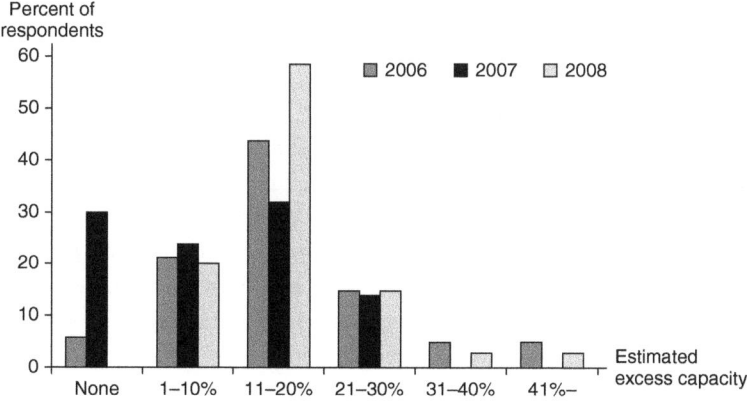

Figure 6.2.
Business executives of the automotive industry about the global excess capacity, 2006–2008
Note: There are six domains of the estimates of excess capacity on the horizontal axis in the year of the survey. The vertical axis shows the distribution of the estimates. For example, in 2007, according to 32 percent of the respondents, the excess capacity was 11 to 20 percent.
Source: KPMG (2009, 15).

The recession has hardly passed, and the number of vehicles sold in Europe since 2008 has fallen from year to year. Yet some giant vehicle manufacturers are still making huge investments, thereby exacerbating further the unused capacity in the vehicle industry as a whole (Piac & Profit 2013).

A fall in the output of the vehicle industry has strong multiplier effects, because its suppliers and their suppliers in the sales chain form a sizable proportion of the economy. There was strong pressure, therefore, to assist the troubled car-making corporations. Huge bailouts were implemented, which increased expectations of a soft budget constraint in future. The factors that impede the process of creative destruction, discussed in Section 2 were vividly exemplified in the automotive industry.

On one side of the scale is the terrible waste that the vast idle capacity of the industry represents. Cars pollute the atmosphere. Traffic accidents are rife. On the other side is the contribution the industry has made in providing rapid, comfortable transportation for a rising proportion of the world's population. The car factories and their suppliers of materials and components offer millions of jobs. The rivalry within the industry is a spur to technical development, making today's vehicles more comfortable, speedier, and safer than they were 20 or 50 years ago. Sooner or later will come a breakthrough that revolutionizes fuel consumption in cars. It is in the "nature" of capitalism for several strong genetic propensities to institute such processes spontaneously, with favorable and unfavorable effects alike.

It is worth drawing another comparison, at this point, between the capitalist surplus economy and the socialist shortage economy. Certainly excess auto-industry capacity and stocks tie down huge resources, but consumers buy cars when they want, and the model they want, assuming they have the money. If they do not wish to pay immediately, the financial sector, the automotive industry, and the salesrooms will offer credit. As opposed to that, vehicle shortage in the socialist countries was depressing. In the Soviet Union and the East European countries at the end of the 1980s, there was a shortage of about four million vehicles—equivalent to about one-third of the surplus capacity that had built up in the capitalist world.[10] There were countries in Eastern Europe where there were waiting lists of 14–16 years for some models (Kornai 1992, 236). It was not just that there was no credit for vehicle purchase; buyers in many countries had to pay all or some of the car price up front. In other words the consumers were extending credit to the producers.

In surplus economies, the development of carmakers advances innovation. The new features appear year after year: from better safety devices to improved heating and cooling, from radar signaling the risk of collision to electronic novelties, from devices to amuse passengers (radios, players, TV) to technical developments that reduce exhaust emissions. In the shortage economies, technical development almost ceased: East German Trabant or Wartburg cars, Soviet Ladas, and other makes scarcely changed for decades. At most, there was a belated introduction of some feature developed in the West, but what could spur technical development if people were ready to wait years for technically obsolete cars?

---

10. The estimate is based on calculations by Zsuzsa Kapitány (Kapitány 2010).

6.10 A STAND IN FAVOR OF CAPITALISM AND THE SURPLUS ECONOMY

The review of the surplus economy and comparison of it with the shortage economy leads to a broader question. What general value judgments can be made about it? To repeat the warning at the beginning of this essay, it covers only one aspect of the operation of capitalism: the demand–supply regime, the choice between a surplus and a shortage economy. This is no small detail but, rather, an analysis of an essential aspect to do with some major virtues and major problems of the capitalist system. To pass judgment on the capitalist system as a whole, however, also means considering, for instance, what tie there is between the capitalist system and the alternative forms of government: democracy and dictatorship; furthermore, what the capitalist system means to the social and economic situation of employees and to the distribution of income. I could easily continue this list of the subjects not covered here.

Still, I do not wish to avoid the problem entirely. I have reached conclusions on other aspects in other writings of mine, always coming out in capitalism's *favor* in relation to the problems discussed there, but expressing no desire to ignore its negative attributes. I have two main arguments for saying I am a believer in the capitalist system in accordance with my system of values.

First, my commitment to democracy is at the top of my list of value priorities. There is no democracy without capitalism. Capitalist economic fundaments do not guarantee the *sufficient* conditions for establishing democracy, and for its successful maintenance and defense against its opponents. However, the dominance of capitalist private ownership and a market economy are *necessary* conditions for the maintenance of democracy. This prime argument in favor of capitalism I can only mention in passing here, but I have expressed it in other writings. (See my collection of studies entitled *From Socialism to Capitalism*, Kornai 2008.)

Second, it stands to capitalism's credit that this system (and no other) is able, through the mechanisms of the surplus economy, to sustain and drive the continual process of modernization, innovation, and rapid technical development. This is a matter of value choices. That second serious argument returns us to the subject of this essay. To my mind it is a *welcome advance* that more and more people are being rescued from famine, deprivation, and paralyzing financial penury, that more and more people are gaining access to technical achievements, that more and more people have a rising standard of living. This advance is made possible by the capitalist system that generates the surplus economy.

All other aspects that I have presented as virtues of the surplus economy rate only third in my eyes. I also take seriously the arguments against the system, but by my system of values, the first two arguments—democracy and technical development—have decided the choice: I choose the capitalist system.

Many others would make the same choice between capitalism and socialism. However, that agreement leaves a number of other important questions open.

Decades ago, I was in Dublin to deliver a lecture in honor of the distinguished Irish statistician Roy C. Geary. I spoke about the shortage economy that appeared in the socialist system and pointed to the suffering this causes to the inhabitants of the socialist countries, but I pointed out that they did not suffer from unemployment. During the subsequent discussion, Professor Geary asked whether Ireland could retain the abundance of goods that appears in a capitalist market economy but "import" from the socialist countries the ability to avoid unemployment. I replied then as this essay points out now: No, it could not. Goods shortage and labor shortage were joint products of the chronic shortage economy, produced together. Conversely, surplus capacity, surplus stocks, and surplus labor appeared concurrently in a surplus economy. Those choosing what they appreciate have to take what they deprecate as well.

I belong to a broad group of economists who are ready to stand up for capitalism while maintaining a sound and "realistic" view of that system. This group is not homogeneous. One subgroup consists of "naive reformers,"[11] convinced that all capitalism's essential woes can be cured, most of them prescribing requisite state intervention as their remedy.

Another subgroup, in which I include myself, does not perceive the woes as wholly curable. Capitalism is an organism burdened with contradictions, with strong good and strong bad characteristics. Both are part of its nature. Its virtues neither are created by the efforts of politicians and bureaucrats or of experts who advise them, nor is it their ill will, selfishness, or stupidity, or the errors of ideologists that bring out the evils. These are immanent propensities of the system, which have developed out of deeply ingrained interests, instincts, and behavioral patterns shaped by evolution.

People have to live with the innate, incurable problems of the system. It has to be acknowledged that where there is a surplus economy, there commercial stocks awaiting buyers will swell, advertisements will proliferate, corruption will appear in connection with public procurement, and so on.

I have found it typical mainly of the American mentality to adopt a naive optimism and expect all problems to have solutions. The European (French?

---

11. Those who have read earlier works of mine will be familiar with the expression. I gave this name long ago to those who expected reform of the *socialist* system to heal all socialism's woes. To my mind some of socialism's negative attributes are "genetic," immanent, innate, and incurable. Likewise, as I pointed out earlier in the study, I see some of capitalism's negative attributes also as "genetic," immanent, innate, and incurable.

Hungarian? Jewish?) mentality is more doubtful, accepting that problems may be *insoluble* as well.

The latter mentality need not lead to passive submission. Much can be done to alleviate the detrimental effects of the surplus economy. Here are a few:

- Improvement of procurement and inventory policies can be developed in each company and the flow of goods among firms made smoother. Think of the just-in-time strategy found widely in Japanese industry. The more widespread the success in this respect, the lower will be the level of surplus in the economy required for a given level of safety and buyer satisfaction.
- The state can regulate and inspect to ensure fair business competition.
- Constitutional methods of criminal investigation need to be deployed against corruption. The frequency can be reduced with measures of deterrence.
- Let me propose what may seem anachronistic: the application of medium and long-term planning. Not the failed socialist system of imperative planning, but updated forms of indicative planning on the lines of those once used in France. After requisite experimentation, this may contribute to better coordination of new capacity and expected demand, and perhaps deter the heads of large corporations from undertaking mammoth investments that only increase the idle capacity in their industries further.

I mention these proposals simply as examples of how sober acknowledgment of capitalism's innate drawbacks can be coupled with constructive thinking and adoption of efficient state regulations and reforms.

6.11 THE SCOPE FOR A THEORETICAL SYNTHESIS AND ITS CONSTRAINTS

The references of this essay branch in many directions. The bibliography contains authors far from each other in their ideas, and the works of schools and subschools of economics spread across orthodoxy and heterodoxy, mainstream and out of mainstream. I handled this multiplicity of intellectual affinities ironically in my earlier writings, describing myself as eclectic. Although still not rejecting that epithet, I have set myself a more ambitious objective in this essay.

I am convinced that in keeping to a *positive* description and explanation of the capitalist and socialist economies, it is possible to *synthesize* the propositions emanating from the various strands of thought. The same reality is seen in the same way by researchers who observe it from differing, sometimes diametrically opposed angles. I am not claiming that every interesting idea so far produced by the economists' profession can be merged into one great common theory. The scope for synthesis is narrower than that. In the area now being discussed, however, there can be a synthesis of the ideas produced by the schools that I mention in this essay. The essay does not carry out that synthesis, but it attempts to outline it.[12] I would call it a *positive synthesis*, positive in the sense that people of differing, even opposed views concerning political endeavors and desirable goals can reach a consensus on understanding and explaining reality.

Table 6.2 is not aimed at completeness. It is not even complete in showing which author or school is referred to in this essay, and it cannot stand for an index of names or subjects. It is deficient particularly in not containing all the works, theories, and propositions that might be incorporated into a new positive synthesis of the theory of the market, but perhaps it can provide an indication of the scope for such a synthesis.

I have not compiled the table to clarify the history of theory or assign "credits." The names in the middle column are not necessarily those who first developed and published some new idea. I have written in names and other indications that may give an idea to readers of the research direction to which I am referring.

The table does not assign a separate row to institutional economics,[13] because I could not fill its third column. It is the position of the *whole study* and theoretical frames of the phenomena that square with the approach of institutional economics. This intellectual affinity, incidentally, runs through my earlier works as well.

Economists with theoretical interests and scholars specializing in the history of economic thought often contrast *orthodox* and *heterodox* thinking. However, there is no agreement on the features on which to base the assignment of economists, past or present, into one of these camps or the other. Those who classify themselves as heterodox (or are so classed by others) usually state clearly the issues on which they disagree with the orthodox. The problem is that the ideas of the various heterodox individuals or small groups differ not only from orthodoxy but also from each other. In better cases, they debate with each other, and in worse, they fail even to read each other's

---

12. I am not the first to see a chance of such a synthesis (see, for instance, Flaschel 2009; Helburn and Bramhall 1986). Authors who refer to synthesis usually seem to characterize it by combining two or three big names (such as Marx, Schumpeter, and Keynes). Or they may use a "neo-" prefix, following Samuelson's example when coining the expression "neoclassical synthesis." Perhaps the attribute "positive" offers a broader characterization. The umbrella of "positive analysis" could cover the contributions of far more strands and schools.

13. Institutional economics dates back a long time. It has taken a high position among schools of economics in recent decades mainly due to the work of Douglass North (1990 and 1991).

Table 6.2. THE ELEMENTS OF POSITIVE SYNTHESIS WITH RESPECT TO THE THEME "SHORTAGE ECONOMY–SURPLUS ECONOMY"

Topic	Author or school	Reference in the present essay (number and title of subsection)
Oligopolistic competition	Theory of imperfect competition	2.2: *Supply-related processes*
Excess capacity	Theory of imperfect competition, Post-Keynesian school	2.2: *Supply-related processes*
Innovation, creative destruction	Schumpeter	2.2: *Supply-related processes*
Reserve stocks	Inventory models of operation research	2.2: *Supply-related processes*
Increasing return to scale	Kaldor, Arthur	2.2: *Supply-related processes*
Process of demand formation	Disequilibrium School	2.3: *Demand-related processes*
Conflict of interest between employer and employee	Marx	2.3: *Demand-related processes*
"Sticky" prices and wages	Keynes, New Keynesian economics	2.4: *The pricing process* 4.3: *Keynesian unemployment*
"Keynesian" unemployment	Keynes, disequilibrium school	4.3: *Keynesian unemployment*
Structural unemployment	Phelps	4.4: *Structural unemployment*
Search	Phelps, search theories, matching theories	4.5: *Mismatched adjustment, frictional unemployment and search*
Efficiency wage	Stiglitz and Shapiro	4.6: *Efficiency wage*
Market is unbalanced	Austrian school	5.1: *The workability of the concept of "equilibrium"*
Effective demand, demand constraint	Keynes, Kalecki	5.2: *Asymmetry*
Evolution of institutions	Nelson and Winter, evolutionary economics	5.5: *Genetic propensities*
"Genetic" propensities	Keynes, behavioral economics, Akerlof and Shiller	5.5: *Genetic propensities*
Aversion to loss	Behavioral economics	5.5: *Genetic propensities*

works.¹⁴ I have to make these comments before stating that a good many of the views expressed in this essay correspond with or resemble those of economists customarily listed as heterodox. The list is a long one. It would start with towering scholars of the past, like Kalecki and Sraffa. I could go on naming contemporaries (in alphabetical order): David Colander, Peter Dorman, Herbert Gintis, Steve Keen, Alan Kirman, and Barkley Rosser. There are essential questions with which I am in agreement with the ideas of those listed, and not with their opponents. However, it would convey little to readers simply to classify my work naming the publications of heterodoxy.

I have tried to emphasize in the table what a quantity of elements I have been able to adopt from other authors when compiling the intellectual edifice of this essay. I regret that even the blueprint is only half-ready, and whole stories of the multistory building's draft are still missing. However, I can state with pleasure that I am not alone in what I have tried to do. There are a good many authors with similar aims seeking to compile some form of a synthesis.

In weighing the possibilities, it seems that the chances for such a positive synthesis are much better for the labor market than for other spheres of the market. This may be because there can be little doubt in relation to the labor market that it is a surplus economy, and in this system it is impossible to ignore the problem of unemployment. There are other phenomena of surplus elsewhere, but they do not cry out so loud as the labor surplus.

The attribute *positive* has appeared several times in this discussion of the scope for synthesis. It is not my policy to stick my head in the sand. The scope for collating and synthesizing ends where positive description gives way to normative analysis, the field of value judgments and policy recommendations. Then the cannons roar, and there comes sharp debate on political ideologies and conflicting views and beliefs of what constitutes a "good society." Then there is no question of objectivity; it is almost impossible for the most phlegmatic of researchers to remain impartial.

Schumpeter was one of the main inspirations of my work, and he was inclined toward conservatism in his political statements. I learned a lot about interpreting the operation of the market from Mises, Hayek, and the later followers of the Austrian school, their political statements belong on the right wing of the political spectrum. Keynes was a liberal politician. Nicholas Kaldor, with whose ideas I feel a strong intellectual affinity, was politically very active on the left wing of the British Labour Party. Most representatives of New Keynesian economics sympathized with the liberal Democrats of the U.S. political spectrum. In the analysis of excess capacity, I have many points of contact with the present-day post-Keynesian school, for instance

---

14. See Rosser, Holt, and Colander (2010). This volume contains an interview conducted by one of the editors, Barkley Rosser, with me about the relationship of Eastern European economists to "heterodox" economics.

with the writings of James Crotty (2001 and 2002); he and the other prominent members of the school are expressly left wing. Finally, at the endpoint of the spectrum this essay takes Marx's position on one or two cardinal questions.

The situation of economists working on the theory of the market resembles that of several doctors examining a patient and reaching the same diagnosis, but then differing sharply on what therapy to follow. One argues for quiet chemotherapy and another for surgical intervention, and a third says there is no point in disturbing the patient with superfluous treatment as he is going to die anyway.[15]

At this point I stop. For example, I do not make any recommendation about what policy today's government should pursue over the recession, although this would tie in closely with the questions dealt with here. I am sure that positive description and explanation of a well-defined scientific field is not only desirable, but also feasible; a broad synthesis of the theories, scientific explanations, and research methods can be achieved.

6.12 THE DEMAND FOR MATHEMATICAL MODELS WITH EXPLANATORY POWER

The list of ideas for incorporating in the proposed synthesis includes theories equipped with a mathematical apparatus and others presented without models. In this respect I do not wish to discriminate among the elements to be built into the positive synthesis. This essay takes a purely verbal approach, but I would consider it useful if it were to inspire those engaged in theoretical mathematical economics to model as many of its ideas as possible.

I am not among those who see mathematical modeling as the *main* culprit in diverting economics onto wrong paths. Nonetheless, I agree that there are many shortcomings in the application of mathematical models and the teaching of mathematical economic theory, and they cause much harm to the discipline. However, it is not within the remit of this essay to study that difficult question comprehensively.

I would not oppose the mathematical modeling of the phenomena discussed here. On the contrary, I would welcome and encourage it. Essential new questions that nobody has posed before are often, if not always, presented in verbal form. Verbal discussion allows a subtle and many-sided description of real phenomena, but that is only the beginning of scientific understanding. There the need will emerge for more exact definitions of the concepts and

---

15. A notable argument in favor of separating the positive from the normative appears in a study by Heilbronner (1986). He argues that the three sharply different action programs recommended by Marx, Schumpeter, and Hayek follow *not* from their great positive descriptions of the situation but from their differing political convictions.

stricter expression of the relations among them, making it logically plain what conditions apply to some statement. This is where mathematical modeling can help.

I have not found in the literature any model applicable to my ideas here. If I did, I would study it eagerly and apply it to check and clarify my propositions. If the mathematical transposition revealed some serious errors, I would subject my ideas to radical revision.

I hardly think the whole problem presented in the essay could be analyzed in a single model. I would be content if separate models examined one or another side of the complex problems. Let me present a few examples.

The subsections of Section 2 of this essay discussing the processes of supply, demand, and price setting present a dynamic system, with interactions among the three. These jointly create the surplus (i.e., the idle capacities and the stocks). My impression is that this could be described by a difference or differential equation system. The models would reveal what combination of parameters leads to the elimination of the surplus or tip the balance of the system into a shortage-economy state, what combination of parameters takes it in the opposite direction to where the system finally "bursts" under its ever-increasing surplus. What attributes of the system modeled will (I guess) make the Walrasian equilibrium unstable and tip the long-lasting state of the market toward a shortage economy or a surplus economy? Perhaps the direction in which to grope forward might be toward utilizing the mathematical apparatus of catastrophe theory and bifurcation theory.

Béla Martos, András Simonovits, Zsuzsa Kapitány, and myself devised models (see Kornai and Martos 1973 and 1981) in which surplus appeared. Indeed the increase and decrease of stocks were the main signals for controlling the process. The mathematical apparatus came from examining difference and differential equations. We were able to confirm that such a system is viable and controllable. However, we simplified things for ourselves by taking technology and the structure of production as constants. This hid from us the ideas central to this essay: the continual change and product-range renewal, and the Schumpeterian problems.

There are important and interesting models compiled in an expressly Schumpeterian fashion—the pioneering work of Aghion and Howitt (1998) should be mentioned—but they only capture the innovation phenomenon to a degree. What they most lack is a presentation of the inner mechanisms by which innovation is motivated and enforced.

I have briefly referred to mathematical models that cover the increasing return to scale (Arthur 1994; Helpman and Krugman 1985). They were big advances, but they have yet to be integrated into examination of the Schumpeterian processes.

The problems seem to be very difficult to handle mathematically. To my lay eyes they appear to show resemblances to physical phenomena such as the flow of liquids or gases, meteorological processes, or the motions of elementary particles. Mention has been made of their obvious resemblance to the evolutionary processes of biology. Perhaps the mathematical instruments of these subjects may offer methods to those inclined to mathematical modeling. Perhaps appropriate mathematical methods can be adopted from the theory of stochastic processes.

Will the genius of a new John von Neumann be needed to build a *new* mathematical apparatus to express precisely the things I have sketched roughly here? Until such a genius appears, nongenius economists can choose between two research courses. One is to confine their choice of subject matter to questions to which the given mathematical knowledge of the economists' profession can reply, thus giving up the modeling of most problems described in this essay. The other is not to duck the very difficult questions but to try to answer them verbally, in the knowledge that the answer is provisional, incomplete, and inexact, but it brings us closer to an understanding. For my part I have chosen the latter course.

SECTION 7

Departures from the General Scheme

Up to this point, the essay marks an attempt at a general scheme of the surplus economy. The sizes, proportions, and distributions of the surpluses clearly differ from country to country. A glance at Table 3.1 is enough to see how the capacity utilization rates of countries cluster around an average of 80 percent. The differences no doubt have several reasons, including the fact that the constituents of the surplus-generating mechanism differ by country in specific details.

This essay does not examine those country differences, important though they may be. As I noted in Section 1, this essay does not deal with the many concurrent variants of capitalism, nor does it employ the typology utilized in the "varieties of capitalism" literature. This section deals with changes *over time* in the state and mechanisms of the surplus economy, dividing up the time according to various criteria.

7.1 FLUCTUATIONS OF THE BUSINESS CYCLE

The fact that the volume of production, at whatever level, is not a constant but, rather, a fluctuating value is generally known. Traditional microeconomics deals in detail with the *short-term* mutual adjustments of demand, supply and prices; our knowledge of these is continually increasing. This essay is not intended to contribute to that.

There is no agreement on fluctuations in the business cycle among schools of economics. This refers to fluctuations in the *medium term*. Agreement has been reached on precise measurement of them and on definitions of some major concepts (e.g., what qualifies as recession), but there has been a debate for a century and a half on the causes of the rises and falls, assessment of the effects, and state economic policy to cope with them. Now the debate is more heated than ever after the recession (or perhaps before the next one). There are opposing views among politicians, economic advisers in the direct service of policy making, and academic economists.

Publicly important and intellectually stimulating though the debate on the fluctuations of the business cycle is, the subject here is not medium-term market movements, but the *permanent*, system-specific character of the capitalist market. When I embarked on this major task, I reckoned with the danger that the best economists would be preoccupied with medium-term problems and intent on giving practical advice on overcoming the recession to politicians and business leaders, but I still went ahead with studying the *long-lasting* phenomena. There is a division of labor among economists; somebody has to deal with these as well. I volunteered for the assignment because my special field—comparison of the socialist and capitalist systems—prepares me for studying the lasting differences between them.

Having stated these reservations, I will confine myself to a couple of comments. I would like to convince my reader that, at a time when attention is focused on the recession, recovery, and problems of cyclical variation, my ideas also have a bearing on these questions. The causes and effects of *medium-term* fluctuations are not divorced from the *long-lasting, continual* demand–supply regime under which they occur.

The general state of the capitalist economy, even amid wild fluctuations, remains within bounds that bear the marks of the surplus economy. (On the bounds, see subsection 5.3.) Not even at the height of strongest boom, when growth fills the order books of leading industries, inventories fall, capacity utilization tightens, unemployment is uncharacteristically low, and labor shortage appears in many places, will the surplus economy flip over into a shortage economy.

Let us turn back to Figure 3.1, showing the utilization of U.S. industrial capacity in 1965–2011. The gray areas mark periods of recession. The curve fluctuates strongly; utilization falls in recession periods to much lower levels. In no single year, however, did it approach full utilization and in only a couple of years did it hit 88–90 percent, and only in two years did it exceed 80 percent. The area above the utilization curve shows a continual presence of surplus, which, in terms of the index of industrial capacity utilization, ranged between 12 and 35 percent.

To put this in general terms, the fluctuations of the business cycle remain within the field of a continual surplus economy. The field has limits. If the economy improves rapidly, it may reach the upper limit, or, breaking previous records, even exceed it.[1] However, when it is near the limit and, still more, when it exceeds it, various protective mechanisms come into force. Some are spontaneous: a "bubble" bursts of its own accord on some market, and its rapid decline pulls other markets down with it, or instances of excess demand

---

1. Let me refer here again to the "corridor" of Leijonhufvud (2009—see note 18 of Section 5). What I call here the limits of the surplus-economy field corresponds to the corridor in which the capitalist macroeconomy moves under normal conditions, according to Leijonhufvud.

cause prices and wages to rise, which prompts intervention through fiscal and monetary policy.

There is a lot of overlap in the *description of the phenomena*, in how Keynesian economists dealing with cyclical fluctuations describe the upward side (a medium-term phenomenon) and in how this study characterizes the surplus economy (a long-term phenomenon).

There is centuries-old debate about how general glut can appear in the economy. The doctrinaire view, citing Say's law, sought to prove the general rule that every supply would create a requisite quantity of demand. If this statement were sound, it would obviously not be compatible with general "glut." When Keynesian macroeconomics appeared, the old debate revived. I would like to emphasize that the polemics there and then were about whether there could be excess production in the whole economy *for a given short period*. The Keynesian approach suggested there could be. This essay goes further, characterizing capitalism as a *continual*, chronic surplus economy.

Even if that temporal aspect is ignored, there is another difference to mention. This essay has avoided the expression *overproduction*. It is possible to refer to continual overproduction (if the meaning of the world is taken seriously), so long as (1) the aggregate capacity in the production sphere would be capable of production much greater than the sum of what all buyers could buy; (2) this excessive capacity is wholly or almost wholly utilized, that is, if the production enabled by the capacity is actually produced; and (3) the growth rate of the economy were such that this disproportion remains permanent. If that happened it would lead to disproportionate expansion of stocks and a steady increase in the ratio of stocks to production. "The coffee stocks are being dumped in the sea" is the nightmare vision that conjures up the Great Depression.

I have sought here to describe the dynamics of the production, consumption, supply, and demand processes more accurately. A sizeable proportion of idle capacity is present permanently (in the form of available machinery, equipment, premises, and labor), but this implies only an unutilized *possibility*, not actual "overproduction." The system operates with sizable stocks that suffice to guarantee buyers a choice, instigate rivalry, and lubricate the machinery to overcome adjustment problems. However, this is not accompanied by continual expansion of the stocks, not least because Schumpeterian creative destruction disposes of some of the production capacity and stocks, now in one place and then in another.[2]

Let us turn to the overlaps in the *causal relations*.

---

2. I hope it will be clear to readers, having reached this far: I am *not* claiming that the capitalist system engenders crises of over*production*. I am not advancing some new version of the old theories of the "crisis of overproduction." "Production" is a real category, whereas "supply" is a mental one. Oversupply is an intention that can be pursued on the resources side, but normally runs up against inadequacy of demand, so that it takes the form of unutilized capacity.

The causal factors used here to explain the *continual* appearance of phenomena of surplus coincide in part with those used to explain *temporary* instances of surplus in certain crisis theories. The way the demand process lags *continually* behind the supply process, as described in this essay is clearly akin to what Keynes and many followers say about the insufficiency of demand as a cause of *temporary* crisis. I hope that, despite the many similarities, I have managed to show that those theories and the ideas in this study are responding to different questions.

The theory presented here does not advance this as a case of a "large" macroeconomic supply hitting a "large" macroeconomic demand constraint. As outlined earlier, I had difficult problems even with the concepts and the measurement of demand and supply at the macro level. I sought to rest my work mainly on microeconomic foundations. In monopolistic competition, the supply proffered by producers or sellers increases while changing in quality and developing technically. Many of them run up frequently against demand constraints on a micro level, especially if they lag technically behind their competitors or lose favor with buyers for other reasons. There may be cases in which shortages develop on the market for a specific innovation, but ultimately the phenomena of surplus become commoner and more intensive than those of shortage.

In the writings of economists who deal with medium-term cyclical fluctuations descriptive–explanatory positive analysis is tied closely to economic policy recommendations. Here I avoid the latter and focus on comprehending the surplus economy generated by capitalism. However, having touched on the problems of cyclical fluctuations, let me say that this study on the regime of the permanent surplus economy may offer some lessons for those devising anticyclical policies.

It is worth thinking deeply about the strong impact of the immanent attributes—the "genetically coded" propensities of the capitalist system on the expansion of production, investment, and credit—and separate that from the weaker influence of policy measures, including the errors and omissions of politicians, governments, central banks, and state regulators. Even if it is conceded that the former are the main forces behind the events, there is no need to take a passive stance toward them. However, actions should be taken in the knowledge that the upswing period of the cycle is driven by vast energies, and, therefore, resistance against them requires great expertise and wisdom.

A still more general remark can be made: accelerating expansion and spinning up is innate to capitalism. When this eventually meets with constraints, contraction will inevitably follow. Ultimately the propensity to cyclic fluctuation is a "genetically coded" intrinsic feature of capitalism. It cannot come as a surprise that the supply of real goods, services, and credit first overshoots, and, as the disproportion becomes conspicuous, "the accelerating increase" abruptly changes its direction and is followed by a fall. We must come to terms with that nature of the signaling system of capitalism.[3]

It does not follow that there is no sense in regulation, but economists who try to assist political decision makers in drafting regulations should have no illusions. The apt expression coined after Hungary's reform debates of the 1960s and 1970s was "the regulation fallacy" *(szabályozási illúzió)*.[4] Governments think they can keep events on course with regulations and occasional hands-on interventions. Meanwhile, lower decision makers at enterprise level learn how to pick holes in the regulations. It is like an arms race, with new weapons being matched by still newer counterweapons.

Perhaps the prime lesson of this is that the effects of economic expansion and contraction are not all harmful or painful. Some are useful and progressive. Pioneer studies by N. D. Kondratiev and others and Schumpeter's great work on the business cycle (1939) showed that technical development accelerated in periods of economic expansion. To use the economic vocabulary of today, each period of accelerating growth generates not only a sequence of events that pave the way for increasingly irresponsible businesses but the same acceleration induces also a process of rapid innovation. That was certainly the case at the time of the "dot-com" bubble: it coincided with unprecedented growth of the infocommunication sector. The innovation process means experimentation, and that means 10 or even a 100 failures for every successful experiment. It is easy with hindsight to say money should not have been given for the failures. A very tight, conservative money market may help to preserve short-term macroeconomic proportions, but it will strangle innovation, which is accompanied by risks, sometimes very great ones.

Anticyclical policy is a double-edged sword on the downward swing of the cycle as well. Section 2 dealt with the way creative destruction involves winding up a lot of earlier production and eliminating a lot of jobs. The urge to defend jobs in times of recession arises out of feelings of human solidarity and desires for political popularity, but it also puts a brake on modernization.

The rivalry of Schumpeter and Keynes is a frequent topic in the history of theory. Keynes's "long term" is long over, and both are dead. It is time to seek what can be squared in their ideas, in what ways they complement each other, and in what ways they are irreconcilable.

Here, again, I must distinguish the positive and the normative approaches. It seems that some ideas of Schumpeter and of Keynes can be synthesized

---

3. Many control devices, such as thermostats to regulate household heating, are designed by engineers in this way. The temperature has to rise above the desired level and reach an upper threshold before the heating switches off. It then switches on again when the temperature falls to a lower threshold temperature of "too cold."

4. The expression was coined by László Antal (1980).

in an attempt to understand the workings of the capitalist market,[5] but no unambiguous conclusions about the tasks can be drawn from the positive synthesis outlined here.

I do not wish on this occasion to go back to the works of the two great thinkers and investigate what policies they were advocating in their time. What I am thinking of now are the contributions of those who put the name of Keynes or of Schumpeter on their banners. This study coincides on some questions with some important Keynesian analyses, but it provides no intellectual support for a "vulgar Keynesian" economic policy ("broaden the aggregate demand constraint at any price to make better use of capacities"). It likewise coincides with some important Schumpeterian analyses, but it gives no intellectual encouragement to a "vulgar Schumpeterian" economic policy ("let the crisis do its deadly work because the destruction is falling behind the creation").

I have arrived at some deep ethical, political, and economic dilemmas. I do not intend to advise the decision makers of Washington, Berlin, or Budapest. All I seek to do is warn the economic advisers of what the line of argument in this study suggests: All the possible methods of intervention will have ambiguous effects.

The study also offers another timely lesson for economic policymakers. The focus during the international debates on the crisis has been on the financial sector. The causes have been sought almost exclusively in the loose regulation of financial-sector actions, the poor structure of the regulating institutions, and the distortions of fiscal and monetary policy. Too little attention has been given to what mechanisms operate in the real sphere, where conspicuously superfluous capacities are being built, and how the proportions among the sectors of the economy can be better coordinated.

7.2 THE WAR ECONOMY

If a country is at war, the conflict can affect all manifestations of its life, including the workings of its economy. Much depends in this respect on how much of the country's resources are being spent on waging the war, for which there are several indicators, notably the proportions of GDP and of labor tied down by direct orders from the military. If the proportion is relatively small, the capitalist economy will remain a surplus economy in which only scattered phenomena of shortage appear. The greater the demands of the military operations on available resources, or the more "total" the war becomes, the greater the tendency for shortage phenomena to build up and become general. Rationing is introduced for households, civilians line up for food, and the

---

5. Synthesizing Keynes and Schumpeter has become fashionable among economists, with a succession of studies announcing such an attempt in their titles.

bureaucracy allocates scarce raw materials or semifinished products to factories. The change is felt ever more strongly as the war drags on, and its destruction spreads from the war zones into the country's industrial hinterland.[6]

World War II gave a taste of the shortage economy to many of the world's countries when capitalism, based on private ownership, continued in the war years. The war economy proves that the "capitalist system → surplus economy" causal connection cannot be applied mechanically or ubiquitously. War temporarily brings conditions that restrict or stop the operation of the mechanism that generates the surplus economy and starts the mechanism that generates the shortage economy.

Historical experience shows that the shortage economy yields to the surplus economy again (rapidly or tardily) once peace is restored, and the surplus economy recovers quickly, as the bases of capitalism remain. For instance, Germany went far toward introducing bureaucratic centralization of economic regulation under Hitler's totalitarian rule and suffered war damage that left supplies very scarce, but it managed, in a few years, to turn its shortage economy into a pattern surplus economy again.

East European countries, where the Communist Party seized power, confiscated private property, and demolished the market economy, hardly had any time to recover from the temporary, war-induced shortage economy before it turned into a chronic shortage economy generated by the socialist system.

7.3 HISTORIC CHANGES AND LASTING TENDENCIES IN MODERN CAPITALISM

Subsection 7.1 dealt with short-term fluctuations and subsection 7.2 with a phenomenon—the shortage economy induced by war—that can last for years but remains temporary. Let us now examine the *lasting tendencies*—changes that occur steadily, continually, in small stages, taking a long time to exert their full effects, but run deep and make essential alterations in the operation of society and economy.[7] The effect is felt on the processes examined in the essay as well.

The growth of the welfare state.—The social services on which a 20th-century welfare state would be based in the developed countries began to appear in some parts of Europe in the latter half of the 19th century. The extent and

---

6. Of the literature on the war economy, following World War II, let me mention particularly Galbraith (1952), Milward (1979), and Olson (1963).

7. The words propensity, inclination, and tendency are almost interchangeable according to dictionary definitions. For the sake of conceptual clarity I used the first two words in the context of the genetically coded inherent properties of capitalism (see Section 5). Now, in Section 7, I reserve the word *tendency* for deep historical changes occurring over long periods, lasting a few decades or more.

expansion of these varied, but they became widespread in all developed countries.

Here I do not want to become embroiled in the conceptual and statistical debates about what constitutes the formation known customarily as the welfare state. There can be no argument about including the services provided gratis or at small cost mainly in the fields of medical care, education, and care of children, the disabled, and the elderly. These activities are publicly funded, that is, from levies that count as taxation or quasitaxation such as compulsory contributions.

Phenomena of shortage appear universally in the allocation and utilization of free or almost-free public services. Most of the economic environment operates as a surplus economy, with all its usual side effects, but, in the sea of surplus, an island that bears the marks of a shortage economy can be seen. The doctor's office is crowded and you may have to wait for hours. The waiting lists for surgery or diagnostic procedure may be months long (Table 7.1). Patients' freedom is severely restricted in choosing a doctor or a hospital. In fact there are health-care systems that deny patients such freedom entirely, so that they have to accept the assigned doctor or health institution. The concept of forced substitution can also apply in medical care, where patients may not obtain the medicine, treatment, or physician they would choose and have to take what they are allocated.

It should be noted that such shortage phenomena are not confined to networks directed and financed directly by the state. Similar experiences may await the customers of large, impersonal, closely regulated private insurance

Table 7.1. WAITING TIME IN WESTERN EUROPEAN HEALTH-CARE SECTORS, 2004 (NUMBER OF WEEKS)

Country	Specialist consultation	Outpatient surgery	Inpatient surgery
Austria	1.8	3.1	7.9
Denmark	5.4	10.2	9.4
France	3.1	3.3	8.1
Germany	1.8	3.1	6.5
Italy	2.9	12.0	9.4
Netherlands	3.5	5.6	11.5
Spain	4.9	17.6	24.1
Sweden	9.7	18.5	28.1

Note: The indicator included in the table is computed based on the data provided by the Survey of Health, Aging and Retirement in Europe (SHARE) conducted in nine European countries on representative samples. The figures summarize the results of the first phase of the survey. The participants were asked the following questions: (1) "How many months did you have to wait for a specialist consultation?" (2) "How many months did you have to wait for your last outpatient surgery?" (3) "How many months did you have to wait for your last inpatient surgery?" The answers to the last two questions are transformed from months to weeks in order to have easily comparable figures.
Sources: Siciliani and Verzulli (2009, 1299–1300); SHARE (2010).

schemes. Here, the U.S. health-care system is instructive. All grades of service exist. At one extreme are the few who can allow themselves to pay out of their own pocket whatever celebrated specialist or expensive private hospital they may choose. There, the usual features of a surplus economy appear: service providers have a strong financial incentive to do excellent work, clients have choice, and so on. At the other extreme are the none-too-few who have no insurance at all. Many of them can resort only to the emergency services available free to all, and may try to do so even if the case is not an emergency. (The number of uninsured will certainly be reduced greatly by President Obama's health-care reform.) This part of the spectrum is a regular shortage economy: crowding, long waits, and often a surly and demeaning reception. Between the two extremes, there are gradations in which surplus-economy and shortage-economy features mingle. Many employers present their employees with a veritable bill of fare, from which to choose their insurance plan. Cheaper options may have lower patient contributions but little or no choice of physician or hospital. The assigned physicians will also be limited in what expensive drugs, diagnostics, surgery, and so forth they may order. The dearer the insurance package chosen, the more completely the potential patient enters the realm of the surplus economy. The most expensive insurance will offer an almost unlimited choice of physicians and hospitals and the insurer will be prepared to pay the fee for service on which doctor and patient agree.

The health-care industry, in the broad sense, includes a substantial for-profit, private sector that is purely commercial, even where the proportion of the state regulated, centrally financed sector is very high. Clearly, part of it consists of the privately owned hospitals, sanitariums, and clinics exclusively for paying patients, the doctors in private practice, and the for-profit diagnostic laboratories. Also included are the pharmaceutical industry and makers of medical equipment, the pharmacies, and so on. The private health sector operates as a regular surplus economy.[8] This is most obvious in the pharmaceutical industry, with its strong, monopolistic competition, dynamic innovation, wide buyer choice, flood of advertising, manipulation of consumers, and frequent covert corruption of the medical practitioners writing the prescriptions.

In contrast to health care, where demands cannot be saturated, the need for some educational services may be saturated. Countries differ in how many years of schooling the law prescribes, but for the age groups covered by the law, the size of their demand for schooling, is known.[9] The problem of the

---

8. Harvard Professor Arnold Relman finds from U.S. experience that "commercialization" of health care and unregulated "entrepreneurialism" (Relman's expressions) produces excess supply and excess capacities (Relman 2010).

9. Yet there may be wide dispersion in supply and demand for less good schools, so that concurrent instances of excess supply and excess demand may appear in the compulsory education sector.

general demand–supply regime appears strongly in higher education. Some well-known symptoms of a shortage economy appear as soon as higher education is free or almost free: there are too many applicants. The number of accepted students is either strictly regulated, or, if the doors are opened wide, it may result in crowding at the universities and overworked teaching staff. Many higher-education institutions become degree factories at the expense of quality. An excessive proportion of the younger age groups receive higher education.[10]

In countries where university education is not a universal right and fees have to be paid for it, the availability of places and services and the number of applicants for them resemble far more closely the usual state of a surplus economy. There might be phenomena of surplus and phenomena of shortage side by side in the same country, for instance a surfeit of applications for universities with high prestige, and at the same time a lack of applicants for less-known universities. The mechanism that produces a surplus economy operates: monopolistic competition, innovation, dynamism on the supply side, and so forth. Those who want a university education and can pay for it will get it. Those who cannot pay or obtain a scholarship lose the chance of such an education. Welfare-state interventions might correct some of these troubles, for example, by state-sponsored fellowships and subsidized student loans.

How far should free welfare-state services extend? What conditions should apply? Selecting them presents some difficult ethical and political dilemmas. On the one hand, there are the demands of efficiency and quality improvement; on the other, considerations of equal human rights and social justice.

I have dealt elsewhere with the normative problems of the welfare state (see primarily Kornai and Eggleston 2001). This essay is confined to the positive analysis of the extremely important historical tendency of the growing welfare state. The greater the depth and breadth with which the free services accompanying the welfare state appear in the economy of a country where otherwise the surplus economy generated by capitalism operates, the greater the likelihood of shortage phenomena developing.

"We have socialism on our backs!" is the cry of conservative opponents of the welfare state intent on alarming fellow citizens. Luckily such slogans only tell half the truth. Certainly, free state services are accompanied by some typical features of the socialist system, with strong effects (good or bad, advantageous or detrimental), including the phenomenon of shortage, as I have sought to show. However, that is not the whole story. The parliamentary

---

10. The output of the "degree factories" exceeds society's demand for graduate labor in many countries. Overqualified staff members are often employed in lowly positions. The free educational service boosts demand for higher education. Under the pressure of high demand, a rise in "output" and a consequent excess supply of graduates occurs.

system does not collapse, nor does the KGB arrive when the state starts to offer free health services or make free education a universal right. The prime feature of the socialist system is repressive and totalitarian political monopoly. The welfare state arrives under constitutional conditions of political democracy and operates in ways compatible with democratic institutions.

Softening the budget constraint.—One major attribute of a socialist economy based on state ownership is the syndrome known as the *soft budget constraint*.[11] This, along with other factors, contributes to the emergence of the shortage economy.

Softness of the budget constraint is not confined to the socialist system. I have mentioned here, several times already, that it crops up under capitalism, too, when the state steps in to rescue firms or nonprofit organizations in deep or mortal financial difficulties, notably hospitals, universities, small farmers, banks, or local government organizations. Such bailouts are normally given wide publicity.

The effects spread beyond the rescued beneficiaries to other participants in the economy. The more frequent and conspicuous the bailout actions, the deeper become corporate managers' expectations that the state will rush in to aid their organization, too, if it should get into difficulties.

My impression from studying the history of capitalism is that softening of the budget constraint is a long-term tendency. Debts were collected with an iron will at the dawn of the capitalist period. Since then, financial rigor seems to have slackened and bailouts proliferated. Fears (rightful ones) that the collapse of a few big corporations, and still more big banks and other financial institutions, may start an avalanche of failures and insolvencies are making state bailouts almost inescapable.

How does such softness of the budget constraint affect the surplus-economy character of the economy?

Two effects can be expected, both in the direction of excess supply. The first is explained in the subsection on supply-related processes of Section 2, which treats the appearance of idle capacities and the decrease in the effect of Schumpeterian creative destruction as a third factor. Even if the budget constraint remained hard, a firm failing to compete and pushed out by innovation would still try to survive for as long as it could. The "rust zones" lingered on long after the spread of plastics, and the smaller size of machines and equipment had relatively reduced the demand for iron and steel products. Owners accepted the dwindling of their profits, and workers put up with lower wages

---

11. A summary of the theory and account of the literature appear in Kornai, Maskin, and Roland (2003). There is a certain overlapping between the issues studied by the theory of the soft budget constraint and contract theory. For an overview of contract theory and its linkages with the theory of the soft budget constraint see Bolton and Dewatripont (2005).

rather than lose their jobs altogether. The urge to survive, which I pointed to earlier, in itself produces unutilized capacity. This is compounded by the pressure applied by owners, employees, and local residents for the state to rescue the doomed production and sustain it artificially. Such pressure often succeeds. In other words, softness of the budget constraint also restrains destruction and the elimination of capacities that have become superfluous.

Many countries encounter a similar situation with agriculture. Competition would squeeze many farms out, especially small ones using obsolete technology. Agricultural lobbies can manage for a long time to sustain those loss-making agricultural units by obtaining state subsidies—softening the budget constraint. This helps to create and maintain high surpluses in agricultural production.

The first effect of the described soft budget constraint is to alter the supply process at *exit*, by *slowing* it, and the second to alter it at *entry*, by *speeding* it.

Here, let me exceed the self-imposed bounds of this essay with a comment on the lending practice of the financial sector. Softening of the budget constraint and repeated confirmation of expectations that troubled banks will be bailed out by the state, through a succession of such rescue operations, makes the banks in their turn less cautious in lending. All too often, easily obtained loans lead to new capacities that prove nonviable and ultimately swell aggregate idle capacity.

Both the lender and the borrowing investor are tempted to be careless if there is a good chance of rescue in a case of failure. Under classic capitalism, the hardness of the budget constraint sets the breaks on the *expansion drive* and *investment hunger* hardens the budget constraint. When this softens under modern capitalism, capitalist companies start entering into risky investment projects with the verve of socialist investment decision makers. It works for many of them. This most-recent recession, too, has seen lifebelts thrown to many huge corporations in the United States and several European countries, in the automotive and other industries, when it turned out that their huge unutilized capacities and sales difficulties were causing financial collapse.

I do not wish here to deal with the "rescue-or-abandon" dilemma in economic policy. There are grave macroeconomic and social problems, and ultimately political and ethical dilemmas, behind every bailout decision. All I want to establish, through a positive approach, is the existence of the tendency here described.

To conclude these remarks on softening the budget constraint, let us return in a sentence to a positive approach: Despite clear signs of a tendency to softening, hardness of the budget constraint has remained dominant in capitalism today.

Globalization.—For simplicity's sake, the study has not so far covered international trade. Yet in dealing with monopolistic competition, for instance, a production firm clearly must cope not only with domestic rivals but, also, with imports (if the product is transportable). There have been exports and imports for millennia. The role of international trade in our time has been enhanced by the complex, comprehensive process known as globalization (Feenstra 1998; Bhagwati 2004).

Examining the possibility of imports, all that has been said so far about immediately available surpluses applies even more. Imported products do not have to be on the shelves or in the warehouses for the domestic producers to cater to the buyers whims, though it is better still if they are. If products of the same quality or better, or cheaper products, are simply *accessible* by import if required, that will suffice to elicit surplus-economy behavior.

One effect of globalization is that the allocation of idle capacities is continually altering in an international frame. The production of many exportable products is burgeoning in China, India, and other developing countries. This brings severe sales difficulties to European and North American firms that have supplied similar products hitherto, but at higher prices. They do not shut up shop straight away. Some change their product ranges and survive, some close sooner or later. In the period of upheaval, however, there stand their capacities, much of them unused.

Many of the once-backward economies now growing very rapidly are building new capacities, mainly with the markets of the developed countries in mind. However, the expansion of these markets is falling short of the investors' expectations, so that idle surplus capacities appear there as well.[12]

The development of information and communication technology.—Before turning to the effect of the rapidly developing information and communication technology on seller–buyer relations, let us reconstruct the situation before the Internet age. This calls for reminders of some topics discussed in Section 4 and studied by various theories of search and matching.[13] Sellers and buyers acquire information about users, sellers about buyers, and *vice versa,* and finally they have to meet. I noted earlier that the problem is not system specific. All systems call for matching producers with consumers, sellers with buyers. All need such information, but the processes are influenced by system-specific effects. The two types of demand–supply regime, surplus economy and shortage economy, differ strongly on which side bears the burden of information acquisition and to what extent.

In a shortage economy, it falls mainly on the buyer to acquire information. Buyers who fail to find the article in short supply that they need in the first store they enter begin touring stores in search of it, and if lucky, they find it. Similarly, the purchasing managers at the production enterprises have to seek out the

---

12. The apt title of one study is "China: The Vicious Circle of Excess Capacity" (Artus 2009).

13. The theories of search and of matching were already discussed in subsection 4.5 on the labor market.

required materials or semifinished products (assuming it is not confined to any single monopoly seller's warehouse).

Some of the information task is done by the bureaucracy, taking on allocation of some cardinal inputs under the system of a command economy. The position of producers or sellers is comfortable from that point of view. They do not have to seek buyers, because the bureaucracy assigns them or the buyers themselves get in touch.

The effort of ensuring the necessary flow of information is divided differently in a surplus economy. The bureaucracy takes no part. Most of the effort comes from the sellers. The vast advertising apparatus uses a plethora of means to convey mainly truthful information to buyers, but of course, as mentioned before, some of the information is one-sided or downright false, and seeks to manipulate consumers.

Not even in the pre-Internet period were buyers in a surplus economy freed entirely of the task of searching for information. Prices are not as uniform as in a socialist economy, where they are set centrally. It is in the buyers' interest to find out where a product can be found most cheaply. Nor do sellers compete only on price. They seek to offer something extra or special, or goods of a different quality, even an entirely new product. What cannot be found in one store can be found in another (or a substitute quite like it, possibly better or cheaper). Indeed the choice available—the outstanding virtue of the surplus economy—is another inducement for buyers to seek and obtain information.[14]

The Internet made a marked change from the accustomed division of labor. Buyers can obtain more information about the supply and far more easily: what is for sale, at what price, and where. There is no need to traipse from store to store, or to phone around, because the bulk of the information can be brought up on a screen. This strengthens the position of buyers, because they can then choose among various products and various sellers. They can exploit this advantage still more if there is an organization (a civil consumer protection organization or a state agency or a professional paper) to conduct objective and professional comparisons between the rival alternatives, and such information is also made available on the Internet.

Sellers have also recognized the scope of choices that the Internet has offered. They use the Web not only to spread information and manipulate buyers, but to pass on more of the burden of finding the right product than ever before. This is done partly with financial incentives, that is, by honest commercial means: Sellers sell the product or service more cheaply if buyers

---

14. When we were commuting regularly between Hungary and the United States in the 1970s and 1980s, my wife always said that we had to tour the stores of Budapest because there was shortage and the product had to be tracked down. The searching took at least as long in America, but it was for the best price, for a bargain sale, or for the best product from a much more varied range.

order it on the Internet. Alongside such correct means of cutting costs there are often less-honest ones: sellers try to pass all the burden of gaining information onto the buyers. Many sellers make it hard for buyers to do business in the antediluvian (pre-Internet) way. This is especially burdensome for those who are not experienced in using the computer or the Internet.

All this—bearing in mind the state of the modern world—adds to the picture of the relative strengths and burdens of seller and buyer (customer sovereignty and manipulation) presented in subsection 6.3.

7.4 MARKET-ORIENTED REFORMS UNDER SOCIALISM AND THE POSTSOCIALIST TRANSITION

There is a huge body of literature describing and analyzing the market-oriented reforms of the social system primarily in Yugoslavia, Hungary, Poland, and China. Successive books and articles deal with the postsocialist transition in the countries east of the Iron Curtain. This transformation in world history is treated here from a single point of view: what change it brought to what I have called the general demand–supply regime.

Let the starting point be 1949, when even Yugoslavia was still a member of the socialist bloc. At that time the shortage economy in its classic form ruled in every communist country from East Germany to China. Then a few countries—first Yugoslavia, then Hungary—began to move slightly away from the utterly centralized system based on planning directives and coordinated by the bureaucratic mechanism, which had produced and was sustaining the shortage economy. At the same time, there began to emerge, from the sea of shortage, a few islands of surplus economy.[15] Anyone, for instance, who went to the great food hall in downtown Budapest in the 1970s could feel there was an abundance of goods almost smothering the buyers, whereas waiting lists in the same city for telephones, private cars, or housing were many years' long.

The political watershed of 1989–1990 brought radical economic changes. The order and pace of change differed by country. Some privatized state-owned enterprises changed at a forced rate, others gradually. Surplus and shortage phenomena coincided throughout. Market liberalization was radical and rapid in some places, protracted in others. More or less in synchrony with the transformation of ownership relations and coordination mechanism were the proportions between the two types of phenomena: instances of excess demand and excess supply, shortage and surplus economy.

---

15. I intentionally use the same metaphor applied previously about an island of shortage economy in a sea of surplus economy, but this time in reverse.

Table 7.2. WAITING LISTS FOR TELEPHONES IN CENTRAL AND EASTERN EUROPEAN COUNTRIES, 1971–2007

	Bulgaria	Czech Republic	Hungary	Poland	Romania	Slovakia
1971–1975	na	25.1	36.6	33.6	na	na
1976–1980	na	30.2	47.2	45.7	na	na
1981–1985	na	11.3	55.5	57.1	na	na
1986–1990	23.5	18.7	59.0	73.2	77.8	na
1991–1995	20.4	25.5	41.7	51.2	98.4	8.8
1996–2000	11.0	7.2	2.9	10.4	56.8	3.8
2001–2005	3.2	0.8	0.5	3.8	23.1	0.4
2006	2.0	1.0	0.5	1.3	6.3	0.2
2007	0.2	0.8	0.5	n. a.	4.9	0.2

Note: The figures show the ratio of the length of the waiting list for connection to fixed line telephone to the number of subscribers of fixed line phones, as a percentage. The second column (under the heading "Czech Republic") presents data for Czechoslovakia with respect to the pre-1990s period. In the case of Bulgaria and Slovakia, the figures shown in the 1986–1990 rows are actually the data for 1990, since pre-1989 data are not available.
Sources: Before the transition period, the data for Czechoslovakia, Poland, and Hungary are taken over from Kornai (1993, 238). The source of all other data: United Nations Statistics Division (2009a and 2009b) and International Telecommunications Union (2006 and 2007).

As the economic transformation came to an end, the surplus economy gained clear dominance. That historical transformation, starting from the classic, Stalinist shortage economy and arriving at a mature surplus economy, may well be the most vivid representation of the ideas expressed in this study.[16] For clarity's sake, let us look at Table 7.2, which returns to the example of telephone services, discussed at the beginning of section 2. It shows what a desperate shortage of telephones there was before the change of system. This is well known to have been one of the most painful instances of the shortage economy, but the shortage ceased soon after 1989–1990 and the use of fixed lines (and of course mobile phones) burgeoned.

While I was collecting data for this study, I had to conclude with regret that, although all inhabitants of the former communist countries had felt the change, there is hardly a time series with the expressive force to convey this. The oft-repeated fluctuations in the developed countries are tracked by a hundred different economic, commercial, and financial indicators, and are

---

16. Djankov and Murrell reviewed the literature that studied the results of the postsocialist transformation empirically, based on statistical data. There is consensus among the most thorough and reliable researchers on the following: One of the big factors behind the reorganization of the business sector and increase in productivity was the development of seller competition (Djankov and Murrell 2002, 20–21).

worth following. However, it has to be said that the East underwent a unique, unrepeated transformation of historic importance as the market switched from shortage economy to surplus economy, but only very few statistical surveys and expressive time-series were made of it.[17] That opportunity will never return.

---

17. One exception consists of the surveys of the obstacles to production done by Kopint-Datorg in Hungary. The time series begins in 1987, before the change of system, and continues without intermission or change of method to the present day, thereby making consistent comparisons over time possible. For a graphic representation, see Figure 3.4, and for the full time series Table A.1.

SECTION 8

A Personal Postscript

I began the study by describing my impressions and I conclude by returning to them.

The problem of shortage first appears in my first book, written over 50 years ago in 1956 for my candidacy degree (Kornai 1994 [1959]). It has remained a preoccupation ever since, forming the main subject of two later books. The vision of it that I gained then has not altered in half a century. All along, I have kept a pair of opposites, a dichotomy before my eyes. I hope that the analytical apparatus with which I describe and explain the phenomena has improved from project to project, making the evaluation of the two states' virtues and vices fuller and more balanced. However, I stand steadfast by my original vision of the problem.

I think most men of the street in the postsocialist region share this impression of the changes which occurred on the market. This observation notwithstanding, I am aware that most professional economists think in terms of other concepts. They see equilibrium where I see that we are not at any, but in a state of having (luckily) tipped from the shortage economy into the surplus economy. One of my favorite comparisons is a drawing by Escher of flying swans. One person sees white swans flying from left to right, the other, in the same picture, black swans flying right to left.

Another metaphor that I would like to express in this line of thought is something that I read in the Domar paper I quoted earlier.[1] According to an old Indian tale, a prince ordered several blind men to examine an elephant and say what it is like. Each examined one part and reported accordingly. One examined its leg, and said the elephant is a thick column. Another touched its

---

1. Domar's title, "The Blind Men and the Elephant: An Essay on Isms" (1989), is exactly on point. He relates how he heard the tale from the noted Indian-American Sovietologist Professor Padma Desai.

trunk, and said the elephant is a soft, thin, and flexible tube. And the blind men fell into quarreling among themselves, each insisting that only he was right.

I am ready for the quarrel, but beforehand let me say with humility that I am blind. The elephant is big and I can only examine one small part of it.

APPENDIX

Table A.1. IMPEDIMENTS TO PRODUCTION IN THE HUNGARIAN INDUSTRY, 1987–2012

Quarter	Time of survey	No hindrance	Insufficient demand	Shortage of labor	Shortage of qualified labor	Insufficient supply of raw materials and spare parts				Shortage of capacity	Financing problems	Unclear economic regulations	Uncertain economic environment
						Domestic origin	Imported	Imported from Roubel area	Imported from dollar area				
1987 Q1	April 1987	13.0	26.0	22.2		41.2	42.6			7.2	31.2	0.0	42.8
1987 Q2	July	10.3	27.4	23.7		42.3	46.7			6.7	24.3	28.5	42.9
1987 Q3	October	11.2	21.3	24.1		46.6	50.4			8.2	22.1	22.0	42.1
1987 Q4	January 1988	17.0	24.1	15.8		39.4	41.8			4.6	20.4	20.4	45.8
1988 Q1	April	10.7	28.0	15.7		50.0		50.0	32.8	6.3	32.7	24.8	45.3
1988 Q2	July	10.8	28.3	24.7		44.1		44.1	35.3	7.9	36.4	27.1	42.2
1988 Q3	October	11.8	27.3	23.0		45.3		45.3	64.0	8.6	35.0	31.2	47.6
1988 Q4	January 1989	16.5	30.7	19.3		38.5		38.5	22.4	6.1	40.1	25.3	46.9
1989 Q1	April	10.8	38.0	21.5		37.6		37.6	17.9	4.7	49.6	23.9	46.6
1989 Q2	July	14.7	40.1	22.0		28.7		28.7	11.8	7.1	46.1	22.0	41.5
1989 Q3	October	12.7	40.4	21.9		27.5		27.5	8.9	5.2	46.8	24.6	42.6
1989 Q4	January 1990	13.6	51.2	13.4		21.4		21.4	6.3	0.7	49.4	21.2	54.6
1990 Q1	April	10.8	51.3	12.1		13.8		13.8	3.9	3.6	57.8	16.4	50.9
1990 Q2	July	8.7	56.1	13.9		13.0		13.0	2.2	3.3	45.2	1.6	47.3

(continued)

Table A.1. (continued)

Quarter	Time of survey	No hindrance	Insufficient demand	Shortage of labor	Shortage of qualified labor	Insufficient supply of raw materials and spare parts — Domestic origin	Imported	Imported from Roubel area	Imported from dollar area	Shortage of capacity	Financing problems	Unclear economic regulations	Uncertain economic environment
1990 Q3	October	6.9	51.0	10.3		15.3		15.3	5.2	2.5	51.9	17.2	54.1
1990 Q4	January 1991	8.9	54.5	4.3		11.3		11.3	3.7	2.7	48.7	20.4	54.7
1991 Q1	April	6.0	60.6	4.3		9.4		9.4	2.6	3.4	53.2	12.6	47.9
1991 Q2	July	5.5	70.1	4.0		7.1		7.1	2.4	1.3	54.1	9.9	43.0
1991 Q3	October	7.0	66.8	3.3		6.2		6.2	2.0	1.8	52.7	13.5	40.4
1991 Q4	January 1992	0.0	65.9	3.0		7.2		7.2	1.0	2.7	47.3	13.7	42.3
1992 Q1	April	7.0	65.1	3.3		5.8		5.8	1.0	2.3	51.0	15.1	47.2
1992 Q2	July	6.9	62.2	7.4		5.9		5.9	1.5	3.7	45.9	15.0	43.0
1992 Q3	October	6.8	56.1	4.4		10.6		10.6	3.1	2.8	47.8	18.2	51.3
1992 Q4	January 1993	9.2	54.5	4.8		8.7		8.7	2.3	3.3	42.9	15.6	45.9
1993 Q1	April	7.4	57.7	2.2		6.1	1.3			2.4	45.5	13.9	40.4
1993 Q2	July	6.4	68.8	3.0		8.0	3.2			3.2	47.3	11.0	44.0
1993 Q3	October	9.6	67.9	3.7		7.5	3.1			4.5	46.6	10.6	42.4
1993 Q4	January 1994	10.9	62.5	4.3		9.4	2.4			4.6	47.3	14.4	46.6
1994 Q1	April	11.4	59.0	4.3		9.5	2.4			4.5	44.7	11.9	38.5
1994 Q2	July	11.7	59.5	6.7		7.1	2.9			6.5	42.4	10.7	39.8
1994 Q3	October	12.7	58.2	6.5		11.1	3.0			7.6	44.4	11.3	41.2
1994 Q4	January 1995	13.2	55.0	7.8		10.1	2.2			5.4	40.0	14.6	40.9
1995 Q1	April	9.8	55.0	4.3		13.5	2.6			6.9	44.8	17.0	46.0
1995 Q2	July	8.1	60.2	7.4		10.2	5.1			7.1	42.4	16.8	43.1
1995 Q3	October	9.8	54.2	8.5		12.9	2.8			4.6	45.0	16.2	45.2
1995 Q4	January 1996	11.1	56.2	4.1		9.4	2.6			6.1	41.0	18.7	45.8
1996 Q1	April	9.9	65.3	5.1	14.4	8.0	4.8			4.1	37.3	13.6	34.6
1996 Q2	July	11.5	65.7	4.6	12.1	5.5	3.2			4.6	36.9	11.8	32.6
1996 Q3	October	12.1	58.0	6.0	17.0	7.4	4.8			5.5	30.8	14.0	36.0
1996 Q4	January 1997	10.9	61.6	3.6	14.9	7.1	2.1			5.0	30.1	17.1	33.6
1997 Q1	April	14.0	61.0	3.7	13.5	7.9	2.8			4.5	30.1	16.0	34.0
1997 Q2	July	15.2	63.0	4.4	15.0	5.3	1.5			4.1	27.9	16.1	30.2

APPENDIX (165)

Table A.1. (continued)

Quarter	Time of survey	No hindrance	Insufficient demand	Shortage of labor	Shortage of qualified labor	Insufficient supply of raw materials and spare parts					Shortage of capacity	Financing problems	Unclear economic regulations	Uncertain economic environment
						Domestic origin	Imported	Imported from Roubel area	Imported from dollar area				
1997 Q3	October	19.0	56.1	6.6	18.2	7.1	2.1			7.9	24.6	11.4	26.0
1997 Q4	January 1998	25.4	53.3	5.5	21.1	8.1	2.3			6.9	23.7	13.0	21.4
1998 Q1	April	21.3	49.5	5.2	20.3	8.0	0.3			7.0	22.4	11.5	17.5
1998 Q2	July	22.5	58.9	5.1	16.1	4.0	1.4			6.5	22.3	11.5	20.3
1998 Q3	October	18.0	57.4	8.9	19.5	3.6	1.9			5.3	22.8	10.6	25.1
1998 Q4	January 1999	24.0	58.4	7.0	19.8	3.3	1.2			6.4	21.6	9.7	22.5
1999 Q1	April	15.7	70.6	4.9	13.0	4.5	0.7			3.8	23.8	10.5	25.5
1999 Q2	July	13.2	71.4	5.0	11.0	3.8	0.6			3.5	23.3	11.0	31.1
1999 Q3	October	16.0	65.7	6.3	14.8	5.2	1.8			5.5	23.6	7.4	24.0
1999 Q4	January 2000	18.0	60.6	4.4	18.6	3.5	2.0			4.7	24.6	9.8	25.2
2000 Q1	April	18.4	63.1	6.1	15.2	3.7	2.0			5.3	22.1	8.6	26.6
2000 Q2	July	16.9	55.1	7.4	18.9	6.8	3.4			10.1	25.0	12.2	21.6
2000 Q3	October	14.8	49.6	9.4	22.2	8.6	3.0			10.2	25.2	10.9	22.6
2000 Q4	January 2001	23.0	53.6	7.9	23.0	7.1	4.4			8.7	23.0	13.9	23.4
2001 Q1	April	17.0	55.8	6.2	19.0	3.5	1.9			8.1	29.8	11.6	32.2
2001 Q2	July	12.1	61.7	6.6	19.1	3.9	2.3			5.5	26.6	13.7	31.6
2001 Q3	October	15.7	64.3	5.5	18.4	6.3	1.2			4.3	24.7	8.2	33.3
2001 Q4	January 2002	14.8	67.0	3.5	15.7	2.6	1.7			2.2	23.0	10.4	30.4
2002 Q1	April	16.1	64.8	3.0	16.6	4.0	1.5			2.5	21.1	8.0	26.1
2002 Q2	July	14.3	67.9	6.3	16.0	3.8	2.5			5.1	23.6	3.4	27.0
2002 Q3	October	16.3	66.1	4.0	20.3	4.0	2.6			5.7	18.5	7.9	25.0
2002 Q4	January 2003	12.2	68.3	3.6	14.5	3.6	1.8			3.6	14.5	9.0	29.9
2003 Q1	April	12.4	70.3	3.2	15.1	4.3	2.2			2.2	21.6	4.9	30.3
2003 Q2	July	8.7	66.9	4.9	12.5	4.2	1.0			7.0	24.0	11.5	37.6
2003 Q3	October	11.7	59.9	7.8	20.8	7.2	3.3			6.8	25.4	17.9	38.1
2003 Q4	January 2004	9.3	64.0	5.4	17.8	5.0	3.9			4.7	23.6	15.9	43.8
2004 Q1	April	16.0	58.0	6.1	16.7	7.9	3.9			5.3	26.8	13.6	37.7
2004 Q2	July	14.0	54.0	7.1	19.9	11.2	6.2			8.3	25.7	11.6	34.4

(continued)

Table A.1. (continued)

Quarter	Time of survey	No hindrance	Insufficient demand	Shortage of labor	Shortage of qualified labor	Insufficient supply of raw materials and spare parts				Shortage of capacity	Financing problems	Unclear economic regulations	Uncertain economic environment
						Domestic origin	Imported	Imported from Roubel area	Imported from dollar area				
2004 Q3	October	13.0	59.8	7.0	24.0	9.2	4.4			6.3	28.4	9.2	33.9
2004 Q4	January 2005	9.1	59.6	7.7	19.7	7.2	4.3			5.3	26.4	15.4	34.6
2005 Q1	April	8.8	65.4	3.2	19.3	4.6	1.8			7.8	27.2	12.9	36.4
2005 Q2	July	8.5	69.7	3.8	23.7	6.6	2.4			5.7	25.6	18.0	37.0
2005 Q3	October	10.9	61.7	7.1	22.4	6.6	3.3			8.2	29.0	16.4	37.2
2005 Q4	January 2006	10.3	60.9	3.3	26.6	4.3	3.8			7.6	28.3	14.7	33.7
2006 Q1	April	12.6	56.5	6.8	26.2	4.7	4.2			8.9	24.1	12.0	34.0
2006 Q2	July	11.7	53.2	8.3	30.2	4.9	5.9			8.3	19.0	21.5	46.3
2006 Q3	October	10.4	52.0	10.4	30.2	9.4	6.9			8.4	23.8	21.3	48.5
2006 Q4	January 2007	9.6	47.8	10.1	30.3	8.4	5.1			9.0	25.3	19.7	44.9
2007 Q1	April	13.9	50.3	11.9	29.1	6.0	6.0			11.3	21.9	15.9	36.4
2007 Q2	Julys	7.3	47.6	9.8	32.7	7.8	3.9			8.3	32.7	26.3	53.2
2007 Q3	October	6.0	56.0	7.5	41.8	5.2	2.2			9.7	29.9	26.1	57.9
2007 Q4	January 2008	8.5	56.8	9.0	36.2	8.5	2.5			7.5	28.1	30.2	48.2
2008 Q1	April	5.3	50.6	8.4	41.6	7.4	4.7			4.7	31.1	27.9	55.3
2008 Q2	July	10.3	49.7	10.8	38.5	5.1	4.6			9.2	27.7	27.2	54.4
2008 Q3	October	3.7	69.4	4.5	20.8	4.2	1.5			3.8	40.0	29.4	66.4
2008 Q4	January 2009	4.5	75.0	2.3	14.0	4.2	1.9			1.1	40.5	35.6	65.9
2009 Q1	April	3.9	78.6	0.9	12.7	4.3	2.2			2.2	39.7		62.4
2009 Q2	July	4.7	76.3	1.4	13.0	4.7	1.4			1.9	39.1	30.7	58.6
2009 Q3	October	4.5	76.8	2.3	11.4	2.3	0.8			3.8	36.4	28.0	64.4
2009 Q4	January 2010	8.0	79.1	1.0	13.9	2.0	0.9			2.5	37.3	30.4	58.9
2010 Q1	April	5.4	78.4	2.7	9.9	3.3	1.6			2.7	39.6	26.1	52.3
2010 Q2	July	3.0	69	2.0	14.1	8.1	2.0			4.0	46.5	24.2	54.5
2010 Q3	October	3.0	66	3.0	8.0	9.0	7.0			3.0	33.0	25.0	47.0
2010 Q4	January 2011	6.0	72	2.0	13.0	6.0	1.0			3.0	37.0	24.0	46.0
2011 Q1	April	4.0	75	0.0	6.0	4.0	3.0			2.0	31.0	38.0	47.0
2011 Q2	July	4.0	70	1.0	13.0	3.0	0.0			1.0	40.0	28.0	60.0

Table A.1. (continued)

Quarter	Time of survey	No hindrance	Insufficient demand	Shortage of labor	Shortage of qualified labor	Insufficient supply of raw materials and spare parts				Shortage of capacity	Financing problems	Unclear economic regulations	Uncertain economic environment
						Domestic origin	Imported	Imported from Roubel area	Imported from dollar area				
2011 Q3	October	5.0	71	0.0	12.0	6.0	0.0			5.0	34.0	40.0	65.0
2011 Q4	January 2012	1.0	79	1.0	11.0	1.0	4.0			0.0	30.0	49.0	67.0
2012 Q1	April	5.0	76	0.0	19.0	4.0	2.0			3.0	30.0	39.0	63.0

Note: The following question was raised to the respondents: "Which factors hinder the most the production of your company?" Several answers were possible: See the heads of the table's columns. The entries of the table show the relative frequency of the answers (total number of respondents = 100).
Source: Direct communication by Kopint-Tárki (Institute for Economic and Market Research, Budapest).
Figure 3.4 represents a graphic image of certain time-series shown in this table.

REFERENCES

Acemoglu, Daron, Philippe Aghion, Claire Lelarge, John Van Reenen, and Fabrizio Zilibotti. 2007. "Technology, Information, and the Decentralization of the Firm." *The Quarterly Journal of Economics* 122(4):1759–1799.
Aghion, Philippe, and Peter P. Howitt. 1998. *Endogenous Growth Theory*. Cambridge, MA: MIT Press.
Akerlof, George A., and Robert J. Shiller. 2009. *Animal Spirits: How Human Psychology Drives the Economy, and Why It Matters for Global Capitalism*. Oxford, UK: Princeton University Press.
Allain, Olivier, and Nicolas Canry. 2008. "Growth, Capital Scrapping, and the Rate of Capacity Utilisation." Working Paper, 12th Conference of the Research Network, Macroeconomics and Macroeconomic Policies, Berlin.
Amann, Ronald, and Julian Cooper. 1982. *Industrial Innovation in the Soviet Union*. New Haven and London: Yale University Press.
Amann, Ronald, Julian Cooper, and R. W. Davies. 1977. *The Technological Level of Soviet Industry*. New Haven and London: Yale University Press.
Antal, László. 1980. "Fejlődés kitérővel. A magyar gazdasági mechanizmus a 70-es években" [Development with a Detour. The Hungarian Economic Mechanism in the 1970s]. *Gazdaság* 14(2):28–56.
Arthur, William Brian. 1994. *Increasing Returns and Path Dependence in the Economy*. Ann Arbor: University of Michigan Press.
Artus, Patrick. 2009. "China: The Vicious Circle of Excess Capacity." *Flash Economics*, no. 115, March 11, 209. Natixis Economic Research. Accessed May 26, 2013. http://cib.natixis.com/flushdoc.aspx?id=45810
Atkin, David J., Tuen-Yu Lau, and Carolyn A. Lin. 2006. "Still on hold? A retrospective analysis of competitive implications of the Telecommunication Act of 1996, on its 10th year anniversary." *Telecommunications Policy* 30(2):80–95.
Azariadis, Costas. 1975. "Implicit contracts and underemployment equilibria." *Journal of Political Economy*. 83(6):1183–1202.
Balcerowicz, Leszek. 1995. *Socialism Capitalism Transformation*. Budapest: Central European University Press.
Ball, Laurence, and Gregory N. Mankiw. 1995. "A Sticky-Price Manifesto." *NBER Working Papers* 4677, National Bureau of Economic Research.
Bartelsman, Eric J., John Haltiwanger, and Stefano Scarpetta. 2004. "Microeconomic Evidence of Creative Destruction in Industrial and Developing Countries." Working Paper. Washington DC: World Bank.
Bauer, Reinhold. 1999. *Pkw-Bau in der DDR: Zur Innovationsschwäche von Zentralverwaltungswirtschaften*. Frankfurt am Main: Peter Lang.
Baumol, William J. 2002. *The Free-Market Innovation Machine: Analyzing the Growth Miracle of Capitalism*. Princeton: Princeton University Press.

Baumol, William J., and Alan S. Blinder. 2009. *Economics: Principles and Policy*. Mason, OH: South-Western Cengage Learning.

Baumol, William J., Robert Litan, and Carl J. Schramm. 2007. *Good Capitalism, Bad Capitalism, and the Economics of Growth and Prosperity*. New Haven and London: Yale University Press.

Baumol, William J., and Melissa A. Schilling. 2008. "Entrepreneurship." In *The New Palgrave Dictionary of Economics*, 2nd ed, edited by S. N. Durlauf and L. W. Blume. London: Palgrave Macmillan.

Benassy, Jean-Pascal. 1982. *The Economics of Market Disequilibrium*. New York: Academic Press.

Berliner, Joseph. 1976. *The Innovation Decision in Soviet Industry*. Cambridge, MA: MIT Press.

Berners-Lee, Tim. 1999. *Weaving the Web*. San Francisco: Harper.

Bhaduri, Amit. 2007. *Growth, Distribution and Innovations*. London and New York: Routledge.

Bhagwati, Jagdish. 2004. *In Defense of Globalization*. Oxford: Oxford University Press.

Bils, Mark, and Peter J. Klenow. 2004. "Some Evidence on the Importance of Sticky Prices." *Journal of Political Economy* 112(5):947–985.

Blanchard, Olivier, and Jordi Gali. 2007. "Real Wage Rigidities and the New Keynesian Model." *Journal of Money, Credit and Banking* 39: Supplement, 35–65.

Blinder, Alan S., Elie R. Canetti, David E. Lebow, and Jeremy B. Rudd. 1998. *Asking about Prices: A New Approach to Understanding Price Stickiness*. New York: Russell Sage Foundation.

Bojár, Gábor. 2007. *The Graphisoft Story: Hungarian Perestroika from an Entrepreneur's Perspective*. Budapest: Manager Könyvkiadó.

Bolton, Patrick, and Mathias Dewatripont. 2005. *Contract Theory*. Cambridge, MA: MIT Press.

Bower, Joseph L., and Clayton M. Christensen. 1995. "Disruptive Technologies: Catching the Wave". *Harvard Business Review* 73(1):43–53.

Bureau of Labor Statistics. 2012. "Job Openings and Labor Turnover Survey (JOLT)." Accessed October 11, 2010. http://www.bls.gov/jlt /#data.

Bygrave, William, and Jeffrey Timmons. 1992. *Venture Capital at the Crossroads*. Boston: Harvard Business School Press.

Castells, Manuel. 1996–98. *The Information Age: Economy, Society, and Culture*. Vols. 1–3. Oxford: Blackwell.

Ceruzzi, Paul E. 2000. *A History of Modern Computing*. Cambridge, MA: MIT Press.

Chamberlin, Edward H. 1962 [1933]. *The Theory of Monopolistic Competition*. Cambridge, MA: Harvard University Press.

Chantrill, Christopher. 2010. "US Government Spending." Accessed November 30, 2010. http://www.usgovernmentspending.com/numbers#usgs302.

Chao, Loretta. 2009. "China Squeezes PC Makers." *Wall Street Journal*, June 8.

Chekhov, Anton. 1973 [1894]). "Letter to Alexei Suvorin, Yalta, March 27, 1894." In *Anton Chekhov's Life and Thought: Selected Letters and Commentary*. Edited and annotated by Simon Karlinsky. Evanston, IL: Northwestern University Press: 261–263.

Chikán, Attila. 1984. *A vállalati készletezési politika* [Inventory Policy of Enterprises]. Budapest: Közgazdasági és Jogi Könyvkiadó.

Chopra, Sunil, and Peter Meindl. 2003. *Supply Chain Management*. Upper Saddle River, NJ: Prentice Hall.

Clavel, Laurent, and Christelle Minodier. 2009. "A Monthly Indicator of the French Business Climate." INSEE, Paris. Accessed January 12, 2011. http://www.insee.fr/fr/publications-et-services/docs_doc_travail/G2009-02.pdf.

Clower, Robert W. 1965. "The Keynesian Counter-Revolution: A Theoretical Appraisal." In *The Theory of Interest Rates*, edited by Frank H. Hahn and P. R. Brechling, 103–125. London: Macmillan.
Clower, Robert W. 1967. "A Reconsideration of the Microfoundations of Monetary Theory." *Western Economic Journal* 6(1):1–8.
Cooper, Julian. 2009. *Russia as a Populous Emerging Economy: A Comparative Perspective*. Birmingham: CREF, University of Birmingham. Draft mimeographed manuscript.
Corrado, Carol, and Joe Mattey. 1997. "Capacity Utilization." *Journal of Economic Perspectives* 11(1):151–167.
Coutts, David A. 2010. "Darwin's Views on Malthus." Accessed December 3, 2010. http://members.optusnet.com.au/exponentialist/Darwin_Malthus.htm.
Cowan, Robin, and Mario J. Rizzo. 1996. "The Genetic-Causal Tradition and Modern Economic Theory." *Kyklos* 49(3):273–317.
Crotty, James. 2001. "Structural Contradictions of Current Capitalism: A Keynes-Marx-Schumpeter Analysis." Accessed December 1, 2010. http://people.umass.edu/crotty/india-rev-May25.pdf.
Crotty, James. 2002. "Why There is Chronic Excess Capacity." *Challenge* 45(6):21–44.
CS Ad Dataset. 2007. "US Internet (online) advertising expenditure in millions of U.S. dollars." Accessed December 1, 2010. http://www.galbithink.org/cs-ad-dataset.xls.
Davila, Tony, Marc J. Epstein, and Robert Shelton. 2006. *Making Innovation Work: How to Manage It, Measure It, and Profit from It*. Philadelphia: Wharton School.
Davis, Christopher, and Wojcieh W. Charemza, eds. 1989. *Models of Disequilibrium and Shortage in Centrally Planned Economies*. London: Chapman and Hall.
Dentsu. 2009. "Advertising Expenditures in Japan 1999–2009." Accessed December 1, 2010. http://www.dentsu.com/marketing/index.html.
Diamond, Peter A. 1982. "Aggregate Demand Management in Search Equilibrium." *Journal of Political Economy* 90(5):881–894.
Djankov, Simeon, and Peter Murrell. 2002. "Enterprise Restructuring in Transition: A Quantitative Survey." *Journal of Economic Literature* 40(3):739–792.
Domar, Evsey D. 1989. "The Blind Men and the Elephant: An Essay on Isms." In *Capitalism, Socialism and Serfdom*, edited by Evsey D. Domar, 29–46. Cambridge: Cambridge University Press.
Drávucz, Péter. 2004. "Ez nagyobb dobás lesz a floppinál" [This is gonna be a greater hit than the floppy]. *Magyar Hírlap*, March 20.
Ehrlich, Éva. 1985. "Economic Development Levels, Proportions and Structures." Manuscript. Budapest: MTA Világgazdasági Kutatóintézet.
Erkel-Rousse, Helene, and Christelle Minodier. 2009. "Do Business Tendency Surveys in Industry and Services Help in Forecasting GDP Growth? A Real-Time Analysis on French Data." INSEE, Paris. Accessed January 12, 2011. http://insee.fr/fr/publications-et-services/docs_doc_travail/G2009-03.pdf.
Etter, Richard, Michael Graff, and Jürg Müller. 2008. "Is 'Normal' Capacity Utilisation Constant Over Time? Analyses with Micro and Macro Data from Business Tendency Surveys." ETH Zurich, KOF Swiss Economic Institute, Zurich. Accessed December 1, 2010. http://www.cesifogroup.de/portal/page/portal/ifoContent/N/event/Conferences/conf_nd/2008-11-20-Third-Workshop-MacroeconomicsandBusinessCycle/work-makro3-graff-m.pdf.
Eurobarometer. 2005. "Special survey on science and technology" (fieldwork: January–February 2005). http://ec.europa.eu/public_opinion/archives/eb_special_240_220_en.htm.

Fallenbuchl, Zbigniew M. 1982. "Employment Policies in Poland." In *Employment Policies in the Soviet Union and Eastern Europe*, edited by Jan Adm. London: Macmillan.

Farkas, Katalin. 1980. "A vállalati készletek szerepváltozása" [The Change in the Role of Inventories]. In *Vállalati magatartás, vállalati környezet*, edited by Márton Tardos. Budapest: Közgazdasági és Jogi Könyvkiadó.

Federal Reserve Bank of St. Louis. 2010. "Federal Reserve Economic Data (Gross domestic product)." Accessed December 3, 2010. http://research.stlouisfed.org/fred2/series/GDPA?cid=106.

Federal Reserve Statistical Release. 2010. "Industrial Production and Capacity Utilization." Accessed December 1, 2010. http://www.federalreserve.gov/releases/g17/current/table11.htm and http://www.federalreserve.gov/releases/g17/current/table12.htm.

Feenstra, Robert C. 1998. "Integration of trade and disintegration of production in the global economy." *Journal of Economic Perspectives* 12(4):31–50.

Finansy i Statistika. 1988. *SSSR i zarubezhnye strany* 1987 [The USSR and foreign countries 1987] Moscow: Finansy i Statistika.

Flaschel, Peter. 2009. *The Macrodynamics of Capitalism: Elements for a Synthesis of Marx, Keynes and Schumpeter*. Heidelberg: Springer.

Francas, David, Mirko Kremer, Stefan Minner, and Markus Friese. 2009. "Strategic process flexibility under lifecycle demand." *International Journal of Production Economics* 121(2):427–440.

Freedom House. 2010. "Freedom in the World: 2010 Survey Release." Accessed December 3, 2010. http://www.freedomhouse.org.

Freeman, C., and Luc Soate. 2003. *The Economics of Industrial Innovation*. Cambridge, MA: MIT Press.

Friedman, Milton. 1968. "The role of monetary policy." *American Economic Review* 58(1):1–17.

Frisch, Walter. 2003. "Co-Evolution of Information Revolution and Spread of Democracy." *Journal of International and Comparative Economics* 33:252–255.

Fuchs, Christian. 2008. *Internet and Society*. New York and London: Routledge.

Galbraith, John K. 1952. *A Theory of Price Control*. Cambridge, MA: Harvard University Press.

Galbraith, John K. 1998 [1958]. *The Affluent Society*. Boston: Houghton Mifflin.

Gomulka, Stanislaw. 1983. "The Incompatibility of Socialism and Rapid Innovation." *Millenium: Journal of International Studies* 13(1):16–26.

Google Company. 2013. "Our History in Depth." Accessed July 23, 2013. http://www.google.com/about/company/history.

Gorodnichenko, Yurij, Jan Svejnar, and Katherine Terrel. 2010. "Globalization and Innovation in Emerging Markets". *American Economic Journal: Macroeconomics* 2:194–226.

Griliches, Zvi. 1957. "Hybrid Corn: An Exploration in the Economics of Technical Change." *Econometrica* 25(4):501–522.

Grossman, Gene M., and Elhanan Helpman. 1991. *Innovation and Growth in the Global Economy*. Cambridge, MA: MIT Press.

Grover, Varun, and Jon Lebeau. 1996. "US Telecommunications: Industries in Transition." *Telematics and Informatics* 13(4):213–231.

Hall, Peter A., and David Soskice, eds. 2001. *Varieties of Capitalism: The Institutional Foundations of Comparative Advantage*. Oxford: Oxford University Press.

Hall, Peter A., and David Soskice, eds. 2003. "Varieties of Capitalism and Institutional Change: A Response to Three Critics." *Comparative European Politics* 1(3):241–250.

Hámori, Balázs, and Katalin Szabó. 2012. *Innovációs verseny. Esélyek és korlátok* [Competition in Innovation: Chances and Constraints]. Budapest: Aula.
Hanson, Philip. 1981. *Trade and Technology in Soviet-Western Relations*. London: Macmillan.
Hanson, Philip, and Keith Pavitt. 1987. *The Comparative Economics of Research Development and Innovation in East and West: A Survey*. Chur, London, Paris, New York, and Melbourne: Harwood.
Harrison, Ian. 2003. *The Book of Firsts*. London: Cassell Illustrated.
Harrison, Ian. 2004. *Book of Inventions*. London: Cassel Illustrated.
Haugh, David, Annabelle Mourougane, and Olivier Chatal. 2010. "The Automobile Industry in and Beyond the Crisis." Working Paper No. 745. OECD Economics Department.
Haug, Wolfgang F. 2003. *High-Tech-Kapitalismus*. Hamburg: Argument.
Hayek, Friedrich. 1948. "The Meaning of Competition." In *Individualism and Economic Order*, edited by Friedrich Hayek, 92–106. Chicago and London: The University of Chicago Press.
Heertje, Arnold. 2006. *Schumpeter on the Economics of Innovation and the Development of Capitalism*. Cheltenham: Elgar.
Heilbronner, Robert L. 1986. "Economics and Political Economy: Marx, Keynes and Schumpeter." In *Marx, Schumpeter, Keynes*, edited by Susanne W. Helburn and David F. Bramhall, 13–25. Armonk, NY: ME Sharpe.
Helburn, Suzanne W., and David F. Bramhall, eds. 1986. *Marx, Schumpeter, and Keynes: A Centenary Celebration of Dissent*. Armonk, NY: ME Sharpe.
Helpman, Elhanan, and Paul R. Krugman. 1985. *Market Structure and Foreign Trade*. Cambridge, MA: MIT Press.
Hirschman, Albert O. 1970. *Exit, Voice and Loyalty*. Cambridge: Harvard University Press.
Hodgson, Geoffrey M. 1993. *Economics and Evolution: Bringing Life Back into Economics*. Cambridge: Polity Press, and Ann Arbor, MI: University of Michigan Press.
Holzmann, Robert. 1990. "Unemployment Benefits during Economic Transition: Background, Concept and Implementation." Manuscript. OECD Conference Paper. Ludwig Boltzman Institut für Ökonomische Analyse, Vienna.
Huang, Haizhou, and Chenggang Xu. 1998. "Soft Budget Constraint and the Optimal Choices of Research and Development Projects Financing." *Journal of Comparative Economics* 26:62–79.
ILO. 2010. "Key Indicators of the Labor Market." EAPEP Database. International Labour Organisation, Genf: International Labour Organization.
ILO. 2012. "Key Indicators of the Labor Market." Accessed May 29. 2013. http://www.ilo.org/empelm/what/WCMS_114240/lang--en/index.htm.
IMF. 2010. "International Financial Statistics (Gross domestic product)." International Monetary Fund. Accessed December 3, 2010. http://www.imfstatistics.org/imf/.
International Telecommunications Union. 2006. *World Telecommunication/ICT Development Report: Measuring ICT for Economic and Social Development*, 104–112. Genf: International Telecommunication Union.
International Telecommunications Union. 2007. "Telecommunication Indicators. Telephones, Cellular Phones, and Computers by Country: 2006." Accessed December 3, 2010. http://www.census.gov/compendia/statab/cats/international_statistics/telecommunications_computers.html.
Isaacson, Walter. 2011. *Steve Jobs*. New York: Simon and Schuster.
Jones, Lamar B. 1989. "Schumpeter versus Darwin: In re Malthus." *Southern Economic Journal* 56(2):410–422.

Kahneman, Daniel, and Amos Tversky. 1979. "Prospect Theory: An Analysis of Decision under Risk." *Econometrica* 47(2):263–291.

Kahneman, Daniel, and Amos Tversky. 1991. "Loss Aversion in Riskless Choice: A Reference-Dependent Model." *The Quarterly Journal of Economics* 106(4):1039–1061.

Kaldor, Nicholas. 1972. "The Irrelevance of Equilibrium Economics." *Economic Journal* 82(328): 1237–1255.

Kaldor, Nicholas. 1981. "The Role of Increasing Returns, Technical Progress and Cumulative Causation." *Economie Appliquée* 34(6):593–617.

Kalecki, Michal. 1971. *Selected Essays on the Dynamics of the Capitalist Economy*. Cambridge: Cambridge University Press.

Kapitány, Zsuzsa. 2010. "Számítások a szocialista gazdaságok 1989 előtti autóhiányáról" [Calculations on car shortage in Eastern Europe before 1989]. Manuscript.

Karvalics, László Z. 2009. "The Information (Society) Race." Manuscript. Budapest: BKE.

Kedzie, Christopher R. 1997a. "Democracy and Network Interconnectivity." In *Culture on the Internet*, edited by S. Kiesler. Mahwah, NJ: Erlbaum.

Kedzie, Christopher R. 1997b. "The Case of the Soviet Union: The Dictator's Dilemma." Chapter 2 in *Communications and Democracy: Coincident Revolutions and the Emergent Dictators*. Rand. Accessed August 31, 2009. http://www.rand.org/pubs/rgs_dissertations/RGSD127/sec2.html.

Keen, Steve. 2002. *Debunking Economics*. New York: Zed Books and St Martin's Press.

Keynes, John M. 1967 [1936]. *The General Theory of Employment, Interest and Money*. London: Macmillan.

King, John L., and Joel West. 2002. "Ma Bell's Orphan: US Cellular Telephony, 1947–1996." *Telecommunications Policy* 26(3–4):189–203.

Kirman, Alan. 1992. "Whom or What Does the Representative Individual Represent?" *Journal of Economic Perspectives* 6(2):117–136.

Kirzner, Israel M. 1973. *Competition and Entrepreneurship*. Chicago and London: University of Chicago Press.

Kirzner, Israel M. 1985. *Discovery and the Capitalist Process*, 119–149. Chicago: University of Chicago Press.

Kornai, János. 1994 [1959]. *Overcentralization in Economic Administration*. Oxford: Oxford University Press.

Kornai, János. 1971. *Anti-Equilibrium*. Amsterdam: North-Holland.

Kornai, János. 1979. "Resource-Constrained versus Demand-Constrained Systems." *Econometrica* 47(4):801–819.

Kornai, János. 1980. *Economics of Shortage*. Amsterdam: North-Holland.

Kornai, János. 1982. *Growth, Shortage and Efficiency*. Oxford: Basil Blackwell, and Berkeley and Los Angeles: University of California Press.

Kornai, János. 1992. *The Socialist System: The Political Economy of Communism*. Princeton: Princeton University Press and Oxford: Oxford University Press.

Kornai, János. 1993. "Transformational Recession: A General Phenomenon Examined through the Example of Hungary's Development." *Economie Appliquée* 46(2):181–227.

Kornai, János. 2001. "Ten Years After The Road to a Free Economy: The Author's Self Evaluation." In *Annual Bank Conference on Development Economics 2000*, edited by B. Pleskovic and N. Stern. Washington, DC: World Bank.

Kornai, János. 2006a. *By Force of Thought: Irregular Memoirs of an Intellectual Journey*. Cambridge, MA: MIT Press.

Kornai, János. 2006b. "The Great Transformation of Central and Eastern Europe: Success and Disappointment." *The Economics of Transition* 14(2):207–244.
Kornai, János. 2008. *From Socialism to Capitalism*. Budapest: Central European University Press.
Kornai, János. 2009a. "Marx through the Eyes of an East European Intellectual." *Social Research* 76(3):965–986.
Kornai, János. 2009b. "The Soft Budget Constraint Syndrome and the Global Financial Crisis: Some Warnings of an East European Economist." http://www.kornai-janos.hu.
Kornai, János. 2010. "Hiánygazdaság – Többletgazdaság" [Shortage Economy – Surplus Economy]. *Közgazdasági Szemle* 57(11–12):925–957, 1021–1044.
Kornai, János, and Karen Eggleston. 2001. *Welfare, Choice and Solidarity in Transition: Reforming the Health Sector in Eastern Europe*. Cambridge: Cambridge University Press.
Kornai, János, and Béla Martos. 1973. "Autonomous Control of Economic Systems." *Econometrica* 41(3):509–528.
Kornai, János, and Béla Martos, eds. 1981. *Non-Price Control*. Amsterdam: North-Holland.
Kornai, János, Eric Maskin, and Gérard Roland. 2003. "Understanding the Soft Budget Constraint." *Journal of Economic Literature* 41(4):1095–1136.
Kornai, János, and Susan Rose-Ackerman, eds. 2004. *Building a Trustworthy State in Post-Socialist Transition*. New York: Palgrave Macmillan.
Kornai, János, Bo Rothstein, and Susan Rose-Ackerman, eds. 2004. *Creating Social Trust in Post-Socialist Transition*. New York: Palgrave Macmillan.
Kovács, Győző. 1999. "Egy elpuskázott találmány. Jánosi Marcell és a kazettás 'floppy'" [A messed up invention: Marcell Jánosi and the cassette-floppy]. Exhibition poster. Budapest.
KPMG. 2009. "Momentum: KPMG's Global Auto Executive Survey 2009." Accessed December 17, 2010. http://www.kpmg.com/Global/en/IssuesAndInsights/ArticlesPublications/Momentum/Documents/Momentum-AutoExec-2009.pdf.
Kürti, Sándor, and Gábor Fabiány, eds. 2008. *20 éves a KÜRT, az Infostrázsa* [20 Years of KÜRT, the Info-Guard]. Budapest: Kürt Információmenedzsment.
Lachmann, Ludwig M. 1976. "From Mises to Shackle: An Essay on Austrian Economics and the Laiic Society." *Journal of Economic Literature* 14(1):54–62.
Laki, Mihály. 1984–85. "Kényszerített innováció" [Forced innovation]. *Szociológia* 12: 45–53.
Laki, Mihály. 2009. "Interjú a Kürti-fivérekkel" [Interview with the Kürti brothers]. Manuscript. MTA Közgazdaságtudományi Intézet, Budapest.
Lange, Oscar. 1968 [1936–37]. "On the Economic Theory of Socialism." In *On the Economic Theory of Socialism*, edited by Benjamin E. Lipincott, 57–143. New York, Toronto, and London: MacGraw Hill.
Latvijas Statistika. 2012. "Population and Social Process Indicators." Accessed December 14, 2010. http://www.csb.gov.lv/node/30604.
Lavoie, Don. 1985. *Rivalry and Central Planning*. Cambridge: Cambridge University Press.
Layard, Richard, Stephen Nickel, and Richard Jackman. 1991. *Unemployment*. Oxford: Oxford University Press.
Lee, Frederic S. 1998. *Post Keynesian Price Theory*. Cambridge: Cambridge University Press.
Leijonhufvud, Axel. 1968. *On Keynesian Economics and the Economics of Keynes*. New York: Oxford University Press.

Leijonhufvud, Axel. 1973. "Effective Demand Failures." *Swedish Journal of Economy* 75(1):27–48.

Leijonhufvud, Axel. 2009. "Out of the Corridor: Keynes and the Crisis." *Cambridge Journal of Economics* 33(4):741–757.

Lovász, László, and Michael D. Plummer. 2009. *Matching Theory*. Providence, RI: American Mathematical Society.

Malinvaud, Edmond. 1977. *The Theory of Unemployment Reconsidered*. Oxford: Blackwell.

Mankiw, Gregory N. 1985. "Small Menu Costs and Large Business Cycles: A Macroeconomic Model of Monopoly." *Quarterly Journal of Economics* 100(2): 529–538.

Mankiw, Gregory N. 2009. *Principles of Economics*. Mason, OH: South-Western Cengage Learning.

Marx, Karl. 1978 [1967–94]. *Capital. Volume 1*. London: Penguin.

Median. 2007. "Internethasználat otthon" [Use of Internet at home]. http://www.median.hu/object.b28bc0d6-0483-4294-b9a5-a006ce40891f.ivy.

McCall, J. J. 1970. "Economics of Information and Job Search." *Quarterly Journal of Economics* 84(1):113–126.

McCraw, Thomas K. 2007. *Prophet of Innovation: Joseph Schumpeter and Creative Destruction*. Cambridge, MA and London: Harvard University Press.

McGraw, A. Peter, Jeff T. Larsen, Daniel Kahneman, and David Schkade. 2010. "Comparing Gains and Losses." *Psychological Science* 21:1438–1445.

Milgrom, Paul, and John Roberts. 1992. *Economics, Organization and Management*. Englewood Cliffs, NJ: Prentice Hall.

Milward, Alan S. 1979. *War, Economy, and Society 1939–1945*. Berkeley: University of California Press.

Morin, Norman, and John J. Stevens. 2004. "Diverging Measures of Capacity Utilization: An Explanation." Working Paper, 3–4. Federal Reserve Board, Finance and Economics Discussion Series, Washington, DC.

Mortensen, Dale T. 1986. "Job Search and Labor Market Analysis." In *Handbook of Labor Economics*, Vol. II, edited by O. Ashensfelder and R. Layard. Amsterdam: Elsevier Science Publishers.

Mortensen, Dale T., and Christopher A. Pissarides. 1994. "Job Creation and Job Destruction in the Theory of Unemployment." *Review of Economic Studies* 61(1):397–415.

Nelson, Richard R., and Sidney G. Winter. 1982. *An Evolutionary Theory of Economic Change*. Cambridge, MA: Harvard University Press.

Nilsson, Ronny. 2001. "Harmonization of Business and Consumer Tendency Surveys World-Wide." Paris: OECD.

North, Douglass C. 1990. *Institutions, Institutional Change and Economic Performance*. Cambridge: Cambridge University Press.

North, Douglass C. 1991. "Institutions." *The Journal of Economic Perspectives* 5(1):97–112.

Nyíri, Kristóf J. 2004. "Review of Castells, The Information Age." In *Manuel Castells*, Vol. 3, edited by F. Webster and B. Dimitriou, 5–34. London: Sage.

OECD. 2003. "Business Tendency Surveys: A Handbook." Accessed December 12, 2010. Accessed December 14, 2011. http://www.oecd.org/dataoecd/29/61/31837055.pdf.

OECD. 2009. "Responding to the Economic Crisis: Fostering Industrial Restructuring and Renewal." Accessed December 14, 2011. http://www.oecd.org/dataoecd/58/35/43387209.pdf.

OECD. 2012. "Registered Unemployment and Job Vacancies." Accessed December 14, 2010. http://stats.oecd.org/Index.aspx?DataSetCode=MEI_LAB_REG1.
Office for National Statistics. 2012. "Job vacancies – ONS Vacancy Survey." Accessed October 13, 2010. http://www.statistics.gov.uk/STATBASE/Product.asp?vlnk=9390.
Olson, Mancur. 1963. *The Economics of Wartime Shortage*. Durham, NC: Duke University Press.
Orsato, Renato J., and Peter Wells. 2006. "U-turn: The Rise and Demise of the Automobile Industry." *Journal of Cleaner Production* 15(11–12):994–1006.
Orwell, George. 1949–50. *Nineteen Eighty-Four*. New York: Penguin.
Phelps, Edmund S. 1968. "Money-Wage Dynamics and Labor-Market Equilibrium." *Journal of Political Economy* 76(4), Part 2:678–711.
Phelps, Edmund S. 2008. "Understanding the Great Changes in the World: Gaining Ground and Losing Ground since World War II." In *Institutional Change and Economic Behaviour*, edited by J. Kornai, M. László, and G. Roland. New York: Palgrave Macmillan.
Phelps, Edmund S., George C. Archibald, and Armen A. Alchian. 1970. *Microeconomic Foundations of Employment and Inflation Theory*. New York: Norton.
Piac & Profit. 2013. "Feje tetejére állt az európai piac" [The European market stood upside down]. *Autoblog*, February 16. Accessed February 16, 2013. http://www.autoblog.hu/hirek/feje-tetejere-allt-az-europai-autopiac/.
Pissarides, Christopher A. 2000. *Equilibrium Unemployment Theory*. Cambridge, MA: MIT Press.
Portes, Richard, Richard E. Quandt, David Winter, and Stephen Yeo. 1987. "Macroeconomic Planning and Disequilibrium: Estimates for Poland, 1955–1980." *Econometrica* 55(1):19–41.
Portes, Richard, and David Winter. 1980. "Disequilibrium Estimates for Consumption Goods Markets in Centrally Planned Economies." *Review of Economic Studies* 47(146):137–159.
Prékopa, András. 1995. *Stochastic Programming*. Budapest: Kluwer.
Qian, Yingyi, and Chenggang Xu. 1998. "Innovation and Bureaucracy under Soft and Hard Budget Constraint." *The Review of Economic Studies* 65(1):151–164.
Ramey, Valerie A., and Kenneth D. West. 1999. "Inventories." In *Handbook of Macroeconomics*, Vol. 1, edited by John B. Taylor and Michael Woodford, 863–923. Amsterdam: Elsevier.
Relman, Arnold. 2010. "Health Care: The Disquieting Truth." *New York Review of Books* 57(14):45–48.
Robinson, Joan V. 1969 [1933]. *The Economics of Imperfect Competition*. London: Macmillan.
Rogers, Everett M. 1995. *Diffusion of Innovations*. New York: The Free Press.
Rose, Richard. 2004. *Insiders and Outsiders: New Europe Barometer 2004*. (Fieldwork: October 1, 2004 – February 27, 2005.) Centre for the Study of Public Policy, University of Aberdeen, Aberdeen. http://www.abdn.ac.uk/cspp/view_item.php?id=404.
Rosser, J. Barkley, Richard P. F. Holt, and David Colander, eds. 2010. *European Economics at a Crossroads*. Cheltenham: Edward Elgar.
Roth, Alvin E. 1982. "The Economics of Matching: Stability and Incentives." *Mathematics of Operations Research* 7(4):617–628.
Samuelson, Paul A. 1980 [1948]. *Economics*. New York and London: McGraw-Hill.
Schumpeter, Joseph A. 1939. *Business Cycles*. New York and London: McGraw-Hill.
Schumpeter, Joseph A. 1954. *History of Economic Analysis*. New York: Oxford University Press.

Schumpeter, Joseph A. 1968 [1912]. *The Theory of Economic Development: An Inquiry into Profits, Capital, Credit, Interest and Business Cycle.* Cambridge: Harvard University Press.

Schumpeter, Joseph A. 2010 [1942]. *Capitalism, Socialism, Democracy.* Milton Park: Routledge.

Scitovsky, Tibor. 1985. "Pricetakers' Plenty: A Neglected Benefit of Capitalism." *Kyklos* 38(4):517–536.

Shapiro, Carl, and Joseph E. Stiglitz. 1984. "Equilibrium Unemployment as a Worker Discipline Device." *American Economic Review* 74(3):433–444.

SHARE. 2010. "Survey of Health, Ageing, and Retirement in Europe." Accessed January 16, 2010. http://www.share-project.org.

Shane, Scott. 1994. *Dismantling Utopia: How Information Ended the Soviet Union.* Chicago: Ivan R. Dee.

Siciliani, Luigi, and Rossella Verzulli. 2009. "Waiting Times and Socioeconomic Status among Elderly Europeans: Evidence from SHARE." *Health Economics* 18(11):1295–1306.

Statistikos Departamentas. 2012. "Population and Social Statistics." Accessed December 14, 2010. http://www.stat.gov.lt/en/pages/view/?id=2326.

Stiglitz, Joseph E., Amartya Sen, and Jean-Paul Fitoussi, eds. 2009. "Report by the Commission on the Measurement of Economic Performance and Social Progress." Accessed September 28, 2012. http://www.stiglitz-sen-fitoussi.fr/documents/rapport_anglais.pdf.

Stokes, Raymond G. 2000. *Constructing Socialism: Technology and Change in East Germany, 1945–1990.* Baltimore: Johns Hopkins University Press.

Stolyarov, Gennady. 2008. *Liberation by Internet.* Auburn, AL: Ludwig von Mises Institute. http://www.mises.org/story/3060.

Szabó, Katalin. 2012. "Az invenciótól az innovációig" [From invention to innovation]. In *Innovációs verseny. Esélyek és korlátok* [Competition in Innovation: Chances and Constraints], edited by B. Hámori and K. Szabó, 21–46. Budapest: Aula.

Szabó, Katalin, and Balázs Hámori. 2006. *Információgazdaság: Digitális kapitalizmus vagy új gazdasági rendszer?* [Information Richness: Digital Capitalism or New Economic System?] Budapest: Akadémiai Kiadó.

Teece, David J., Gary Pisano, and Amy Shun. 1997. "Dynamic Capabilities and Strategic Management." *Strategic Management Journal* 18(7):509–533.

Thomke, Stefan. 2003. *Experimentation Matters: Unlocking the Potential of New Technologies for Innovation.* Boston, MA: Harvard Business School Press.

Timmer, John. 2009. "China to Mandate Web Filtering Software on All New PCs." *Ars Technica.* Accessed July 27, 2009. http://arstechnica.com/tech-policy/news/2009/06/china-to-mandate-web-filtering-software-on-all-new-pcs.ars.

Toomey, John W. 2000. *Inventory Management: Principles, Concepts and Techniques.* Norwell, MA: Kluwer.

Transparency International. 2010. "The 2010 Corruption Perception Index." Accessed December 3, 2010. http://www.transparency.org/policy_research/surveys_indices/cpi/2010.

U.S. Census Bureau. 2012. "Vacancy Rates for the United States: 1965 to 2010." Accessed February 15, 2010. http://www.census.gov/hhes/www/housing/hvs/qtr210/files/tab1.xls.

United Nations Statistics Division. 2009a. "Fixed telephone lines per 100 inhabitants." Accessed December 3, 2010. http://data.un.org/Data.aspx?q=telephone&d=ITU&f=ind1Code%3aI91.

United Nations Statistics Division. 2009b. "Industrial Commodity Statistics Database (radio, television and communication equipment and apparatus)." Accessed July 16, 2009. http://data.un.org/Data.aspx?d=ICS&f=cmID%3a47220-1.

Vahabi, Mehrdad. 2004. *The Political Economy of Destructive Power*. Cheltenham: Edward Elgar.

Vámos, T. 2009. "Social, organizational and individual impacts of automation." In *Handbook of Automation*, edited by Shimon Y. Nof, 71–92. New York: Springer.

van Brabant, Jozef M. 1990. "Socialist Economics: The Disequilibrium School and the Shortage Economy." *Journal of Economic Perspectives* 4(2):157–175.

Veblen, Thorstein B. 1898. "Why Is Economics Not an Evolutionary Science." *Quarterly Journal of Economics* 12(4):373–397.

Veblen, Thorstein B. 1975 [1899]. *The Theory of the Leisure Class*. New York and London: Macmillan.

WARC. 2007. "World Advertising Trends (Advertising Expenditures)." Accessed July 21, 2011. http://www.warc.com/LandingPages/Data/AdspendByCountry.ask.

Webster, Frank, Raimo Blom, Erkki Karvonen, Harri Malin, Kaarle Nordenstreng, and Ensio Puoskari, eds. 2004. *The Information Society Reader*. London: Routledge.

Weitzman, Martin. 2000. "On Buyers' and Sellers' Markets under Capitalism and Socialism." In *Planning, Shortage, and Transformation*, edited by Eric Maskin and András Simonovits, 127–140. Cambridge, MA: MIT Press.

Wikipedia. 2009a. "Google." Accessed July 23, 2009. http://en.wikipedia.org/wiki/Google.

Wikipedia. 2009b. "Internet censorship." Accessed August 19, 2009. http://en.wikipedia.org/wiki/Internet_censorship.

Wikipedia. 2012a: "Shortage economy." Accessed September 28, 2012. http://en.wikipedia.org/wiki/Shortage_economy.

Wikipedia. 2012b. "Eastern Bloc economies." Accessed September 15, 2012. http://en.wikipedia.org/wiki/Eastern_Bloc_economies#Shortages.

World Bank. 2008. *World Development Indicators*. Washington, DC: World Bank.

World Bank. 2009. *Doing Business 2009*. World Bank International Finance Corporation. Washington, DC: Palgrave Macmillan.

World Bank. 2010. "World Development Indicators and Global Development Finance (Gross Domestic Product per capita)." Accessed November 12, 2010. http://databank.worldbank.org/ddp/home.do?Step=2&id=4&DisplayAggregation=N&SdmxSupported=Y&CNO=2&SET_BRANDING=YES.

World Bank. 2012. *World Development Indicators*. Washington, DC: World Bank. Accessed June 25, 2012. http://databank.worldbank.org/ddp/home.do?Step=2&id=4&DisplayAggregation=N&SdmxSupported=Y&CNO=2&SET_BRANDING=YES.

INDEX

Acemoglu, Daron, 15n14
activity rate, 91, 93, 94
adaptation, 19, 31, 64, 99, 127, 129
    mutual ~ between producer and
        consumer, 128
    ~ friction, 100, 121
    See also adjustment
adjustment, 32, 72, 104, 108, 114, 146
    forced ~, 109
    lasting ~ of production to consumer
        needs, 127
    mal~, 121
    mismatched ~, 100
    mutual ~ of supply and demand,
        76–78, 81, 144
    price ~, 120
    wage ~, 120
    ~ process, 77
    See also adaptation
advertisement, 128, 136
aggregation, 19, 78, 84–85, 112
Aghion, Philippe, 39, 142
agriculture, 97, 99, 155
Akerlof, George A., 66, 123n19, 139
Allain, Olivier, 75
Amann, Ronald, 11, 12, 13
analysis, causal ~, 103n10, 106–124
animal spirit, 66, 97, 123n19
Apple mouse, 6, 15n16
approach
    normative ~, 108, 148
    positive ~, 125, 155
Arrow, Kenneth, 108
Arthur, William Brian, 65n13, 139, 142
asymmetry, 111–113, 115–117, 124, 139
    ~ic information, 112n10
Atkin, David J., 57
automobile, automotive
    ~ industry, 26, 65, 132–134, 155

Austrian school, 39, 107, 108, 139, 140
aversion to loss, 124, 139
Azariadis, Costas, 68n18

bailout, 34, 97, 134, 154, 155
Bakunin, Mikhail Alexandrovich,
    104n14
Balcerowicz, Leszek, 39
Ball, Laurence, 69
Bartelsman, Eric J., 32, 33
Bauer, Reinhold, 22n28
Baumol, William J., 10n5, 14n10, 39,
    126n2
Bechtolsheim, Andy, 16
Benassy, Jean-Pascal, 77, 98n5, 112
benefits, of science, 37
Berliner, Joseph, 19n22
Berners-Lee, Tim, 17
Bhaduri, Amit, 68n20
Bhagwati, Jagdish, 156
Bils, Mark, 69
Blanchard, Olivier, 98
Blinder, Alan S., 39n4, 69
Bolton, Patrick, 154n11
Bojár, Gábor, 26
Bower, Joseph L., 9n3
Brabant von, Jozef M., 84n17
Bramhall, David F., 138n12
Brin, Sergey, 14, 15
British Labour Party, 140
bubble formation, 16n19
budget constraint
    hard ~, 68, 97, 120, 154–155
    soft ~, 34, 64, 68, 97, 101, 134,
        154–155
bureaucracy, bureaucratic, 21, 30, 35,
    55, 97, 123, 157, 158
    ~ centralization, 4, 17, 19, 20, 100,
        122, 150

bureaucracy, bureaucratic (*continued*)
~ coordination, 21, 122
business
~ cycle, 90, 144–149
~ privacy, 11
~ research, 35, 77n9, 79, 87, 133
buyer
~s' market, 111, 112n10
~s' competition, 112
Bygrave, William D., 16

Canry, Nicolas, 75
capacity, 64, 71, 72, 76, 79, 101, 128, 129, 133, 137, 146
allocation of ~, 156
excess ~, 53, 59, 61, 64, 65, 85, 119, 120, 132–134, 139, 140, 146
practical ~, 71, 72, 73, 74, 75, 80
rate of ~ utilization, 74, 75, 84, 144
reserves of ~, ~reserves, 52, 62n8, 63, 108, 127
spare ~, 52, 104, 127
surplus ~, 65n13, 68, 84, 132, 134, 136
theoretical ~, 71
~ utilization, 61, 62, 71n3, 86, 126, 127, 145, 146n2, 155
capital
reserve ~, 16
venture ~, 16
capitalism, capitalist
anti-capitalist views, 35, 38, 42
capitalist market, 52, 55, 60, 69, 117, 145, 149
varieties of capitalism, 53, 144–160
Castells, Manuel, 10n4, 47
causal chain, 42, 118–122
causal relationship, 23, 30, 31, 36–39, 41, 42, 56, 98, 106, 125, 146–147, 150
Central Europe, 22, 40, 43–44, 45, 92
waiting lists in Central and East European countries, 134, 159
centralization, 19, 20, 22, 46, 63
bureaucratic ~, 4, 17, 100, 122, 150, 158
censorship, 22, 45
Ceruzzi, Paul E., 9
Chamberlin, Edward H., 61
change of system, 42, 60n2, 79–80, 87n18, 92–95, 122, 159, 160n17
See also transition

Chantrill, Christopher, 127
Chao, Loretta, 45n8
Charemza, Wojcieh W., 84n17
Chekhov, Anton Pavlovich, 131n6
Chikán, Attila, 82, 83
China, 31, 45, 51, 99, 131, 156, 158
Chopra, Sunil, 62n8
Christensen, Clayton M., 9n3
Clavel, Laurent, 87
Clower, Robert W., 78
Colander, David, 140n14
communication, 17, 99
information and ~ technology, 6, 10, 17, 22, 24, 28–30, 38, 42, 44n7, 45, 47, 148, 156
communism, communist, 45, 150
~ dictatorship, 22, 45
~ countries, 11, 32, 158, 159
company, 6–9, 10, 14, 15, 18–21, 58, 26, 66, 67, 72–73, 79–80, 85, 107, 109, 132, 137, 155
small ~, 31
large ~, 15, 31, 32, 66
competition, 4, 15, 17, 18, 20, 27, 64, 66, 126, 132–134, 137, 155
imperfect ~, 61, 139
monopolistic ~, 57, 61, 63, 65, 69, 120, 126, 147, 152, 153, 155
oligopolistic ~, 139
perfect ~, 57, 61
sellers' ~, 64, 112, 125, 126, 132, 159n16
composite index, 86, 87, 113, 115
concept, conceptual
~ clarification, 53, 54, 86, 87
~ apparatus, 70–87, 53, 85–88
conflict of interest
~ between employers and employees, 67–68, 139
~ between owners and managers, 66
conservatism, 34, 35, 140, 148, 153
constitutionalism, 125, 137, 154
constraint
dominant ~, 111
hard budget ~, 68, 97, 120, 154, 155
soft budget ~, 34, 64, 68, 97, 134, 154, 155
~s of production, 65, 78–81, 97, 98
consumer
manipulation of the ~, 127, 128
sovereignty of the ~, 127, 128

~ism, 130n5
~ society, 126, 130
contract theory, 68n18, 154n11
control
    state ~, 97
    ~ on prices, price, 97
    ~ on wages, 97
Cooper, Julian, 11–13, 30
coordination, 64, 107, 128, 129, 149
    bureaucratic ~, 21, 55, 122, 158
    market ~, 4, 21, 55, 120, 122, 137
    ~ mechanisms, 111, 158
Corrado, Carol, 75
corridor theory (Leijonhufvud), 122n18, 145n1
corruption, 86, 87, 131, 132, 136, 137, 152
cost, marginal, 60, 65
Coutts, David A., 110
Cowan, Robin, 107n2
creative destruction, 31–35, 58, 63, 98n7, 99, 120, 124, 134, 139, 146, 148, 154
crisis
    ~ and bailouts, 133, 134, 154
    ~ and bubble formation, 16n19, 145
    ~ and multiplier effect, 133
Crotty, James, 141
cycle
    fluctuations in the business ~, 90, 144–149

Davies, Robert W., 11, 12, 13
Davis, Christopher, 84n17
Davila, Tony, 22n27
Debreu, Gerard, 108
decentralization, 4, 15, 17, 20, 46, 63, 109
demand, 17, 27, 30, 53, 58, 60, 62–65, 68, 69, 70–73, 79–81, 86, 97–99, 100–102, 108, 110, 120, 127, 137, 139, 142, 146, 147, 149, 152, 153n10, 154
    excess ~, 60, 78, 80, 82, 84–86, 104, 110, 121, 145, 152n8, 158
    excess-~ economy vs. excess-supply economy, 53, 54, 85, 111
    mutual adjustment of supply and ~, 76–78, 81, 144
    net excess ~, 84, 113

~-constrained vs. supply-constrained system, 111
~ related processes, 67–68, 139
~-supply regime, 113–117, 124, 125, 130, 131, 135, 145, 153, 156, 158
democracy, 42–46, 125, 135, 136, 154
    multiparty ~, 4
deregulation, 35
Desai, Padma, 161n1
description, positive ~, 34, 106–124, 137, 140, 141
destruction, creative, 31–35, 58, 63, 98n7, 99, 120, 124, 134, 139, 146, 148, 154
development, economic, 21, 93, 94, 98, 99
Dewatripont, Mathias, 154n11
Diamond, Peter A., 100
dichotomy, 161
dictatorship, 4, 22, 45, 46, 135
diffusion of innovation, 11, 12, 27–31
disequilibrium, 54, 106
    ~ model, 84n17, 98n5, 112
    ~ school, 77, 139
discrimination, 105
distribution
    ~ of income, 15, 40, 41, 118, 129, 130, 135
    ~ of wealth, 129, 130
Djankov, Simeon, 159n16
Domar, Evsey, 61n4, 161
Dorman, Peter, 140
dot-com
    ~ bubble, 148
    ~ firms, 34
Drávucz, Péter, 19n21
dynamism, dynamic, 3, 9, 25, 31, 32, 39, 41, 57, 60, 61, 67, 69, 77, 85, 98, 99, 107, 129, 142, 152, 153
    steady state ~, 107, 109
    ~ system, 107, 142

East Europe, 22, 40, 42, 43–45, 160
East European socialist countries, 13, 30, 59, 76n8, 92, 93, 96, 104, 122, 134, 150
    waiting lists in Central and East European countries, 134, 159

economics, 3, 9n3, 23, 31, 39–41, 51, 52, 53, 54, 55, 62, 69n21, 86, 89, 92, 98, 104, 106, 109, 110, 117, 119n15, 141, 144, 145, 147, 161
  behavioral ~, 66n14, 124, 139
  comparative ~, 12, 39, 47
  equilibrium ~, 108n3
  heterodox theories in ~, 137, 140n14
  institutional ~, 138
  mainstream ~, 39, 40, 52, 53, 54, 61, 128, 137
  standard micro ~, 53, 64, 84, 111
economies of scale, 64, 65
education, higher, 22n28, 44, 127, 153
efficiency wage, 103–105
Eggleston, Karen, 153
Ehrlich, Éva, 93
e-mail, 17, 23, 44
employment, 20, 89, 97, 98, 103n11, 104, 109
  natural rate of ~, 52
  full ~, 92, 95, 105
Engelbart, Douglas, 15n16
entrepreneur, entrepreneurship, 12–22, 25–27, 30, 31, 35, 39, 66, 120, 152n8
entry, 31–34, 57, 58, 60, 155
Epstein, Marc J., 22n27
equilibrium, 52, 54, 60, 69, 84, 106–112, 115, 116, 119n15, 122, 139, 142, 161
  competitive ~, 112
  market ~, 52, 108
  unemployment ~, 109, 112, 116
  Walrasian ~, 108, 112–114, 142
  ~ economics, 108n3
  ~ unemployment, 103
Erkel-Rousse, Helene, 87
Escher, Maurits Cornelis, 161
espionage, industrial, 11
establishment, political, 42
Etter, Richard, 74
evolution, evolutionary, 33, 109, 110, 136, 139, 143
  ~ biology, 109, 110
  ~ economics, 139
excess, 53, 54, 59, 60, 61, 64, 66–68, 70–74, 76, 78, 80–82, 85, 86, 104, 110, 111, 121, 125, 131, 145, 146, 152n8, 154, 158
  net ~ demand, 84, 85, 113

  net ~ supply, 84
  ~ capacity, 53, 59, 61, 85, 108, 119–121, 125, 132–134, 139, 140, 152n8
  ~ demand, 60, 78, 80, 82, 86, 104, 110, 121, 145, 152n9, 158
  ~ supply, 53–54, 59, 61, 61n4, 64–66, 68–74, 76, 78, 80, 80n12, 81–86, 121, 131, 152nn8–9, 153n10, 154, 158
exit, 31–34, 57, 58, 60, 64, 65, 99, 128, 155
expansion drive, 66, 97, 120, 155
expectations, 37, 87, 109n4, 134, 154–156

Fabiány, Gábor, 27
factor
  political ~, 22, 23
  ~ analysis, 87
Fallenbuchl, Zbigniew, 95
famine, 131, 135
Farkas, Katalin, 83
Fed (Federal Reserve Bank), 71
Feenstra, Robert C., 156
financial sector, 34, 47, 55, 134, 149, 155
firm, 33, 61, 65, 69
  small ~, 14, 15
  large ~, 14, 65
Fitoussi, Jean-Paul, 41n5
Flaschel, Peter, 138n12
fluctuation
  ~ in the business cycle, 144–149
Francas, David, 133
Freedom House, 86
Freeman, Christopher, 10, 14n11, 22n27
friction
  ~al unemployment, 98n7, 100–102, 139
Friedman, Milton, 104n12
Frisch, Walter, 45

Galbraith, John K., 127, 130n5, 150n6
Gali, Jordi, 98
GDP, 28–30, 40, 45, 93, 94, 127, 128, 149
  ~ growth rate, 40
  the "gap" between actual and potential ~, 85

Geary, Roy, 136
Gintis, Herbert, 140
glasnost (openness), 23
globalization, 47, 99, 155, 156
glut, 51n3, 146
Gomulka, Stanislaw, 19n22
Gorbachev, Mikhail Sergeyevich, 23
Gorodnichenko, Yurij, 27n1
Graff, Michael, 74
Graphisoft, 26
Griliches, Zvi, 22n27
Grossman, Gene M., 39
Grover, Varun, 57

Hall, Peter A., 53
Haltiwanger, John, 32
Hámori, Balázs, 10n5, 47
Harrison, Ian, 9
Haug, Wolfgang Fritz, 47
Haugh, David, 132n8
Hayek, Friedrich, 107, 140, 141n15
health care, 90, 130, 151, 152
    fee for service in ~, 152
    waiting time in ~, 151
Heertje, Arnold, 14n10
Heilbronner, Robert L., 141n15
Helburn, Susanne W., 138n12
Helpman, Elhanan, 39, 65n13, 142
heterogeneity, 67n16, 77, 84, 85
high-tech sector, 11n7, 47
Hirschman, Albert O., 127
Hitler, Adolf, 150
Hodgson, Geoffrey M., 110n8
Holzmann, Robert, 95
honesty, 35, 104, 127, 131n7, 157, 158
housing sector, 76
Howitt, Peter P., 39, 142
Huang, Haizhou, 21n26
Hungary, 13, 19, 26–29, 31–33, 37, 39, 41, 43, 44, 59, 79, 80, 83, 87, 93, 94, 96, 148, 157n14, 158, 159, 160n17

income distribution, 15, 40, 41, 118, 129, 130, 135
index
    composite ~, 86, 87
    synthetic ~, 87n18
    ~ on shortages, 87n18

indicator, 28–30, 40, 41, 44, 64, 85–91, 95, 96, 101, 102, 113–116, 128, 149, 151, 159
industry
    ~ial espionage, 11
    reserve army of ~ial workers, 104
inequality, 40, 44n7, 129, 130
information
    age of ~, 47
    asymmetric ~, 112n10
    ~ and communication technology, 10, 17, 22, 24, 38, 42, 45, 47, 99, 156
    ~-flow, 100
    ~ society, 10
    ~ Society Index, 31
innovation
    diffusion of ~, 11, 12, 27–31
    revolutionary ~, 5, 6–11, 14, 17, 18, 20, 22n28, 23, 25, 27, 31, 66n15
    ~ process
innovator, 10, 11, 14, 15n16, 16, 18, 25–27, 31, 35, 63, 66n15
input stock, 83
interconnectivity, 42–46
internet, 8, 14, 16, 23, 27, 28, 29, 30, 31, 37, 38, 40, 42, 44, 45, 131, 156, 157, 158
inventory, 62, 82, 126, 137, 139
    just-in-time ~ strategy, 82n15, 137
    See also stock
investment, 55, 58, 64, 121n17, 133, 137, 147
    rigidity of ~ allocation, 21
    ~ hunger, 97, 155
iPhone, iPad, 58, 66n15
Isaacson, Walter, 66n15

Jackman, Richard, 112
Jánosi, Marcell, 19, 26
job vacancy, 91, 94–96, 101, 113, 116n12
Joffe, Abram, 18
Jones, Lamar, 110

Kádár-era, 26
Kahneman, Daniel, 124
Kaldor, Nicholas, 65n13, 108n3, 111, 139, 140
Kalecki, Michal, 97, 104n13, 139, 140

Kapitány, Zsuzsa, 142
Karpinski, Jacek, 18
Karvalics, Z. László, 31n4
Kautsky, Karl, 104n14
Kedzie, Christopher R., 23, 44, 45
Keen, Steve, 69n21, 140
Keynes, John Maynard, 66, 97, 98,
    111, 123n19, 138n12, 139, 140,
    147–149
  New ~ian economics, 139, 140
  post-~ian, 69, 111, 139, 140
  ~ian unemployment, 95–98
KGB, 110, 154
King, John L., 57
Kirman, Alan, 67n16, 140
Kirzner, Israel M., 39, 107
Klenow, Peter J., 69
Kondratiev, Nikolai Dmitriyevich, 148
  ~-cycle, 148
Kovács, Győző, 19n21
Köllő, János, 93, 95
Krugman, Paul R., 65n13, 142
Kürti, János, 26
Kürti, Sándor, 26, 27

labor
  child ~, 88
  surplus ~, 112, 116n12, 120, 136
  ~ force, out of force, 90, 91, 95, 121
  ~ market, 55, 62n9, 63n10, 67n17,
    88–105, 109, 116, 117, 121,
    140
  ~ productivity, 97, 99
  ~ shortage, 88, 92, 94, 95, 97, 98,
    103, 104, 105, 116n12, 121,
    136, 145
Lachmann, Ludwig M., 107
Laki, Mihály, 20, 27
Lange, Oscar, 84
Lau, Tuen-Yu, 57
Lavoie, Don, 107n2
Layard, Richard, 112
Lebeau, Jon, 57
Lee, Frederic S., 69
Leijonhufvud, Axel, 78, 122n18, 145n1
Lenin, Vladimir I., 22, 23, 104n14
Lin, Carolyn A., 57
Litan, Robert E., 39
loss, aversion to ~, 124, 139
Lotka–Voltera model, 110n5
Lovász, László, 117

Ma, Yun, 31
macro-level analysis, 85
mainstream economics, 39, 40, 52–54,
    61, 128, 137
maladjustment, 121
Malinvaud, Edmond, 98n5, 112
Malthus, Thomas R., 110
Mankiw, Gregory N., 39, 69
Mao, Zedong, 131
margin, 58, 67
  ~al cost, 60, 65
market
  external ~, 32
  internal ~, 32
  labor ~, 55, 62n9, 63n10, 67n17,
    88–105, 109, 116, 117, 121,
    140
  sellers' ~, 111
  ~ for goods and services, 55, 57–69,
    70–87, 121
  ~ monopoly, 30, 57, 61n4, 69, 157
  ~ research, 59, 77, 79, 86
  ~ structure, 57, 61
Marshall, Alfred, 109
Martos, Béla, 142
Marx, Karl, 23, 68, 104, 110, 138n12,
    139, 141
  ~ism, ~ist, 68, 103
  ~-Leninist ideology, 4, 45
Maskin, Eric, 34, 154n11
match, 14, 52, 99, 117, 148, 156
  mis~ed adjustment, 100–102, 139
  ~ing problem, 99, 100, 101, 107
  ~ing theory, 62n9, 100, 117, 139,
    156
mathematical models, 62n8, 66, 107,
    108, 111, 116, 117, 119n15, 123,
    124, 141–143
Mattey, Joe, 75
McCall, John J., 100
McCraw, Thomas K., 14
McGraw, A. Peter, 124
measurement, 28, 29, 30, 40, 41, 54,
    70–105, 144, 147
Meindl, Peter, 62n8
microeconomics, 39, 53, 62n8, 64, 84,
    108, 111, 144, 147
Microsoft, 6, 16, 26
Milgrom, Paul, 103n10
Milward, Alan S., 150n6
minicomputer, 18

Minodier, Christelle, 87
Mises von, Ludwig Heinrich, 107, 140
model, mathematical, 62n8, 66, 107, 108, 111, 116, 117, 119n15, 123, 124, 141–143
modernization, 4, 41, 126, 135, 148
monetary policy, 55, 56, 68, 69, 118, 121, 122, 146, 149
monitoring, 103
monopoly, 15, 20, 30, 45, 57, 122, 154, 157
   ~istic competition, 57, 61, 63, 65, 69, 120, 126, 147, 152, 153, 155
   ~istic rent, 15
Morin, Norman, 71n3
Mortensen, Dale T., 100, 116
motivation, 54, 66
   for-profit ~, 152
Müller, Jürg, 74
multiplier effect, 78, 133
Murrell, Peter, 159n16

naive
   ~ optimism, 136
   ~ reformers, 136
natural selection, 34, 109
Nelson, Richard R., 110, 139
neoclassical synthesis, 138
net
   ~ excess demand, 84, 85, 113
   ~ excess supply, 84
Neumann, János, 108, 143
   ~'s growth model, 108
Newton's physics, 109
Nickell, Stephen, 112
Nokia, 16, 21
North, Douglas C., 138n13
Nyíri, J. Kristóf, 47

Obama, Barack, 152
OECD countries, 60
Olson, Mancur, 150n6
operations research, 62, 63, 82
Orsato, Renato J., 132n8
Orwell, George, 45
output, 13, 21, 32, 33, 41, 80, 103, 133, 153n10
   ~ stock, 83
   sustainable maximum ~, 71
overemployment, 32, 103

Page, Larry, 14, 15
patent, 11, 19
penetration of modern technology, 13, 28–30
pensioners, 89
Phelps, Edmund S., 39, 100, 104n12, 139
phone, mobile, 21, 23, 27–30, 37, 38, 42, 58, 159
Pisano, Gary, 15n17
Pissarides, Christopher A., 100, 112, 116
planning
   indicative, ~ 137
   medium- and long-term ~, 137
   system of imperative ~, 137
Plummer, Michael D., 117
Poland, 13, 28, 29, 37, 41, 43, 44, 51, 59, 76, 83, 92–96, 158, 159
police, 110
policy, 3, 17, 34, 41, 63, 95, 140, 141, 147
   anticyclical ~, 148
   economic ~, 98, 105, 118, 121, 122, 132, 144, 145, 147, 155
   fiscal ~, 55, 56, 68, 118, 121, 122, 146, 149
   inventory ~, 62, 63, 82
   monetary ~, 55, 56, 68, 69, 118, 121, 122, 146, 149
   pricing ~, 130
   "vulgar Keynesian" economic ~, 149
   "vulgar Schumpeterian" economic ~, 149
politician 41–42, 136, 145, 147
politics, political
   ~ factors, 22
population
   economically active, ~ 90–94, 101–102, 102n9, See also labor force
   economically inactive, ~ 89–92, 101–102, 102n9
populism, populist, 42
Portes, Richard, 84n17, 112
Prékopa, András, 62n8
pressure, 111
price, prices
   price setting, pricing process, 68–69, 84, 121, 124, 139, 142
   sticky, ~ 69, 120, 139
   ~ adjustment, 120, 144

price, prices (continued)
  ~ control, 97
  ~-maker, 69n21
  ~-taker, 69n21
production function, 71n3
productivity
  constraints on, ~ 78
profit-maximization, 60–61, 65–67
propensity
  genetic ~, 122, 124, 147
  system-specific ~, 99, 123n19
  ~ to enterprise, 25, 123
property, system-specific, 3, 40

Qian, Yingi, 19n23
queuing, 86

racism, 105
Ramey, Valerie A., 62
R&D activity, 21
rationing, 110, 149
recession, 32, 34–35, 132–133, 141, 144–145, 148, 155
  transformational ~, 32
reform, reformer, 26, 45, 136n11, 137, 148, 152, 158
  naive ~, 136
  ~ of the socialist system, 136, 158
regulation, 21, 35, 123, 137, 148–150, 163–167
  over ~, 35
  ~ fallacy, 148
Relman, Arnold, 152n8
reserve, 82, 90, 97, 97n4, 104, 132, 139
  ~ army of industrial workers, 104
  ~ capital, 16
  ~ of capacity, capacity, ~ 52, 62n8, 63, 108, 120, 127
responsibility
  ~ of economists, 39
  ~ of politicians, 41, 42
reward, 15, 15n16, 16, 20, 35, 104, 129
rights, 48, 86
  human ~, 125, 127, 153
  universal ~, 153–154
rivalry, 30, 64, 112, 119, 120, 124, 134, 146, 148
Rizzo, Mario J., 107n2
Roberts, John, 103n10
Robinson, Joan, 61
Rogers, Everett M., 14n11, 22n27

Roland, Gérard, 34, 154n11
Rose, Richard, 43, 44
Rose-Ackerman, Susan, 131n7
Rosser, J. Barkley Jr., 140
Roth, Alvin E., 100
Rothstein, Bo, 131n7
Rubik, Ernő, 8, 18
rule, 34–35, 69n21, 81n14, 84, 146
  ~ of the shorter side, 72, 78
Russia, 28, 30, 31, 43, 44, 94, 122

safety level, 62, 62n7, 63
Samuelson, Paul A., 53, 138n12
satellite, 17, 42
Say, Jean-Baptiste, 146
  ~'s Law, 146
saturation of demand, 152
scale
  constant return to ~, 73
  decreasing return to ~, 65
  economies of ~, 64, 65
  increasing return to ~, 58, 65, 65n13, 73, 139, 142
Scarpetta, Stefano, 32
Schilling, Melissa A., 14n9
Schramm, Carl J., 39
Schumpeter, Joseph A., 14, 16n19, 22n27, 31, 39, 51, 52, 64, 108, 110, 138n12, 139, 140, 141n15, 148, 149
  non-~ian innovation, 17–18
  ~ian innovation, 9, 18, 20, 27, 31, 34, 35, 39
  ~ian growth theory, 39, 148
  ~ian vision, 51–52
Scitovsky, Tibor, 69n21
search
  ~ theory, 62n9, 100, 116, 117n14, 139, 156, 156n13
  ~ engine, 6, 14
selling effort, 61n6
semiconductor, 18
Sen, Amartya, 41n5
Shane, Scott, 23
Shapiro, Carl, 103, 139
Shelton, Robert, 22n27
Shiller, Robert J., 66, 123n19, 139
shirking, 103
shortage, 20, 54, 79, 83, 86–87, 88, 91, 102, 111, 113–116, 117n13, 118, 121, 122, 128, 130, 132n9, 134,

147, 149, 151, 153, 157n14, 158, 159, 161
~ economy, 20, 30, 51–53, 60, 63, 63n10, 80, 83, 85, 87n18, 92, 109–116, 118, 119, 119nn15–16, 122, 126–131, 134–136, 139, 142, 145, 150–154, 156, 158–161
~ economy vs. surplus economy, 49, 80, 85, 94, 111, 114, 126, 128, 131, 139, 142
~ of goods, 20, 38n1, 76n8, 79–81, 83, 134, 136, 157n14
~ of labor, 79–80, 81n13, 88, 91–95, 97, 97n4, 98, 100, 101, 103–105, 121, 136, 145, 163
Shun, Amy, 15n17
Siciliani, Luigi, 151
Simonovits, András, 142
slack, 51n3, 82, 154
Soate, Luc, 10, 14n11, 22n27
socialism, socialist
   market-oriented reforms under ~, 158
   ~ shortage economy, 52, 80, 134
   ~ command economy, 19, 157
   ~ system, 3, 10–12, 17, 19, 20n25, 21, 23, 27, 42, 44, 51–54, 55n5, 55n7, 63, 76n8, 79, 83, 93, 97, 97n4, 98, 100, 116, 118, 119, 121, 122, 136, 136n11, 137, 145, 150, 153, 154
social psychology, 89
society, 10, 31n4, 40, 47, 48, 52, 105, 123, 126, 127, 130, 130n5, 131, 140, 150, 153
sociology, 89
Soskice, David, 53
South Europe, 29
Soviet Union, 5, 11, 13, 17, 18, 20, 23, 28, 30, 40, 45, 59, 76n8, 83, 92, 104, 134
Sovereignty, 127, 158
Sraffa, Piero, 140
Stalin, Iosif Vissarionovich, 18n20, 46, 131
   ~ist–Maoist period, 122
state
   normal ~, 124
   welfare ~, 102, 130n4, 150, 151, 153, 154

~ control, 97
~ regulation, 123, 137
~ ownership, 4, 97, 122, 154
stealing intellectual property, 11, 11n7
Stevens, John J., 71n3
Stiglitz, Joseph E., 41n5, 103, 139
Stokes, Raymond G., 22n28
Stolyarov, Gennady, 23
structural unemployment, 98–100, 105, 139
substitution, forced, 78, 81, 127, 151
suction, 111
supply, 27, 30, 38n1, 52, 53, 58, 60, 62n9, 63, 64, 67–70, 70n2, 71–73, 77, 77n10, 80, 81, 85, 97, 99, 100, 103, 108, 110, 111, 113, 115, 117, 120, 124, 127, 130, 132, 142, 146, 146n2, 147, 152n9, 153, 155, 157, 163–167
~ related processes, 60, 66–67, 121, 139, 154
demand-~ regime, 113, 115, 118, 125, 131, 135, 145, 153, 156, 158
excess ~, 53–54, 59, 61, 61n4, 64–66, 68–74, 76, 78, 80, 80n12, 81–86, 121, 131, 152n8–9, 153n10, 154, 158
excess ~ multiplier effect, 78
mutual adjustment of ~ and demand, 76, 81, 144
net excess ~, 84
stock
   ratio of input and output ~s, 83
   safety level of ~s, 62, 63
   turnover of ~s, 82, 86
   See also inventory
surplus, 51, 51n3, 54, 61, 62, 64, 68, 74, 82, 84, 86–87, 87n18, 88, 90, 91, 93, 98–105, 112–115, 117–118, 120–122, 124, 126, 130, 131, 132n9, 142, 144, 155, 156, 158
   islands of ~ economy, 158
   reproduction of ~, 57, 64, 88
   ~ capacity, 65n13, 84, 132, 134, 136, 156
   ~ economy, 51–53, 60, 63, 65, 67, 69, 70, 77, 80, 85, 92, 110–116, 118–119, 121, 122, 125–147, 149–161

surplus (*continued*)
~ economy vs. shortage economy, 49, 51–53, 60, 63, 65, 67, 69, 70, 76, 77, 80, 85, 92, 110–116, 118, 120, 122, 125–132, 134–137, 139, 140, 142, 144, 145, 145n1, 146, 147, 149–154, 156–160
Svejnar, Jan, 27n1
synthesis, positive, 138, 138n12, 139–141, 149
system of imperative planning, 137
Szabó, Katalin, 10, 47

tâtonnement theories, 69
technical development, technical progress, 3–5, 16, 17, 21–27, 30–32, 34, 38–42, 45, 47, 63, 100, 107, 109, 126, 134–136, 148
brakes on ~, 100
technology, 13, 19, 23, 32, 37, 46, 48, 100, 109, 142, 155
information and communication ~, 18, 22, 24, 27–30, 38, 42, 44, 45, 47, 57, 156
Teece, David J., 15n17
Terrel, Katherine, 27n1
telephone sector, 27, 28, 30, 38n1, 59, 60, 126, 159
American ~, 57–60
theory
contract ~, 68n18, 154n11
corridor ~, 122n18, 145n1
Schumpeterian growth ~, 39
matching ~, 62n9, 100, 117
search ~, 62n9, 100, 116, 117n14
Thomke, Stefan H., 16n18
time
waiting ~, 151
~-lag, 11, 12
Timmer, John, 45n8, 46n9
Timmons, Jeffrey A., 16
Tolstoy, Lev Nikolayevich, 131n6
Toomey, John W., 62n8
transformation, postsocialist, 3, 4, 25–35, 95, 158, 159, 160
transition, 4, 30, 32, 38, 41, 42, 158–160
~ economy, 25, 27, 32, 33, 43, 44
See also change of system

Trotsky, Lev Davidovich, 23
trust, 131n7
Tversky, Amos, 124

unemployment, 32, 90, 92, 94, 95, 103, 104, 116, 121, 136, 140, 145
chronic ~, 67, 105
equilibrium ~, ~ equilibrium, 103, 109, 112, 116
frictional ~, 98n7, 100–102, 139
Keynesian ~, 95–98, 139
natural rate of ~, 92, 104n12
rate of ~, 91, 96–98, 101, 102, 105, 116
structural ~, 98–100, 105, 139
~ within the factory gates, 95n3
~ outside of the factory, 95n3
unemployed, 89, 90, 91, 92, 94, 95, 102, 105, 113
registered ~, 88–90, 98

vacancy
~ of jobs, 88, 91, 94–95, 96, 101, 113, 116
~ in hotels, 70–71
~ of homes, 76
Vahabi, Mehrdad, 64n12, 110n7
value 2n, 87, 125, 126, 130, 131, 135, 136
~ judgments, 23, 24, 28, 106, 125, 126, 135, 140
Vámos, Tibor, 9
varieties of capitalism, 53, 144–160
Veblen, Thorstein B., 110, 130n5
venture capital, 16
Verzulli, Rossella, 151
Vietnam, 45
vision (Schumpeterian), 51–52

wages, 67, 68, 98n6, 101, 130, 146, 154
sticky ~, 68, 98, 120, 139
efficiency wage, 67n17, 103–105, 123, 139
wage adjustment, 120
wage control, 97
waiting
~ time, 27, 86, 151
~ lists, 59, 113, 126, 134, 151, 158, 159

Walras, Léon, 108, 109
war, 20n25, 90
   ~ economy, 149, 150
Weber, Max, 53
Webster, Frank, 47
Weitzman, Martin, 61n6
welfare state, 102, 150–154
Wells, Peter, 132n8
West, Joel, 57
West, Kenneth D., 62

Wikipedia, 51
Winter, David, 84n17, 112
Winter, Sidney G., 110, 139
worker
   discouraged ~, 63n10, 89
   ~s' aristocracy, 104
World Bank, 35
World Wide Web, 17

Xu, Chenggang, 19n23, 21n26